TEXAS WOMEN

ARE ON THE MONEY:

Three Centuries of Female Entrepreneurs in the Lone Star State

CYNTHIA DEVLIN

First Edition

Book Design: Tolina Rowlands

ISBN: 978-1-62288-272-4

For more information:
Stephen F. Austin State University Press
P.O. Box 13007 SFA Station
Nacogdoches, Texas 75962
sfapress@sfasu.edu
936-468-1078

Distributed by the Texas A&M University Press Book Consortium
www.tamupress.com

Acknowledgments

People from the East and from the South traversed the Red River or headed west across the Sabine into a rugged land known as Texas. Rugged men with rugged women forged a country out of the vast environmentally divergent land mass dotted with ample places where living was sometimes beyond the pale. Whether from the East or the South or from foreign countries, the people transformed themselves into Texans where individualism and determination reigned, and women of the formation era set the template meant to inspire future females of Texas to become the entrepreneurs of the twenty-first century. This book reveals how women of the state evolved into first rate businesswomen.

The person I thank most for his contribution to this effort on Texas Women at Work is Dr. Scott Sosebee, Executive Director of the East Texas Historical Association and history professor at Stephen F. Austin State University. Scott represents the spirit of the Panhandle and the wide open, unbridled West Texas skies. I was born overlooking the Gulf of Mexico, spending part of my early youth in the old state capital of Velasco where we lived in a Dow Chemical rent house, and everything was painted in diluted Army green after World War Two. Eventually we progressed to a purchased home in Lake Jackson and moved to Port Arthur after Hurricane Carla. As Texans, we inhabit land that was a country that became the Lone Star State, and we believe that female settlers established the model for women who followed because of their strong work ethic and skills to further the growth, development, and wealth of the state from its inception to the present. Scott gave his time, with his wife Leslie joining us as a sounding board for one of the several meetings on the endeavor. His enthusiasm abounded as he rattled off ideas and suggestions, one after the other that either explain history or that question the status quo. I wrote furiously trying to capture his ideas, hoping I could read the scribble later.

We spent about five years discussing how to focus on the path women took, evolving from mamas to owners of successful businesses, finding that women of the past had done a variety of everything needed to broaden the state's advancements against all odds. The project began as a joint effort and has finished with Scott graciously giving me sole authorship as I never let go of the need to write about how Texas women helped forge a successful state. I am forever grateful for his generosity and his writing of the preface.

My husband Philip kept me on track by asking, "Why aren't you writing today?" He never complained if supper came late or may have been only a sandwich. Others to whom I am ever grateful include the interviewees that cooperated so generously with their truth and their time. My sister Kay Ryan has a certain knack for getting the point and was helpful, along with my retired teacher mom Janiece Marshall who patiently listened to me when I read passages of the book, seeking ways to improve the text Sadly, both my husband and mother have passed away before publication. I appreciate the mentorship provided by Dr. Mark Barringer from SFA who sat in the conference room and spent time improving my writing skills when I was a graduate student in the years 2003-2005. Dr. Troy Davis from SFA trusted me to teach history and opened the door to my academic career that began late in life for me as I came from an aviation background. Every professor in the department taught me much history over time while standing at the coffee pot or talking in the hallways.

I also convey my personal gratitude to Kimberly Verhines, Director of the Stephen F. Austin University Press and her whole staff, including any graduate students that may have been involved, for making this book a reality. I thank Tolina Rowlands for her expert editing. I truly savor my relationship with SFA because the path I have been able to take was the direction I wanted to go.

CONTENTS

Preface

Some years ago, more than either of us will admit, Cynthia Devlin and I were on the faculty together at Stephen F. Austin State University and as we often did when we were colleagues, we began to chat about current events and other "hot-button" topics. Cynthia mentioned some of the ongoing activities in Saudi Arabia and Iran and how those nation's current regimes were so oppressive in their policies toward women. We remarked how egregious it would be if—particularly in the case of Saudi Arabia and its oil wealth and power—either of those nations or any other country that followed such an ideology, were to accumulate such prosperity that they could inflict such ideas on the rest of the world. I replied that I would never worry about that happening because any society that habitually denied half their population economic freedom would never accomplish such a feat.

We discussed the state of the Western economy, particularly how dynamic the United States' wealth boomed in the post-World War II years. We both lamented how it is often forgotten by many commentators, pundits, and especially politicians—but not among economic and gender historians—that much of that vitality was directly due to more and more women entering the workplace and becoming entrepreneurs and professionals. It only makes sense that if a large sector of the population begins to inject money and talent into an economy it will grow by leaps and bounds.

I forgot about our conversation, but it lit a fire under Ms. Devlin, resulting in this wonderful volume. Some women have always been a part of the economy and, even in the postwar years, those women have persevered against great odds and barriers. Cynthia Devlin has, in this work, demonstrated how women in Texas overcame those obstacles and became true economic actors. She gave insight into how thirteen Texas female entrepreneurs made such strides and found success in a society and system that often tried to restrict their triumphs. The work you will read is well-researched and written and provides a much-needed insight into how Texas women, by either force, circumstance, or pure pluck (or a combination of all three) have become successful and become role models for those who came after them. It is a story of underdogs, yes, but also of how society becomes more positive and powerful when it allows all its citizens to participate. Ms. Devlin's narrative aptly shows the struggle and initiative these women engaged in, and how Texas is a better place because of their grit. I think you will find it a worthy and engrossing read, and I am very proud to have played a very small part in its genesis.

M. Scott Sosebee

Introduction

Texas, at the start of 2019, ranked number one for female business startups; the state represents a great place for women to do business by skirting the traditional paths to the boardroom.[1] Between 2007 and 2018, Texas tied for the number two position, where female-owned firms increased their economic clout; and by 2018, San Antonio, Austin, and Dallas were cities where women-owned businesses flourished.[2] Texas also ranked number one in Gross Domestic Product growth for the second quarter of 2018.[3] Three reasons support why Texas women are presently in businesses formed and directed by women; and those reasons include: a need to circumvent male-dominated work environments, an atypical circumventing of the traditional Feminist Movement, and a business environment that could easily facilitate the formation of companies. Women bypassed the Glass Ceiling as they carved out business niches to suit their specific needs over an expanse of time in a state that can historically be described as distinctly masculine, because cotton, cattle, and oil formed the original foundation of the state's economy. Women work for the same reason that men do—they want to earn money. Texas, because of its sheer size, its varied geographic regions, and its unique history under Spanish/Mexican occupation where community property law provided a more equal playing field for women, provided a different path to economic success than many other areas of the United States.

While most of the history of working women has addressed the issues of balancing family life within the context of the business world, a less discussed reason that women faced, when attempting to exploit their talents in Texas spotlights,was a Texas-styled second wave of feminism that flourished differently than traditionally examined case studies of those generated by Betty Friedan's seminal post-WWII Feminist Movement. The characteristics and roots of the Texas-styled movement resulted from a

Southern culture that emphasized exaggerated feminine nurturing patterns and an extraordinarily embedded cultural worldview that promoted male dominance, resulting from a warrior ethic that amplified perceptions by men that women possessed little, if any, business acumen. Coupling that underlying attitude with a male-driven economy, based on cotton, cattle, and oil, the bloody history of Texas produced euphoric feelings of overall superiority by men that permeated workplace attitudes for many years. However, the state government has presently encouraged the growth of corporations giving women an open door to success, because Texas is the number one place to do business in the United States and has held that position for the last fourteen years.[4]

Texas-style feminism began in earnest after the Korean War ended in 1953. It ramped up in the 1960s and culminated in many victories by the turn of the century and beyond. Women of the state have now bypassed tradition and are, in many instances, foregoing the process known as Cracking the Glass Ceiling. As a long-term soft coup, the movement spanned a couple of centuries as the Southern-styled upbringing had taught, trained, and expected young women to speak softly, tread lightly, be overly courteous, and deliver multi-babies, while supporting their husbands' dreams of success instead of their own. Such demure women were reticent to verbalize their frustrations unless among themselves, or to even ponder picketing or protesting in the land of cotton, cattle, and oil. As Texas Ranger Daniel Roberts stated, "I was reared and almost rocked in the cradle of war in Texas."[5] Texas was forged by strong men with a propensity for war. With war, rough men stood ready to fight; women held the home front as necessary, whether on the frontier during the Texas Revolution or during the many following wars and conflicts around the world. Men cut a wide path and made their way confrontationally, while exercising force over reason in the treatment of women, whose frontier lives were intertwined with sewing bonnets, tending babies, and baking biscuits.

Women promoted the economic growth of the United States from its inception. As societal mores evolved, as technological advances flourished, and as political changes occurred, women flowed into the workplace. Women in America contributed ample goods and services to the overall gross domestic product that propelled the United States to the number one financial position in the world by 1900. Texas women, throughout time, have worked diligently to propel the state to the forefront of economic strength and power.

Cultural, legal, ethno-racial, and demographic pressures have formed the history of females as participants in the American labor force. Women in Colonial and preindustrial America worked to improve their family situation mostly through unpaid domestic labor. The legal status of women, unless provisions were made through special circumstances, added to the negative work environs women encountered during the industrial age. Married women could not own property, sign legal contracts, or even claim their own pay, as they had no separate identity from their spouse. As cash became an important avenue for the overall wellbeing of the American family, more women entered the labor pool. Men continued as the main "breadwinners" and only through time and changes in the legal system would women "bring home the bacon" and fry it in their own pan.

The economy of the Northeast flourished during the preindustrial and the industrial age partly because of the labor force participation of immigrant women from all parts of the globe over time. Young females filled the needs of the textile manufacturers, abandoning their rural roots for a paycheck. Home-based jobs and family businesses provided jobs for some immigrant women, but many worked as maids, laundresses, and cooks. Women workers dominated in the burgeoning garment district of New York by the twentieth century. Because of the invention of the typewriter and the Dictaphone, women increasingly entered the work force as clerks and secretaries. An expanding retail sector employed young women as sales associates. As educational opportunities increased, middle-class women had opportunities as nurses, teachers, librarians, and eventually from an assortment of occupations.

The over-arching thesis of this effort focuses on the economic contributions of Texas women over time and how they have, in the past and in the present, remained crucial to the gross domestic product of the world's twelfth largest economy. Women have always worked with their husbands, their fathers, their bosses, and with each other for the promotion of capitalism and the growth of the economic riches of the state. Unbridled Texas women created wealth and assisted with the expansion of businesses across the Lone Star state. Many issues concerning working women have long been lamented and discussed in books, articles, and lectures that focused on entrenched mind-sets, old-fashioned "Big Daddy" biases, intransigent bosses, the problems of working while rearing children, and the disparities between male and female wages. This rendering concentrates on presenting examples of the efforts of some outstanding women in Texas' history that contributed their work efforts to building an economically successful state over time.

Chapter One
Colliding Cultures: Women in Spanish/Mexican Texas, 1700-1830

"The Roman, Visigothic, Jewish, Arabic and Catholic influences during Spain's long history had combined to make the Spanish woman one of the most sub-ordinated in all of Europe."[6] After Spanish laws of matrimony had been codified in the Siete Partidas during the Middle Ages, the purpose of marriage was childbearing and child-rearing by the mother while the father dealt with business and financial matters.[7] Marriage accordingly references matrimony, not patrimony, to "honor" women.[8] Yet in Spanish—and later Mexican—Texas, natives and US settlers, in conjunction with time and space, separated the strict laws that defined women's roles as laws of local custom mostly prevailed in the largely unoccupied expanse of land. The harsh realities of life on the frontier dictated how closely marital laws remained intact. In some circumstances, a demographic shortage of women placed a higher value on a woman's importance in Texas to those that came in with the empresarios. While the standard daily "work" performed by women remained ubiquitous for the women of Mexico and Texas during the incipient stages of development, a bifurcated social system—resulting from the eventual Texas Revolution—gradually allowed the women of Texas the opportunity to extricate themselves from the matrimonial laws of Mexico with the Texas Constitution of 1836, along with adjustments made in 1845. However, the basic precept that a woman's place was in the home remained entrenched in the state for almost 140 years. However, these pioneer women extended their domestic duties by assisting their husbands in solidifying the success of the farm or the ranch.

Mexico under Spanish rule was never homogenous and social status dictated whether women worked outside the home. The country was highly multiracial and miscegenation in various locales occurred regularly.[9] Elite women did not work outside the home and usually had servants to assist them.[10] Widows, singles, those of mixed racial background, and those of low social status, ran small shops and various businesses and conducted legal transactions.[11] Many low-caste women provided foodstuffs for towns and villages. Women often had children outside of marriage because of various social mores that occurred outside of the dictates of the Catholic Church.[12] For some, marriage was not a socially acceptable lifestyle.[13] Before the Spanish occupation, natives married in their early teens and regardless of the introduction of Christianity, the ages of brides mostly remained in the teens for all social groups.[14] The females coming to Texas rejected some of the customs of Mexico. While youthful marriages became common, marriage remained important for Texas women. Cultures collided over family and marriage laws when Texas became a republic.

The period after the American Revolution led to less ethnic identity in the United States because of the new market economy underpinned by capitalism and the exercise of freedom and liberty unleashed by the independence of a new-styled republic; while the Catholic-directed Spanish mission system had declined precipitously. During this decade, Spain ceded Florida to the United States with the Adams-Onis Treaty in 1821 and in exchange, America agreed not to claim Texas after the execution of the Louisiana Purchase of 1803 by President Thomas Jefferson.[15] President James Monroe issued his Monroe Doctrine on December 2, 1823, warning European nations not to attempt any recolonization in the Americas.[16] Twenty-three states made up the United States with a population of over nine million and Americans realized that tomatoes were not poison and coffee in an English teacup energized them as much as tea. After a tumultuous state of unrest, Mexico separated from Spain via a revolution in 1821, and while delegates did write a constitution that reflected the US document, the government never stabilized under old Spanish Civil Laws that represented a jurisprudence system antithetical to English Common Law. Republican Motherhood, an overall phrase for the role of women after the American Revolution set the parameters for women that included the home as their sphere with a responsibility to teach children the importance of citizenship and patriotism. Women throughout the nation, given their home or farm was their castle, will demand the necessities to make the drudgery of their daily lives bearable. While unable to speak in public, to vote, or to own property in most states, nevertheless women will work diligently to benefit the family and the nation as the adventurous among them moved onto a vast frontier, forging a country from sea to shining sea. A wild Texas beckoned settlers with cheap land, wild horses, longhorn cattle, and herds of bison on the western plains and these ladies worked with their spouses to create ranches and farms to sustain their families through wars, hurricanes, droughts, and ice storms.

Long before English-speaking Anglos entered Texas, the Spaniards from the 1500s settled their northern frontier by intermarriage between Mexican and Indian women to establish missions and towns under a policy of unidad doméstica.[17] While consensus on the depopulation of Indigenous peoples greatly varies, demographers figure that rate is between eighty to ninety percent.[18] Between 1544 and 1737, Spanish priests recorded seventeen major epidemics that ravaged New Spain, including measles, mumps, smallpox and influenza.[19] From 1545 to 1548, hemorrhagic fever killed five to fifteen million natives resulting in one of the worst demographic calamities in human history.[20] Approximately every fifteen to twenty years, smallpox devastated Mexico with three major outbreaks in the eighteenth century, with massive death rates and one colossal eruption from 1779 to 1780.[21] At various times, families simply perished because potential caretakers succumbed simultaneously. No one could cook and provide hydration for the ill. The Spanish mission system forced people from their traditionally grown corn fields that contradicted the rules of ecology, thereby creating an unnatural and unhappy economic paradigm doomed for failure. According to Father Hidalgo's "Grito," by 1810 the Spanish dreams of an educated country had failed as only about two million citizens were literate out of a population of over thirteen million. Female literacy rates barely reached twenty percent.[22]

Correspondingly, with the depopulation of Mexico and most of New Spain from disease, the Europeans introduced pastoral agriculture, a combination of gardening and herding. Corn remained important along with grapes, olives, and wheat as these became standard produce, while cattle and chickens were introduced and a strong emphasis on silver mining continued.[23] Cattle and sheep herding allowed a new mixed-blood population to establish the hacienda or ranchero economic system of the 1700s and 1800s.[24] After the dust settled in 1714 from the War of Spanish Succession, King Philip V, a Bourbon dynasty member, diligently sought to "renationalize" New Spain.[25] Thus, the push to garner wealth from their land resulted in an increase in taxes, and they proved to be astute in the collection of duties. Taxes were needed to fund wars in Europe. "A series of statistics calculated by Richard Garner shows that the share of Mexican output or estimated GDP taken by taxes grew by 167 percent between 1700 and 1800. The number of duties collected by the Royal Treasury increased from 34 to 112 between 1760 and 1810."[26]

Women in Spanish Texas survived as most women around the world did— they adapted to the dictates of men living within patriarchal parameters. Distinct gender roles existed on South Texas ranches during the 1750s and beyond, and over sixty land grants were awarded to women.[27] Forty-five percent of the total population, excluding Native Americans, were female.[28] Within the mission system, women produced candles, soap, and clothing, along with the preparation of food, including dried meats.[29] Whether of the patrón class or the peón class, both groups of women exercised the same duties as homemakers, cooks, gardeners, and caretakers of their children. As producers in an economic system, women worked as tailors, peddlers, servants, laundresses, and cooks, among other professions.[30] Women acted as healers using household remedies made from herbs popular at that time. As midwives, they delivered most of the children. Women acted as folk chiropractors using massage methods for sprains, broken bones, and bad bruises. Women, too, saw to the education of the children. The yearly dances given by the wealthy ranchers represented the only form of entertainment shared by both men and women. However, the women socialized separately from the men who enjoyed horse races, gambling, and cock fights. Women provided spiritual guidance for the family, as priests usually visited the ranch only once a year. Women came of age at fifteen and at the appointed time of their visit, priests conducted weddings, baptisms, and on occasion, funerals.[31]

While most women in Spanish Texas lived in the same domestic sphere as their sisters in the United States, some conducted business on behalf of their husbands when necessary. Occasionally, American husbands trusted wives to conduct business too, but the practice proved uncommon throughout the United States. One major difference between America and New Spain focused on inheritance rights. The concept of community property allowed women in Spanish/Mexican Texas more control over their lives. Indeed they had to have a male represent them in legal issues and special laws of honor ruled the conjugal relationship; however, there were women like Maria Ana Cubelo, a widow in 1770, who owned and operated a ranch in Bexar with 300 head of cattle.[32] Rosa María Hinojosa de Ballí owned much of the lower Rio Grande valley.[33] Much has been documented by attorneys and historians that ancient Visigoths codified community property laws that stood the test of time even after they fell to the Moors in 711 A.D. Women were permitted to own property and to inherit property from a marriage. Ferdinand and Isabella embraced the idea in the late 1400s that enabled the holding of large expanses of Spanish territory while consolidating power through the Great Diaspora by expelling Jews and Muslims from Spain and through the tragic Spanish Inquisition as Spain unified under the Catholic papacy. Modern legal and historical explanations indicate that Anglos from Louisiana to California bestowed these corresponding rights on the female populations of those eventual states through the legal system or, as in the case of Texas, through its constitution. Other considerations account for the adoption of Spanish ganancial civil law and those include a propensity for fauna-driven herding societies to treat women better than flora-driven sedentary societies;[34] and a drastic male-female demographic imbalance in Texas and the Great Southwest. Women were in short supply and were treated better because men competed for their hands in marriage. Young men desired to marry and have families; therefore, generous property rights could and would entice women to go to raw, uncivilized land on the frontier. Texans repealed all Spanish/Mexican laws before they debated the adoption of the 1845 Constitution. The Texans understood English common law and Spanish civil law had become diluted and convoluted over time. Also, in 1803 during the fading years of Spanish hegemony, a new royal edict diluted the rights of women when the decree allowed only pledges of marriage in writing as legal. This new requirement entered the republican civil codes, thereby negating the colonial custom among the people that a verbal declaration of intended marriage would suffice. The verbal declaration by the male to the female allowed her to lose her virginity to him.[35] The Catholic Church and civil courts ensured that a deflowered maiden would soon be married because the suitor needed to fulfill his declaration of love through marriage or provide compensation to the jilted and hopeful bride. Unfortunately for the female, her honor was lost if a promise of marriage was never fulfilled. Women, it seems, had no redress in the legal system if they accepted verbal declarations of intentions to marry and the man walked away after she lost her virginity. Mexico passed some protective laws concerning women; however, many of them were simply ignored over time. No one calculated the monetary benefit of women's work to the country's GDP, and the United States also failed to place a value on what women contributed to the wealth of the nation. Women in both countries shouldered the domestic chores, and in Mexico, those duties were written in the laws of 1917.

The history by which Anglos ventured into Texas began in 1821; while Spain's control of the area was tenuous at best and soon to be lost, a decision was made to allow foreigners into the state.[36] Moses Austin planned colonization by bringing in settlers. Mexico, independent from Spain, promoted a liberal colonization policy in 1823.[37] However, Mexico revoked the law and passed another one in 1824. Through a special accommodation, Austin received a contract. After Austin's untimely death, his son Stephen F. Austin will painstakingly increase his efforts to fulfill his father's dream. He will learn Spanish, read the laws, and endeavor to understand the culture and the Catholic religion. Mexico remained in flux with dictators demanding constant changes in government authorities and laws. For Austin, nothing went smoothly as the convoluted system in Mexico City required that his grant needed further approval. He worked through the chaos to obtain a decree that secured the grant.

Anglos receiving Spanish Land Grants in Texas from the influx of settlers, as facilitated by Stephen F. Austin and other empresarios, copied the Spanish/Mexican methods of ranching but eventually added many English strategies as well. Austin became a citizen of Mexico on March 9, 1824.[38] From September of that year, 272 land titles were issued and seventeen titles were granted to single men who formed a family when ten of them joined to obtain one league of land per title.[39] By 1830, the approximate population of Texas equaled 14,000 and men outnumbered women by ten to one.[40] Irish and Germans came into Texas along with many Southerners, as well as others from the Northeast.

The whole system of ranching duplicated itself in Texas, creating a true replica of the Spanish ranching system that provided an economic base for its citizens.[41] The model for ranches in Texas commenced with the arrival of Spanish cattle that would become known as Texas Longhorns, and Spanish/Mexican vaqueros morphed into American cowboys. Longhorns never provided juicy, tasty, and tender beef, so crossbreeding with short-horned breeds accomplished the goal of better beef desired by future markets in the Midwest and Northeast.[42] Women supported men in their efforts to maintain their cattle kingdoms. Ranches eventually existed in most areas of the state, however each faced unique challenges depending on climate, topography, and soil type. Open-range ranching produced inconsistent profits because of unstable markets and Indian attacks. Ranches were the result of an adaptive strategy that enabled a few men to control huge land masses. Various ethnic groups lived in Texas at the time and men continued to outnumber women.[43] A few of those were Spaniards from Spain. Most were mestizos, or mixed race, and made their living with herd animals.[44] Cattle, sheep, hogs, and goats provided the economic base and the king allowed 4,428.4 acres which equaled one league of land for raising large herd animals. To be granted land, a fee was necessary with an application. However, in Texas, standards proved informal.[45] Families formed rancheros, living in basic utilitarian housing in the area west of San Antonio to the Guadalupe River and south of the Nueces River to the Rio Grande.[46] Nacogdoches proved an excellent environment for breeding fine horses.[47] For maximum exploitation, men, their wives, and their children worked from sunup to sundown.[48] They faced attacks from Native American tribes in the area along with hot summers and sometimes brutal winters. At the time of Anglo settlement, forty families could form towns. Although only a dearth of information concerning the worth of women's labor on farms and ranches existed before 1900, this labor was a proclamation that isolated women did not suffer a proclivity toward insanity, more so than their city counterparts. The logic at the time stemmed from the fact that they were much too busy to focus on their seclusion because of the many varied quotidian duties, regardless of the drudgery. Women had little time to enjoy amusements and were certainly not expected to "contemplate the universe." [49]

The abdication of the Bourbons to Napoleon Bonaparte in 1808 spurred the uprising of peasants in Mexico and destroyed the mining industry, resulting in a paralysis of the economy and the deaths of many rebels. By the time of their victory in 1821, Mexico borrowed heavily from London the money to forestay another invasion by Spain and would default on the loan, leaving the country in chaos for many decades with no access to international markets and capital.[50] Such depletion of funds left the country unable to stabilize and would precipitate the government's later effort to occupy their northern territories by inviting Americans to come in and make Texas their new home. While rules and parameters would demand loyalty and Mexican citizenship, the two cultures never melded. Cultures tend to accept what works and reject ideas that do not coincide with long-established practices that are deeply rooted in the psyche of a people. Texans decidedly remained fiercely independent, were seldom team players, and spoke their minds without filters.[51] New Spain remained socially stratified, laggard economically, and resistant to change. Also, a major difference in the societies stemmed from the acceptance by America of different religious practices while Mexico demanded the practice of Catholicism with social controls and dictates exercised by the local priests. The whole empresario idea fostered and implemented by the Spanish, and later the Mexicans, simply proved a fait accompli—doomed to fail by means of a bloody confrontation that would upend Mexico's hold on land they could not occupy, hold, or control culturally, economically, or militarily. In practice, Mexico proved strongly centralized, and every local official eventually reported up the chain of command to the "supreme executive."[52] Decisions never came quickly, and some remained unclear.

There were a limited quantity of females in early Texas; their role remained the same for many years to come. Those on ranches tended to work side by side with their husbands and those on farms maintained a more English-styled identity. Regardless, women pioneers faced many struggles, and their efforts need the remembrances and contributions awarded to the men of the Texas frontier.

Chapter Two
Babies, Biscuits, Scarecrows and Slaves: The Texas Revolution to Statehood: 1830-1845

During the fifteen years from 1830 to 1845, huge changes occurred in both the United States and Texas. Texas, when a republic, will be referred to as "The Republic of Porkdom" because of the amount of ham and bacon consumed in the country.[53] Eggs were for breakfast if one could protect their chickens from predators; young live girls would stand in fields as scarecrows,[54] and lettuce was viewed as useless because it provided little energy, and where it was grown was often seen as too close to where outhouses were purged.[55] Women cooked and men eagerly ate. Calorie intake has been estimated at 4,500 calories per day.[56] Women provided sustenance for the fighting men of Texas, as no soldier fights long on an empty stomach. A price tag for those efforts cannot be estimated. President Andrew Jackson overwhelmed Henry Clay in the presidential election to earn a second term and he was sworn in on March 3, 1833. The US population reached almost thirteen million and poet Emily Dickinson was born in Massachusetts.[57] Cyrus McCormick requested a patent for his mechanical reaper that would allow better rations for President Lincoln's Union Army in the eventual Civil War of 1861. In 1838, Cherokee Indians were forced from their homeland in a death march called the "Trail of Tears" where thousands died reaching the new Indian Territory of Oklahoma.[58] The circus was born as P.T. Barnum took his show on the road entertaining American families.[59] For women at the time, Sarah Levitt in her book, Victorians Unbuttoned, noted: "Nearly all women wore stays; they were essential for decency, and to go without them was to risk being considered a 'loose woman'."[60] Elizabeth Cady Stanton, treated poorly at the World Anti-slavery Convention in London, returned to the US and along with Lucia Mott, organized a women's rights convention held in 1840 at Seneca Falls, New York.[61] Along with Susan B. Anthony, the ladies expressed themselves with the "Declaration of Sentiments" requiring equal rights with men and new laws regarding property rights, divorce, and child custody.[62] Women should have opportunities opened to them that included professions in law, medicine, education, and the ministry.[63] Voting rights topped their wish list and the long fight began.

If indeed there is any credence to the belief that a "moving frontier" such as promoted by Frederick Jackson Tuner's "Frontier Thesis,"[64] created a new man—the American,[65] then one can conclude that frontier Texas created a new man—the Texan; and correspondingly, one can also surmise that the state also forged a new woman, equally Texan. Women of Texas, during its formative years, laid a lengthy and impressive predicate for those to come. One today cannot put a dollar value to their efforts in building the state, but logic dictates that their efforts proved necessary to the eventual success and wealth of the state. While in the modern sense, they were not fashioned as entrepreneurs, in every sense, however, they did business. The colonists coming mostly from the South had stepped into a situation where their beliefs, institutions, and culture shaped the varied landscapes of the huge landmass in harmony with their own patterns while living under the jurisdiction of a foreign government; that of Mexico after that country's break from Spain. Other American frontier settlers faced dangers when settling the territories of the Louisiana Purchase; however, they lived under the umbrella of the United States with the assistance of the government through the protection of forts, the use of the National Road, the eventual Homestead Act of 1862, and the benefit of railroads. Their fights with the Indians proved ferocious, but Texans would forcibly extricate themselves from Mexico with a revolution, fight the Indians, and forge a republic, however tenuous. Texans had "married" Mexico with a vow promising that each settler would learn Spanish, become Catholic, obey the messy legal system, and be loyal to their adopted country through cultural assimilation. Stephen F. Austin tried, however, cultural diffusion, forced by the Mexicans, failed to inculcate local customs and the quite dissimilar Spanish civil law system irritated the people who genuinely believed that anyone would be happier and more prosperous in a United States-styled government where power originated with the people. Many laws failed to be published, much less translated and produced coherently. Trouble loomed and friction grew.

Living in Texas before the revolution challenged women in many ways, including the marriage process. Priests were not readily available to marry couples.[66] Instead of a religious ceremony, Austin devised a marriage bond that would "legalize" the couple's commitment until a priest arrived.[67] Usually, the couple had about five or six children before they said their vows.[68] While Texans disliked the system, the men did not make a fuss.[69] One can imagine that perhaps the women hoped they would have vociferously insisted that Mexican authorities find, at minimum, one traveling priest. Women worked hard and deserved some attention. With the varied landscapes of Texas, women's lives and duties depended on the location and type of lifestyle. General duties included planting the garden, washing and ironing clothes, sewing, cooking, carding wool, knitting, quilt making, butter churning, soap making, cow milking, corn shucking, pea picking, potato digging, and tallow rendering.[70] Hog killing usually took place by early December or as cold weather began. Stephen F. Austin's first cousin, Mary Austin Holley believed ladies should have cultivated, inquiring minds, however, most Texas women had little time to play backgammon, a game she enjoyed.[71] Coastal cities endured hissing snakes, horseflies, and wolves howling at night.[72] At times mosquitoes devoured the women as they placed clothes on the line. Women took salt baths, if possible. Their frontier lives were intertwined with sewing bonnets, tending babies, and baking biscuits whether on a farm or a ranch. Breakfast might be chicken, or eggs, if available, biscuits, and coffee. Cholera remained rampant at various times. Well-to-do people did, on special occasions, eat cake and drink Champagne. However, high poverty levels forced many children to work alongside their moms in supporting the family. On the coast, seafood included turtles, crabs, shrimp, crawfish, and oysters. Deer, duck, pork, and turkey were favored meats, along with beef. Women on ranches performed many of the same tasks, however, they lived a more isolated life than those in port coastal areas, such as Galveston or Velasco, where boarding houses, hotels, the customs house, and trading posts existed. Regardless of female contributions to the advancement of better lives, it was not until the late 1800s that men decided that women in isolated areas were not more inclined toward insanity than urban females.[73] About 25,000 folks entered Texas through Velasco until cholera in 1832 destroyed the population.[74] Women were the caretakers and nurses, doing all possible to make comfortable those in their care.

Women of Early Texas

Truly, the early Texas women could be labeled necessity entrepreneurs. With her portly Chihuahua by her side, Madam Candelaria greeted guests at her hotel in San Antonio in the 1800s.[75] Sam Houston, Jim Bowie, and other Texians frequented her place of business.[76] She had a reputation as a nurse, supported the Texians in rebellion against Mexico, and later ran a Fandango.[77] Samuel Augustus Maverick of South Carolina went to Texas in 1835 where he joined the Texas Volunteer Army.[78] On a trip to Alabama, he picked up a dropped handkerchief of the lovely Mary Ann Adams.[79] They married after four months of courtship and he moved her to the dangerous city of San Antonio.[80] She was eighteen and he was thirty-three years of age as was the custom of many Texas marriages during those times.[81] She had her ten children, had access to books and novels, ate noon meals, and enjoyed siestas (naps).[82] She rode horses with elite Texans carrying her gun and Bowie knife, and she managed the affairs of her family after her husband's death.[83] She contributed to the development of the Alamo as a memorial, helped build a local church, and was known as a great administrator.[84] Maverick's observations noted that a fourteen-year-old lovely Mexican girl married Greek, Roque Catahdie who bought her an old piano that she mastered, entertaining locals with her immense talent.[85] While one cannot assume the level of her talent reached a professional level, one could accept that she could have given lessons for pay. The belief was that Catahdie obtained the piano to ensure his bride stayed home because of his jealous streak.[86] After an Indian attack, an injured Lieutenant Thompson recovered at Madam Santita's house, indicating that she was a nurse or caretaker in San Antonio. Another sought-after nurse, Mrs. Jacques, ran a boarding house at Commerce Street and Yturri Street. She served a special Easter Sunday meal of simple elegance for many Texan families.

Independence for Mexico in 1821 resulted only in a political victory, certainly not a demographic or social triumph. Three centuries of colonial domination left the country in ruin. An estimate of 200,000 people of African origins had been delivered into Mexico over time. By the eighteenth century, because of dire economic circumstances, slavery had decreased because labor was too cheap.[87] Slaves ran away, or they voiced their discontent through the church and within the Spanish civil legal system. Those of mixed Afro-Mexican origins formed communities and numbered more than one-half million by 1810 and "constituted the largest group of free blacks in the Western hemisphere."[88] Therefore, Mexicans asked the Texans to give up their slaves, and along with Mexico's propensities to ignore the idea of a speedy trial, to ignore any true rule of law or any semblance of individual freedoms, trouble brewed early on. Slavery remained antithetical to the freedoms Mexicans had gleaned from their victory. Texas viewed slavery as essential to their way of life. Current research indicates that Southern parents gave slaves to their daughters as gifts.[89] "One woman, Martha Gibbs, even took enslaved people to Texas and forced them to work for her at gunpoint until 1866, a year after slavery's formal abolition."[90] Women who owned slaves most likely became more attractive brides. New data challenges the common perception of a Southern Belle as the "gentler sex" as some certainly considered their financial stability with the ownership of slaves. The decision by the framers of the 1845 Texas Constitution drew on English common law, rejecting all Spanish Civil Law concepts except for Spanish/Mexican community property laws because women owned large numbers of slaves as their separate property, thus protecting them from irresponsible husbands.[91] During 1836 the estimated population of Texas was 38,470 of which 5,000 were slaves[92]. By the time of statehood in 1845, 30,000 slaves resided in Texas.[93] Most worked on cotton and sugar plantations, but others worked in various urban homes.

Summing up the period leading to statehood for Texas, all attempts by the government of Mexico to control and conform the Texas settlers proved futile. They, unable to stem immigration, unable to abolish slavery, unable to force Catholicism, unable to maintain a stable government, and unable to extinguish English common law found themselves with a mighty insurrection whereby the Texans won independence in 1836. During the revolution, after the terrible defeats at the Alamo and Goliad, men and women living in Central Texas communities fled in what became known as the "Runaway Scrape" to avoid Santa Anna's advancing army.[94] After the Alamo and Goliad, Texans realized that Mexicans showed no quarter, so panic ensued and running seemed logical.[95] Not enough wagons were available to load household goods or to allow women and children to ride instead of walking.[96] Some left meals on the table, gathered what they could handle, and ran, joining other families or women whose husbands were already fighting for independence. Texans won their independence at the Battle of San Jacinto in 1836.

Texas remained an unstable republic, unable to sustain itself financially, and hopeful for a marriage with the United States; and that finally came on December 29th, 1845, when President James K. Polk signed the Annexation Act. Texas, with a new state constitution, became the twenty-eighth star on the US flag. From about 1821 to the Texas Revolution, what few women who resided in Texas found themselves living beyond the pale in a Darwinian state of chaos, and they did so with much grace under unrelenting pressure. While true that women in Texas had not acted as warriors in the Texas Revolution of 1836, they defended their farms, ranches, and towns from Native American attacks.

In preparation for the first anniversary of the victory at San Jacinto, Sam Houston and others prepared to celebrate. The agenda of activities included an evening dance that barely happened because of a shortage of women. Constant dangers abounded in the state after independence and during the fall of 1839, six horse riders from Houston rode to San Antonio—four men and two women—each armed with a pistol and Bowie knives.[97] Never for a moment did they not believe that Native American warriors watched from thick forest near river bottoms.[98] The Comanches and Apache had attacked Spanish Texas for three hundred years, therefore no reason existed that the attacks would stop because the land was now the Republic of Texas.[99] During a confrontation with sixty-five Comanches in March of 1840, who came to San Antonio for a council meeting at the courthouse with military authorities, a huge melee broke out and a female cook working for the Mary Maverick household put herself between an Indian warrior and all the children.[100] She picked up a rock, placed it above her head, and cried out to him, "If you don't go 'way from here I'll mash your head with this rock!"[101] The Comanche ran quickly toward the bank of the nearby river.[102] Dangers from attacks by Native Americans existed all over the state. Ranch life and plantation life continued in the environmentally bifurcated state until the nation broke into a nasty civil war, the worst any nation could fight. Texas would make a fateful decision to join the Confederacy against the advice of their founding father, Sam Houston. Women supported the war efforts during the Mexican-American War after Texas won its independence, and they will do so later in the Civil War.

Chapter Three
Texas Women Adapting and Surviving: 1846-1865

Texans faced major issues between the years of 1846 and 1865, suffering through two wars, two hurricanes, a major ice storm during the winter of 1863–64, and a pink-eye epidemic that temporarily blinded victims during the Civil War.[103] Women formed strong circles of confidence, bound with determination to overcome extremely difficult times that pushed the threshold for survival. Their financial worth inextricably depended on the laws of Texas, written by men. The writing of the Texas Constitution established community property rights that enhanced a woman's ability to control an estate after the death of a spouse, along with her ability to hold separate property.[104] A major issue with Mexico over the exact location of the border between them erupted, leading to a war between Mexico and the United States. In the huge two-day Battle of Buena Vista, General Zachary Taylor's 4,800 men defeated the 15,000-man force under General Santa Anna. The 1849 Treaty of Guadalupe Hidalgo ended the Mexican-American War.[105] Mexico gave up about 500,000 square miles of land in exchange for $15 million while settling $3.25 million in American claims.[106] At President Zachary Taylor's death, Millard Fillmore was sworn in as President on July 9, 1850; he was America's thirteenth leader of thirty states with a population of approximately 23,000,000. The country suffered a financial recession by 1857 as it approached the eve of a civil war with the election of President Abraham Lincoln in 1860. Piecework created steady employment for urban Northeast women, and many young women filled the needs of the textile mills.[107] As immigration increased, the labor pool grew and companies centralized; as a result, piecework decreased while society embraced the ideal woman as homebound without an expectation toward any monetary contribution to family finances. Texas women lived lives that did not conjunct with the increased industrialization of their urban sisters. Many females worked side-by-side with their husbands on farms and ranches in rural Texas creating worth for the family. Texans produced 405,100 bales of cotton from 42,891 farms, with a population of 604,000 by 1860.[108] The burden of survival at the advent of the Civil War changed the landscape for many Texas women as they would fend for themselves and their children during immensely trying times.

Texas, by the 1850s, represented a frontier state confirming outstanding growth as home-seekers sought to improve land either by sod housing, costing just a few dollars, or a substantially improved home that could cost upwards of $250.[109] Plowing forty acres costs about $120 and fencing and other improved farmland could reach slightly over $525. Couples married young and families needed strong sons to plow the land.[110] Population growth in Texas increased as unoccupied, arable lands remained available. Internal expansion slowed at this juncture and Texans continued to move to ranching lands in West Texas. By 1860, the South represented forty-two percent of the improved land in the United States.[111] The area produced 54 percent of the cattle, 43 percent of the corn, 26 percent of the wheat, 36 percent of the dairy cattle, 54 percent of the hogs, 27 percent of the sheep, and 43 percent of horses and mules. The South also produced cotton, rice, and sugar, along with most of the tobacco in the country.[112] Female slaves and female settlers provided much of the labor for this economic growth during the Antebellum period.

Texas' Founding Fathers embraced the concept of community property, and most importantly, they legalized the ownership of separate property for females. Texas represents the only state that protected women's property rights within the constitution, preventing legislatures from adjusting those basic rights without amendments to the constitution. Louisiana established property laws under both French and Spanish hegemony with the idea of the "common fund" coming directly from the Spanish.[113] The Spanish code, according to legal scholars, greatly influenced the laws in Texas. Men in the state did not uniformly relinquish their dominance over women; however, some astute and wise lawyers and various delegates in Texas copied the laws from Louisiana. Spain controlled Louisiana for only thirty-nine years from 1763 to 1802,[114] and the lawmakers absorbed the ideas of community property mostly from French occupation, however, Spanish laws of inheritance were practiced.[115] Lawyers coming to Texas from Louisiana either used Louisiana law books, had trained there, or had become familiar with Spanish and French property laws.[116] Two attorneys, Edward Clark and Philip Cuny, both from Louisiana, became delegates to the 1845 Texas Constitution convention.[117] Louisiana laws on property had been in effect since 1769 and had been recorded in the Louisiana Digest of 1808, and later redone in the 1825 Civil Code. The Anglo-Americans settling in Texas in the 1820s and 1830s believed that Mexican law replicated Louisiana law, and while much of it did, it was by no means thorough. Texas permitted the property laws of Louisiana after the Texas Revolution.

Louisiana appears as the prime mover for community property; however, Texas certainly appears as the fons et origo for the adoption of community property across the Southwest after the results of Manifest Destiny. Therefore, Texas represented the prototype as to how community property for women became the standard in states from Texas to California. As the delegates gathered to write the states' constitutions, the discussion did not necessarily reflect a viable connection to and knowledge of ancient Visigothic law and such was the case with Texas. Mexican laws were repealed before negotiations took place. The notes taken by reporter William F. Weeks during the debates surrounding the writing of the Texas Constitution of 1845 provided insights as to the allowance of community property rights for women. Delegate Armstrong expressed his views that husbands and wives should have equal rights.[118] Delegate Hemphill expressed that by Texas law women are considered "distinct persons, at least so far as their estates or property are concerned."[119] Although it was expressed that Spanish law had ample provisions for all possible contingencies as to how property should be managed in a marriage; "This system has been abolished, and all the regulations about the subject, have been swept off."[120] Even by the current law, before the constitution was finished, a Texas husband had total control of property and any slaves owned by the wife. Discussions extended to husbands that could "lay waste" to a wife's property or fraudulently mismanage the estate. The discussions occurred between majority and minority committees with men who favored community property and men who believed English common law should have been applied. Women, by law, were entitled to one-half of all the property acquired during the marriage. The minority thought it useful to change the portion to one-third of her spouse's estate, at widowhood. Expressed too, the importance of inducements to the "gentler sex" would deny destitution. Some delegates considered the possibility of "tyrannical husbands" who could refuse their spouse support through their wills. The hope by one member desired that no such allowance so "ungracious" be allowed in the Texas Constitution or its laws.[121] The vote supported the addition of Section 18 in the judiciary department. By a tally of thirty ayes in favor of community property protection, over nineteen noes were recorded.[122] Still, those men who wanted the adoption of English common law introduced Mr. Everts, who offered reasons for the vote to be reassessed.[123] His reasoning surrounded his recollection of a case where a man had purchased large amounts of land, acquired a great deal of personal wealth and died, leaving his second wife who was in her early twenties with his fortune and his six-to-seven children received a balance that left them "beggars."[124] Since she supposedly came to the marriage with nothing but her personal clothing, Everts contended that many such cases existed. He argued that although civil law had existed in earlier settlements, the current population understood common law.[125] He insisted that people of French and Spanish descent should hold no sway in Texas. Others argued passionately that a wife's property should be protected in the constitution and beyond the whims of a fickle legislative session that can void a wife's rights, leaving her in tears as her gambler husband loses their property.

James Davis, soldier, politician, and landowner from Liberty County expressed a new mode of thinking about women in a marriage. He logically stated that he favored a separation of the property a wife brought to the marriage. No forced sale of such property should place a woman at the "drudgery of the wash tub, to which the vices or improvidence of her husband may reduce her."[126] "The days have passed away when women were beasts of burden, and as intelligence increases, they will be placed upon the high and elevated ground which rightfully belongs to them. And it is the opinion of the age, that women should be protected in their property."[127] Therefore, English common law should be avoided.[128] Personal property of the females means the following:

> All property, both real and personal, of the wife, owned or claimed by her before marriage, and that acquired afterwards by gift, devise, or descent, shall be her separate property: and laws shall be passed more clearly defining the rights of the wife in relation as well to her separate property as that held in common with her husband. Laws shall also be passed providing for the registration of the wife's separate property.[129]

Arguments by the delegates continued concerning many aspects of the community property laws. The basis of discontent among those who preferred civil law centered around the wife's separate property as subject to confiscation by debtor companies when the husband owed money. If a wife's separate property could be taken, then her financial viability remained in jeopardy. Mississippi had, in 1819, legally permitted white women to own slaves.[130] Some families came into Texas with wives who owned slaves, and the wives maintained separate ownership. Fortunately, Article VII, Section 22 of the Texas Constitution of 1845, protected women in an important way as the delegates agreed to the following:

> The legislature shall have power to protect by law, from forced sale, a certain portion of the property of all heads of families. The homestead of a family, not to exceed two hundred acres of land, (not included in a town or city, or any town or city lot or lots), in value not to exceed two thousand dollars, shall not be subject to forced sale for any debt's hereafter contracted; nor shall the owner, if a married man, be at liberty to alienate the same, unless by the consent of the wife, in such manner as the legislature may hereafter point out.[131]

Texas is home to an environment so varied that farming proved easier in the eastern half while ranching fared better as an adaptive strategy in the western half. By the late 1800s, cattle occupying the Southern part of the United States accounted for one-third of all cattle in the US[132] Because most of that Southern cattle was based in Texas, the state occupied an economic sector described as Western.[133] Texas historians enjoy bantering back and forth over whether the state is Southern or Western. As the iconic and revered Texas historian Walter Prescott Webb argued, "perhaps the most distinctive institution American has produced: the range and ranch cattle industry."[134] In Southwest Texas with horses, longhorns, and Spanish techniques, herding cattle as a method of environmental adaptation spread across the greater Southwest in about one decade.[135] Regardless of cultural differences, all three colonial powers, Spain, France, and England would employ the ranch as the method to control and hold immense expanses of terrain with the fewest humans.[136] Texas is bifurcated environmentally; and Southerners with some Northerners, along with Irish, German, and Swedish émigrés, helped build the state with the initial blessings of the Mexican government, and later with the approval of the Texas government. Texas blossomed with an ethnic milieu that forged the untamed, lawless territory into an eventual, although shaky, republic that finally resulted in its adoption by the United States in 1845 when Texas became the twenty-eighth star on the American flag.[137] Texas ranching helped reinforce the acceptance of community property and a woman's separate property rights and Texas is Southwestern in that respect. Herding, nomadic societies treated women better than sedentary, flora-driven societies. Men seeking domination over previous conquerors and indigenous peoples within challenging environments resulted in the enhanced value of potential brides where greater demographic imbalances existed. As anthropologist Ester Boserup argued when explaining the origin of gender roles, men who plowed continued to dominate women because they became the breadwinners while women retreated to the home as mothers in charge of domestic duties.[138] What may have been a perceived enhancement of male strength became an entrenched reality and men, as "breadwinners," became the "boss" of the family. The whole cultural system of dominance over women evolved over time whereby the treatment of women was institutionalized and became the norm when the economy was agriculturally based. East Texas produced corn, cotton, and a variety of crops. A conclusion may be drawn that if Texas had been a "flora-only" state, women may not have gained property rights. At the intersection of environmental absolutes, legal precedents, and basic human requisites, community property rights for women flourished in the Great Southwest during the time period of confluence and conflict between England, France, and Spain, from exploration to the times of Manifest Destiny.

The Mexican American War 1846-1848

In 1844, a powerful hurricane struck Texas on August 6 at the mouth of the Rio Grande; all homes were destroyed, and seventy people at Brazos Santiago lost their lives, metaphorically representing future events from statehood to war.[139] The presidential election that year launched the fight for Texas to become the twenty-eighth star on the American flag. In an extremely close election, expansionist James K. Polk won over Henry Clay and his "American System."[140] The plots and machinations employed to win the annexation of the Lone Star State ignited divisive political arguments, lasting from President John Tyler's administration to the final adoption of the state in December of 1845. The Mexican's refused to settle the border at the Rio Grande and did not agree to sell California to the US War began quickly and women entered the fray in support roles, titled as camp followers. Women from both countries followed their husbands, doing all the chores and nursing duties necessary to maintain the cleanliness and health of the soldiers.[141] For each unit of about sixty-five men, there were four laundresses who washed clothing, receiving pay based on the quantity finished each day.[142] Illustrations of brave dedication included Sara Bowman who, with other women, filled sandbags at the battle of Fort Texas.[143] Orders placed them in underground weapon storage for protection; however, she refused to obey, instead serving water and food to the troops.[144] Remembered as the "Heroine of Fort Brown," with the title of Colonel Bowman, she was given full military honors at her death.[145] While the actual monetary worth of her efforts and the work of others cannot be quantified, the women brought a touch of home and even though oxymoronic, a bit of civility to war.

The Civil War 1861-1865

Southerners were crushed in the American Civil War by the overwhelming forces of President Lincoln's Union Army, as "the right side won for the right reasons."[146] Because the primary purpose of this endeavor remains economic in nature, a look at how Texans gained access to war matériel proves necessary. While few industries flourished in the state at the start of the Civil War, innovation quickly established new endeavors, including the manufacture of guns, ammunition, uniforms, iron, and salt, among other necessities of war goods.[147] The sale of cotton produced by slaves was transported to Mexico and sold abroad, solving some of the currency issues. However, the Texas Confederate script issued for war purposes continued to lose value as the war continued and near the end, inflation ran rampant.[148] An example of pre-war production quantities on the Levi Jordan Plantation located near the Brazos River in Brazoria County showed that about 134 slaves in 1860 on 600 acres produced 3,000 bushels of corn, 77 bales of cotton, and 193 hogsheads of sugar.[149] By 1860, according to the census, Levi Jordan had 134 slaves.[150] That year, the plantation comprised 600 improved acres and produced 3,000 bushels of corn, 77 bales of cotton, and 193 hogsheads of sugar.[151]

Women living in transitory times between war and peace in Texas had existed beyond the pale, fighting a zero-sum game in a Hobbesian world where civilization remained a distant goal and their dreams remained locked in their minds.[152] However, they remained resilient and determined and they survived using their talents and ingenuity to either earn their livings or act as economic support staff to their husbands. The Civil War had placed women in great jeopardy as they had found themselves keepers of the important "ways of life" while their men were off to war. Texas women had sent hoopskirts to men who failed to fight for the Confederates, while some women had worn symbols of Confederate cockades to show support.[153]

The war years left women with the burden of survival, including the education of children, the growing of foodstuffs and other crops, and the maintenance of their communities, among many other concerns. Women also managed businesses and ran cattle ranches in both east and west Texas. Pork and cornbread fed many during this time. Letters written during wartime by soldiers, wives, daughters, and sisters shed light on home-front life. Weather issues made life miserable for many Southeast Texans, both soldiers and civilians, during the period from December 1863 to January 1864.[154] Sergeant Connor of Spaight's Battalion returned to Texas from battles in Louisiana.[155] On the road to Houston on December 16th, the icy rain started to fall. Impossible to remain on horses, the men walked, feet frostbitten as they proceeded.[156] The horses suffered cuts and bloody legs. The ice and cold persisted until January 6th, 1864.[157] Men and animals perished from the long voyage over icy rivers with ice-water depths from six inches to four feet.[158] Food was scarce, and blankets froze solid, along with saddles and horses.[159] Arrival in Houston found bakeries and liquor shops with no supply.[160] One can conclude that many women and children suffered during this anomalous cold spell.

Women survived in what many called the War of Northern Aggression after their homes and lives were destroyed by consummate warrior, William Tecumseh Sherman on his march to the sea. Destruction and disruption of Southern society, as directed by President Lincoln and Ulysses S. Grant in a joint decision to force the concept of total warfare, placed women in dangerous situations. While Texas escaped the brunt of the Union Army, women in Texas shared their homes with those from Arkansas, Louisiana, and the city of Galveston as people who fled from those war-torn areas poured in, many with their slaves. Women paid high taxes, taught school, and Texans fought bandits in the Hill Country as crimes rose in Houston.

Cornbread sustained many, but malnutrition resulted in severe diarrhea and major outbreaks of whooping cough among children.[161]

An example of Texas grit was Mollie Mann, a bride for only eight months before her new husband Rufus left for the war, leaving her to manage their home in Mount Vernon.[162] While supporting her newborn son and extended female family, she took over the duties of her husband. Blockades of the Mississippi River and along the Gulf of Mexico stifled the arrival of supplies, creating a severe shortage of normally used basics. Soldiers needed clothing and Texas women sewed for them while maintaining gardens and preserving food. The slave population needed food as well. Mollie, along with other females, contracted pink eye that blinded her for twenty days, accompanied by the most horrendous pain she had ever experienced, and considering she had gone through childbirth, one can only imagine. She lamented in a letter to Rufus that there occurred an abundance of illness in one year, more than in many years.[163]

Women in the state whether innately or by necessity were and are tough, tenacious, and as untamed as the Spanish Longhorns that wandered into the state from Mexico long ago. Yet they remained submissive for generations. Chivalry died slowly in Texas, where men used force over logic, and women once dropped their lace hankies, hoping to snare a man who not only struck their fancy but could provide and protect them. Amelia Edith Huddleson Barr came to an untamed Texas with her husband, not suspecting how her life would unfold.[164] The couple could have easily chosen to stay in New York, but he chose to move to a dangerous place. Another destructive hurricane had struck Matagorda, moving northwest toward Columbus, destroying all structures in 1854.[165] She lost two children in infancy during the Civil War. Born in England in 1831, after her father's death, she went to Downham Market to take her "place among the workers of the world."[166] Later as a boarding schoolteacher, she met the wealthy Robert Barr whom she married in 1850.[167] He was swindled by a friend, ending up poor.[168] She lamented that husbands should confide in their wives.[169] They left Scotland for America and ended up in both Austin and Galveston, Texas, beginning in 1856.[170] Ten years in Austin sustained the young couple as she savored the smell of the China trees while watching couples in frontier fashion stroll along the wide highway.[171] On June 24, 1865, in Austin, the local sheriff read the Emancipation Proclamation to the public.[172] Many newly freed Negroes expressed shock that trumpets were not heard, nor cannons fired at such fantastic news.[173] Barr offered her former slave a salary to stay, but Harriet left with her young daughter, choosing to exercise her new-found freedom by seeking more money elsewhere.[174] Until the Union Army arrived during Reconstruction it was noted in Austin that only the women worked. "Men loafed on the streets, or made little camps in the corn fields, for the young ears were ripe and milky and good to eat."[175] The Barr family suffered in Reconstruction, as her husband needed work. After receiving an offer from a cotton company in Galveston, the family moved in hopes of a better life.[176] Instead, Yellow Fever consumed the island.[177] Barr inhaled the salty Gulf of Mexico waters that in no way could wash away the misery of an island shrouded in death. Her husband succumbed with some of her children, however three daughters survived.[178] Texas held no future for the saddened widow, so she moved her family to New York in the fall of 1868.[179] With her heretofore untapped natural talent for writing, she sold an article about Texas.[180] She wrote hundreds of works, including about eighty novels, and then she penned her most famous book, All the Days of My Life.[181] Barr represented in those past times a necessity entrepreneur and an opportunity entrepreneur. She had first doubted her talent, perhaps due to low self-esteem from the perception by males that women had few talents outside of housekeeping. She kept writing until she died in 1919.[182]

Confederates came home in ripped and soiled grey jackets, hungry and exhausted, finding their farms and ranches in states of decay with herds scattered and cattle stolen by Indians. Money proved worthless and real estate values remained depressed. The close of the Civil War found two percent of the US population deceased with twenty-five percent of Southern military-age soldiers either dead or disabled.[183] General Gordon Granger arrived with his Union Forces in Galveston to ensure that Texans would express loyalty to the United States, would free their slaves, and would admit that succession from the Union was illegal.[184] Life for women proved tedious as many widows had to support their families and newly freed black women had to do the same with little assistance. Governor Richard Coke, a former Confederate officer, in a contentious election, beat the Republican Reconstruction Governor E.J. Davis. Texas experienced Reconstruction until the state re-entered the Union with Reconstruction ending on January 17, 1874.[185]

Chapter Four
Transitory Times: An Orphan, A Huntress & Sculptress, A Knitter & Cotton Picker, A Midwife, and Two Cattle & Sheep Divas, 1865-1900

The population of the United States by 1870 was 38,558,371 and the National Weather Service issued its first report in the fall of 1871.[186] Nothing proved so important as weather to Texans as they awakened early to contemplate quotidian chores. At least fifteen major weather disturbances occurred in the Lone Star State from 1867–1899.[187] Some Southern states remained under military occupation within the parameters of Republican Reconstruction until the chaotic election of 1876, when the presidential election led to a showdown in Congress; whereby a compromise placed Republican Rutherford B. Hays in the presidency. The election of Hays precipitated the exodus of occupying Union forces and Texas Democrats wrote another constitution more suited to their independent nature. The dangerous corset-driven fashions with multi-layered petticoats of the Civil War era gave rise to ideas that clothing represented metaphors for gender constraints.[188] All Texans eventually found themselves adjusting to a new paradigm after the Civil War with the necessity to re-establish the state within the Union. In conjunction with the fight for citizenship equality, women in the postbellum period operated as necessity entrepreneurs. Besides new railroad construction and new industries, the state remained mostly agrarian with sharecropping for many of the former slaves. A gradual economic recovery in the Lone Star State eventually allowed women a little more financial security; however, avenues to financial stability remained difficult, tedious, and many times were without true fulfillment, leaving dreams that remained locked within their souls.

The economic role of women in the state expanded some in small towns and growing cities while limited opportunities existed for rural women to enter market-driven jobs. Women operated in an orbit of male-dominated economic activities, revolving around cattle, cotton, and timber. Labor data during the postbellum years adhered to divisions among races.[189] In the overall South, Blacks equaled 1,344,000 of the labor force by 1900, and of those, about a half million were female.[190] Female workers, overall, equaled 663,000, and only 19,000 of them worked outside the South; about 77 percent were black.[191] By 1880, about 12 percent of women in Texas worked as boardinghouse keepers, dressmakers, domestic services, hotel workers, and restaurant workers; however, most worked in agriculture.[192] Many female orphans worked from a young age in the homes of the more well-to-do Texans without recompense or proper human consideration. While few white females sought work outside the home, many black women worked as servants and laundresses.[193] Teaching became a female profession, and they outnumbered males by 1895. On average each month, a female earned $35.50 while a male earned $49.20.[194] A demand for teachers increased as the number of black high schools in Texas outstripped other Southern states.[195] The position of Postmistress allowed women in rural East Texas to exercise financial skills. Some women worked as midwives and dentists; however male doctors began to deliver many of the new Texans at the approach of the new century. A few determined women drove cattle and some managed ranches. The frontier shook the obsolete Victorian Code of subservience as cultured Anglo women gave up the English sidesaddle riding rules, adopting the necessities dictated by the environment.[196] By 1900, the population of Texas reached 3,048,710,[197] and 82.9 percent of those resided and worked in rural settings.[198]

Also, for the women of Texas, the economic catastrophe rendered by the Civil War triggered changes in marriage patterns that influenced the direction of their financial futures. The emphasis on "getting married" at this time in history illustrated the absolute social and psychological significance of this community construct, and the anxiety that shook the souls of women and many men when the war disrupted lives, while deaths by war resulted in a marriage squeeze. When economic opportunities in the Northeast rose for young females, marriage ages increased, and data may be interpreted that Southern Anglo women married earlier because of the lack of any chances outside an agricultural, male-dominated society.[199] Couples in America traditionally married in their early to mid-twenties, after attaining some financial wealth and the ability to purchase land and construct some type of dwelling. Texans, because of cheap land and a lack of females, tended to marry younger. When considering the importance of marriage to both men and women during the Civil War, one must note that "getting married" and forming families remained a top priority. Gossip about marriages and engagements prevailed throughout the war.[200] Diaries, memoirs, and letters revealed that the fear of spinsterhood had provoked much anxiety; however, data conveys that in the long term, their overall fears proved unfounded.[201] Churches, during the war, married couples at night before men left for war. Men worried that sweethearts would replace them with non-fighting men. Some women chose to marry beneath their social status postbellum to attain the prestige of being "married ladies."[202]

Data from the 1880 census revealed that many war widows remained as such, therefore, their financial security and that of their children remained difficult even with small pensions allowed by Texas law in 1899. For these women, earning a living and supporting their children remained paramount and crucial, therefore they embraced entrepreneurial avenues in various forms. As widows, sometimes with as many as ten children, they survived by any means possible. In the West and on the Texas Frontier, men outnumbered women, therefore the prevalent sex competed for brides during the great migration period. Even with many bachelors in early Texas to choose from, some women had little discretion as to whom they married. Simply attaining a home sufficed as logic to marry any man who desired to marry them. Most women made their lives work within the orbit of their husbands' methods of earning money. The greatest change came for newly freed black women as they were now able to legally marry, have choices of potential husbands, and form traditional families. Antebellum rules prevented slaves from the opportunity to enter contracts, as they were considered morally unfit for legal marriages.[203] Having their marriages legalized informed their overall citizenship rights. As conversations and gossip concerning courting, engagements, and the fear of spinsterhood proved so relevant for white women during the Civil War, the Reconstruction period found that legally sanctioned weddings provided the strength and dignity black women so embraced and relished during the transition from female slave to female citizen.[204] Such realities reinforced that basic human connections formed in marriage represented the primary foundation from which dreams could flourish, although many decades passed before black women had open access to the fulfillment of those hopes and aspirations.

An Orphan

Women worked hard and tirelessly, as exemplified by orphaned Mathilda Doebbler Gruen Wagner, who provided a record of her heartbreaking life story as a child given no comfort by those who used and abused her in the Fredericksburg/San Antonio area. Born August 29th, 1856, she worked her whole life from childhood and continued quilting up to the age of eighty-one.[205] After what could be described as a most miserable childhood, she never felt that the work ethic should be abandoned, even when taking time to heal during sickness. Her contributions to the foundation of Texas deserve accolades. Her family originated in Germany and her father, a stonemason, built a two-room house on some farmland near Fredericksburg. After another little sister was born, and while Mathilda was young and small, her mother suffered a nosebleed, and then a fly infected her nose, causing a painful death. For whatever reasons, her father proved unable to care for his daughters, and the children were split up between other families. Her sister worked in a sugar press, crushing her fingers. The treatment included wrapping the whole hand in bandages. Unfortunately, the fingers grew together, and the hand proved useless later. Mathilda seldom saw her family during these times.[206]

Mathilda reflected on life in Fredericksburg in the 1800s as a period in which Texans, especially the women, had troubled times. Indians came to Fredericksburg to trade beads and pecans for needed goods. She remembered they mostly wanted to obtain food and other necessities; however, some scalped two girls and cut their breasts off, fomenting anger by the locals. Mathilda's father remarried a "mean" woman who ruled the roost with an iron skillet. He gathered his daughters, bringing them home, however, Mathilda's life failed to substantially improve. Fortunately, plentiful meat fed the family, and coffee, in good supply, sustained them at all meals and in between. Flour encased in sheets was stored in barrels and grain was sold in town. She wore dresses made from cloth that farmers' overalls were sewn. Her stepmother had two sons and additional children were born, one of which Mathilda had little choice but to become his caretaker. Forced to cut sugar cane while also responsible for the toddler, she failed to keep the boy from walking on hot coals under the molasses boiler. The stepmother struck her with a plank of wood causing serious pain and refused the young girl food that day. Another incident where the boy slammed his hands in the heavy door of the smokehouse caused the stepmother to deny food to her. Her father attempted to cook some eggs in a skillet, however, the stepmother jerked it off the chimney fire and threw the pan and all out the door. Many times, the children went to bed hungry.[207]

Mathilda found herself sent away once more to live and work with a family in San Antonio. Again, she did housework and ran errands. For one dollar a month, she attended school where only German was spoken while learning reading, writing, spelling, and arithmetic. Never allowed to play after church on Sundays, when other kids were out, she did household chores. While running errands, people sometimes gave her material for a dress, which excited her because she sometimes had more than two dresses that she desperately tried to keep clean. She remembered the cholera outbreak in San Antonio, most likely the one that occurred in 1866 that killed an estimated 293 out of a population of about 12,000.[208] More orphans will attempt to survive. The deceased had been mostly wrapped in sheets and buried in trenches. In the summer, Mathilda traveled to New Braunfels, on orders of the family she lived with, to pick cotton where the noon meal was cornbread and buttermilk. Daily, she walked a long distance to the cotton fields and slept on the floor with a small pillow and no coverlet. The twenty-five cents she was paid, for each hundred pounds of cotton, went to the family she lived with and not a dime was shared with Mathilda.[209]

When she was older, Mathilda worked for the wife of the mayor of San Antonio; she cleaned all the pots and pans that hung in the kitchen every Saturday, rubbing them with ashes. The mayor's wife obsessed over her oleander bushes and required that all leaves had to be washed "leaf by leaf." Contracting typhoid fever required that Mathilda's long, thick hair had to be cut. Her hair represented her pride, and cutting it devastated her. Never given a proper Christmas gift, she occasionally received a few nuts or a small bag of candy. When older, she seemed to forgive her father as she stated, "My father sent his little children away so if they had to suffer, he would not see it."[210] She wondered whether a search for her would have been undertaken had she gone missing when a heavy rain filled irrigation ditches and two Mexican children were lost and the mayor organized a search party. Mathilda questioned her self-worth. Again, when she was fourteen years of age, her father reached out for her and returned her to his home. She met twenty-seven-year-old Fredrick William Gruen, and they married in her fifteenth year. He was not exactly her choice of husband, but at least she would live in a home as a wife. Her life was like so many others during those times, filled with activities such as baking, working in the fields, candle-making, soap-making, sewing, and any other of the numerous tasks necessary to sustain life. By 1890, the family sold their land and moved to Kerrville. Making a living proved difficult so the family took in boarders. However, a pregnant Mathilda worked to sustain the family because cultural practices dictated that the female complete the indoor work necessary to run the boarding house. Her husband absolutely refused to assist, as social mores dictated. After he accidentally shot and killed himself, she later married again after spending many years in San Antonio running another boarding house with her six children, who also worked to support the family. Overall, she had eight children and helped rear two stepchildren.[211]

Mathilda Doebbler Gruen Wagner's life in Texas resembled that of part slave and part servant. Few orphanages existed in the area during those times, and one doubts that her life would have been better in an institutionalized setting. She contributed life skills to her family, to those whose homes she worked, and to the collective growth of Texas as one of many women who helped establish the state. While impossible to place a dollar value on her contributions, she adapted to various environments and suffered indignities, but taught her children the same work ethic that made her feel guilty when she broke her hip and could not continue sewing at eighty-one. Texas was a tough place for a woman, but she was a tough woman who made her way under stressful circumstances.

A Huntress and a Sculptress

During the great cattle drives from Texas northward during the open range days, cattle divas from various ranches worked alongside their husbands and the hired cowboys to maintain homes and market their herds, thereby enriching their families. Unlike some frontier women who found the wild lands "hard, unlovely, unrelieved, unbeautified,"[212] and laced with "greed, godlessness, and profanity" whereby children turned into "debased imitations of men and women,"[213] these "grit to the backbone"[214] Texas ladies embraced the struggles on the plains of Texas, enduring rain, heat, cold, tornadoes, hurricanes, sandstorms, stampedes, Indian attacks, scorpion stings, rattlesnake bites, brush fires, and sickness. Ella Elgar Bird Dumont, originally from Mississippi, came to Texas after the Civil War with other relatives in covered wagons. After several moves, the family settled in Young County in the Panhandle of the state, occupied by more Indians than settlers.[215] What happened that changed her life seemed unlikely on the sparsely populated plains. She recorded the actions that changed her life. "My brother-in-law, Willie Fite, opened the door, and there I beheld, mounted on the most beautiful big black horse I had ever seen, a man, yes, a man, in full Western attire, that of a Texas Ranger, gallant, and brave in appearance."[216] Married in 1876, she was a young teenager, and he was about twenty-nine years of age; the couple settled on land alongside buffalo, antelope, deer, and other wild animals.[217] Her husband gave her his prized Winchester so he could teach her to shoot. Together, they earned a living shooting buffalo and sending the hides to market. Fascinated by gyp rock in the area, she whittled shapes out of the rock. She considered her home in the wilds "a real little love nest" and the marriage proved happy. She enjoyed the art of carving gyp rock and shooting her rifle. After Indian attacks, snow-driven winters, and the decimation of the buffalo, the Birds sought new ways to earn their living, including selling the hides of other animals. Ella used her talents to make vests and gloves needed by cowboys. Payment came in the form of cattle, and a small herd was formed. In 1881, Ella delivered a son and the family decided that her husband would become a ranch hand. Living in what amounted to a dugout suited her as most never expected anything fancier on the frontier. While caring for her baby, she spent hours alone on the ranch while the men worked the cattle. Since no dinner table existed, she figured rightfully so that she could make a table with all the saws, hammers, and wood available. Ella worked quickly while the child slept and by the evening meal, a tablecloth adorned her creation. The three cowhands teased her rather incredulously—a woman made a table! At that juncture, she wished she "had never heard of a table." [218]

As nomads, the Birds moved to another ranch when the previous one sold. Food proved plentiful as they raised chickens, kept cows, and ate much turkey meat. She preserved plums, berries, and grapes. Her husband returned to their first home together, where Ella had left her father's book collection and her sixty pieces of art carvings—and they had been stolen, all her work never found! "I wanted to be a sculptor."[219] Happiness came when a six-pound little girl entered their lives. During the coming years, the Birds moved from ranch to ranch, losing their daughter to a fever. The son survived and another daughter came in 1886. As the Birds thought of settling in a permanent home, the husband's health began to fail and, on a journey, to scout the mountains of New Mexico, he died alone in the wilderness. Ella shook in pain as her heart broke with the news of her beloved husband's death. After nine years of sewing gloves, beading vests for cowboys, and tending her cattle with the help of ranchers in the area, she married August Dumont, a businessman and sheriff in Paducah, Texas. Only for a short while had she worked as a sculptor for a monument company in Dallas before returning to Paducah to marry and live her days in a white Victorian home. She lost one of two sons with Dumont and her only surviving daughter died as a teen of a fall from a horse.[220] She survived all the grand adventures and trials and tribulations, hopeful that her children could experience life in a more civilized Texas. As happy as she had been, especially with her first marriage, Ella never fulfilled her dream of becoming a professional artist. Perhaps, in another time, we might have been viewing her sculptures in a garden far from the Panhandle of Texas.

A Knitter and Cotton Picker

As a child, Mrs. Mose "Granny" Jones provided freshly knitted socks for a cat so it could romp in the snow in Texas.[221] With her family, she moved from Missouri to Texas on March 18, 1850, later moving to Lamar County by 1858.[222] After marrying Mose Jones, the family moved a couple of times to various West Texas counties.[223] During the Civil War, her knitting skills served her well as she made over 159 pairs of socks eventually delivered to Confederate soldiers. Her education came from a McGuffey's Reader and a Blue Back speller.[224] Each fall, she picked cotton and separated the seeds with a rudimentary cotton gin concocted by her father, as the Eli Whitney cotton gin had not yet arrived in Texas.[225] "Granny" Jones represented a pioneer spirit that moved Texas forward with her community spirit, which garnered her a special 100th birthday party on Sunday, March 18th, 1950, when 430 celebrants came to Plainview to honor her for her great generosity and overall kindness.[226] Three birthday cakes and dinner for 200 capped off a great celebration.[227] She attributed her few gray hairs to her lye soap shampoo.[228] Although the date is unclear, "Granny" was featured on a Friday morning on an NBC radio program titled "Breakfast in Hollywood," where she gladly gave advice for living, "Be yourself and find trust in God."[229] Showered with many flowers and gifts, she celebrated with her eight children, twenty-five grandchildren, thirty great-grandchildren, and eleven great-great-grandchildren, most of whom were Texans from all over the state.[230] "Granny" moved Texas forward, leaving a loving and most likely productive progeny that continued her good name and promotion of the soul and worth of Texas.

A Midwife's Tale of Birthing Babies and Roping Cows

The history of midwifery in the United States and in the South illustrated that the system of child delivery by females dominated until the late 1800s and early 1900s when the practice of medicine became professionalized.[231] Doctors gradually introduced childbirth into their duties between 1910 and 1920, as the practice enriched the training of new doctors at newly established charity hospitals. In raw Texas and on early Spanish ranches, midwives contributed their skills to the process.[232] With the arrival of slaves into Texas, female slaves known as "granny midwives" assisted with deliveries of both black and poor whites unable to pay a doctor. Generally, midwives received nominal compensation, or a chicken, or household goods.[233] At the age of thirteen, Mary Holmsley began assisting her father, a frontier doctor living in Runnels County Texas in 1893 after he lost a section of an arm and suffered an accident that damaged his remaining hand.[234] After her marriage to Joe Holmes Neely, the family moved to Hudspeth County, where she ministered to people on both sides of the Rio Grande, acting not only as a midwife but also as a medic.[235] She roped and milked wild cows to feed her family.[236] She and her husband managed ranches and eventually purchased land for their ranch. Standing almost five feet tall, she tackled heavy ranch work, later reading daily to her children as a believer in education.[237] After gaining a good reputation, people referred to her as Grandma Neely. Cattle rustlers roamed the area, along with panthers and rattlesnakes. As a self-taught intellectual, she read Einstein, Plato, and Solzhenitsyn from her later well-stocked library, and she had the time to relish her growth because she lived to 105.[238] Her birthday, December 28, 1985, became Mary Neely Day, as proclaimed by former governor Mark White.[239] Known to cuss up a storm when herding her goats,[240] she had spent her life bounding wounds, nourishing souls, and delivering future Texans and Mexicans, living a grand life of giving to her community.

Cattle and Sheep Divas

Both cattle and sheep formed a financial foundation for Texas. Growth after the Civil War came from thousands of miles of new railroad tracks that launched new cities and delivered new immigrants to the state.[241] Railcars moved cattle, crops, and timber to market. Women accompanied and worked on some of these endurance cattle drives, and they managed sheep ranches, selling their wool to Northeast buyers eager for good quality products. Ranchers with hired hands drove Texas Longhorns sometimes as far north as Canada to sell herds to those hungry for beef in the times after the Civil War. Although the cowboy history is short-lived due to the invention of barbed wire and other factors, the mystique established during those times earned Texans a reputation for dogged determination and fierce independence. Two such women included Johanna Carolyn Wilhelm, known as the "Sheep Queen of West Texas," and Lizzie Johnson Williams, known as a Texas "Cattle Queen," and businesswoman.[242]

As the bride of Johan Wilhelm, Johanna Carolyn Wilhelm, born in Germany in 1850, arrived in Texas at the age of eighteen in 1868.[243] She and her husband originally held about 40,000 acres in West Texas where they grew sheep, sold wool and raised cattle as well.[244] Life for her proved difficult as she lost her husband in 1890 when a cattle rustler shot and killed him.[245] Her eldest son died on the range about a year later and she had nine children to provide for alone.[246] She owned about 10,000 sheep in both Menard and McCulloch counties, making her the woman with the most sheep in Texas as compared to other women.[247] The extraordinary contribution of Johanna Wilhelm remains amplified because her daughter Kuhne Gunda Wilhelmina Wilhelm carried on her mother's legacy of selling wool that achieved top-quality status in Texas.[248] Emil Haby was born January 15, 1867, in San Antonio, Texas and he married Kuhne Wilhelm in 1897, the union produced four children.[249] Emil came to Lampasas in 1906 from Smithville where he purchased the ice plant and rebuilt it.[250] He sold it in 1926 to the Texas Power and Light Company and moved with his family to his wife's estate where he engaged in ranching activities, buying additional ranch land.[251] Walter Haby, after receiving his degree from Texas A&M in animal husbandry operated the ranch for fifty-seven years.[252] Again, the family produced fine-quality mohair and wool. After Walter Haby's death, his nephew William McFarland ran what was now called Calf Creek Ranch.[253] He passed in 1996, leaving his wife and daughters to manage the working ranch, presently a cattle ranch, that modified their business plan to include hunting leases for deer, dove, and turkey.[254] Johanna Carolyn Wilhelm laid a strong business platform for her dedicated progeny. She helped create a financially successful Texas.

Lizzie Johnson Williams, the Texas titan of business and lady who traveled with her cattle up the Chisholm Trail, in some ways replicated the financial story of Hetty Green the Northeastern female investor known as the "Witch of Wall Street."[255] The women contemporaries lived in the 1800s, with Williams dying in 1924 while Green passed in 1916.[256] Unlike Carnegie, Rockefeller, and others hailed historically as brilliant businessmen, regardless of the descriptive term "Robber Barons," the female anomaly's brainpower equated a comparison with a witch during America's great financial rise. Green outsmarted many speculators, bankers, and Wall Street geniuses. Both Lizzie and Hetty had insatiable appetites for knowledge. While Green read everything possible about the stock market, Williams began her career as a strict, demanding teacher with an eye for minute details.[257] Both women married men who seemed unfit for them, and both must have had some reservations concerning their choice of mates because both chose to have strong prenuptial agreements whereby their husbands could not infringe legally on the wealth the ladies accumulated. For maven Williams, the decision to prevent her husband from claiming any portion of her property defied the Community Property Laws of the state of Texas yet affirmed her business knowledge and independence.[258] However, she had been smitten with the handsome Hezekiah Williams, an excessive drinker and preacher.[259] Both women bailed their husbands out of financial disasters.[260] Each became known for specific life habits that rendered them eccentric by the social standards of the times. Williams flavored her life with expensive diamonds and extraordinary outfits while negotiating with a local diner to keep her soup and crackers at the same price, even when other diners paid more.[261] Williams built up her herds and she exercised good business acumen as to when she should buy or sell. Her several trips on the trail with her husband while riding in a buggy took place between 1879 and 1889.[262] Instead of her fancy, expensive clothing, she chose calico skirts with petticoats and as custom of the day, a bonnet on her head and a shawl if needed.[263] Lizzie drew much attention on the trail and she relished every gift of "wild fruit, prairie chicken, and antelope's tongue."[264] Her meticulous record-keeping would make an accounting professor smile. Paying her cowhands at the end of the trail, she kept daily tallies of hours and subtracted overhead costs[265]. She kept a keen eye on profits. After her husband died when she was seventy, Lizzie continued her real estate business and other endeavors, however, she lost the zeal for life without Hezekiah.[266] Nevertheless, she remained resolute and strong and was known as the queen of cattle ranching. She died a wealthy frontier rancher who had stunned bankers when she paid off notes with cash stuffed in a red bandana. She broke a mold that only men could borrow money, make money, build an empire, and drive cattle.

The end of the century found about fifteen percent of Texan females receiving pay for their labor, while most remained within the confines of the home.[267] Woman suffrage failed to muster enough concern by the Texas House of Representatives to be released from committee.[268] Almost eighty-three percent of Texans remained in rural areas,[269] earning their livings from cotton, corn, timber, ranching, and the start-up of the oil industry. Women assisted in all areas of the economic growth of the state, either as employees or as foundational family support, allowing their husbands to earn a living. The loss of slave labor did not marginalize the cotton industry in Texas as Mexican labor picked the valuable crop around many parts of the state.[270] At the close of the century, cotton production grew from 350,628 bales in 1869 to 3.5 million bales.[271] Coastal Texans had lived through an 1867 hurricane that came inland south of Galveston, ravishing the entire coast from the Sabine to the Rio Grande.[272] Towns at the mouth of the Rio Grande simply vanished. Galveston flooded, and the damage proved substantial.[273] Texans managed to survive the Recession of 1873 and suffered through five more hurricanes leading up to the turn of the century, one of those inundated land about twenty miles inland in Jefferson County with every home shaken from their foundations and 150 dead.[274] As a journal stated, the first thing entered every day was the weather conditions because the weather was the single controlling factor in any family's ability to live and survive.[275] Weather patterns on February 14th and 15th, 1895, resulted in a massive cold spell that brought snow and ice to the whole Texas coast with over fifteen inches of snow in Galveston.[276] Cattle froze in place and would freeze again during the freeze of February 1899.[277] The temperature in Brownsville remained sixteen degrees Fahrenheit for two days, triggering the destruction of crops.[278] Texans remained resilient and determined. Many women across the state continued in planting and hoeing gardens, washing and ironing clothing, cooking all meals, knitting socks, carding wool, rendering tallow, making quilts, and milking cows while the division of labor found men branding cattle, butchering and curing meat, plowing, planting, hauling manure, cutting and curing hay, gathering watermelons, and digging potatoes.[279] Some crossover occurred, depending on family circumstances. Overall, in 1898, the United States had annexed Hawaii and fought and won the Spanish-American War with the assistance of many former Texas Rangers organized in the state by future president Theodore Roosevelt.[280]

The advent of the new century metaphorically finalized the transition of the creation of a new people—the Americans, the Texans that became Americans but insisted on embracing their exclusive brand of identity, and the "free range" ranch women and housebound females on the numerous farms who, together, assisted in the transformation. All had occurred by forced adaptations, changing cultural patterns, an amalgamation of peoples from numerous countries, and the reshaping of institutions and legal systems. The frontier had been settled by 1890 as Texas, and the women who helped build the state, faced the next set of challenges.

Chapter Five
A New Century of Texas Women: Chatelaines to Bread Makers and Beyond

Joseph Draper Sayers governed the state of Texas when the September 8, 1900 hurricane—the deadliest natural disaster in the United States history—devastated the island of Galveston, killing upwards of 8,000 people.[281] The population of the country totaled 76,212,168, and the population of Texas was 3,896,542. President William McKinley died from an assassin's bullet on September 14, 1901, at 2:15 A.M.; and later that day, Theodore Roosevelt took the presidential oath, introducing the Progressive Era.[282] Orville and Wilbur Wright took flight at Kitty Hawk, North Carolina on December 17, 1903.[283] At the 1904 World's Fair and Exposition in St. Louis, a Texas-originated soft drink, Dr Pepper, received accolades.[284] Varied by the weather and topography of the massive state, twenty-seven cultural groups calling the state home created a fusion of foods that became known as Texas Cuisine.[285] Fashions for women transitioned from the Victorian styles to the Edwardian Era, and before its sinking in 1912, the RMS Titanic set the stage for opulence that quickly faded at the start of World War I in 1914.[286] Men collected Japanese swords and women embraced silks. Young, well-to-do women embraced the new silhouette of a long tube shape topped with wide, decorated hats. The narrow skirts prevented women from taking long strides that metaphorically equated to the tiny steps in the fight to enact fully defined civil rights for all women. Twenty-one percent of Texas women worked outside the home, with thirty percent working in major cities by 1910.[287] While much of the state remained rural and women supported the farm or city home, females of all cultural backgrounds did business in Texas. The following examples explore the efforts of women to earn money and to support the state economy in changing times as the Industrial Revolution transformed the direction of Western Civilization and the world.

The Chatelaine of Boquillas

Maria "Chata" Sada operated a motel, restaurant, and trading post on the Texas side of the border across the Rio Grande in the Big Bend area.[288] Born in Mexico in 1884, she married Juan Sada in 1901. Leaving her husband but not her marriage, "Chata" settled in Boquillas, where she sold fresh tortillas included in a twenty-five-cent meal. Newspaper men visited her adobe establishment, enjoying fiery tamales and tasty chili served on a table set with ironed and starched flour sacks. Due to the opening of Big Bend National Park in 1944, and after the death of her husband, she relocated to Del Rio, living with one of the many orphans the couple had cared for during their lifetime. Her many talents included acting as a teacher, priest, judge, midwife, and medic.[289] Reports indicated that food critic Duncan Hines recommended "Chata's" outpost cuisine.[290] She reigned as 'the Chatelaine of Boquillas, Texas," according to Fort Worth reporter Presley Bryant.[291]

A Strong East Texas Woman

The aftermath of crises had fertilized the growing hope that women would be treated more equally, however, realization of those hopes proved more elusive between the years of 1865 and the start of the twentieth century. The Franklins and the Drivers left Alabama after the Civil War for new land and a new start.[292] Both male patriarchs had served in the Confederacy.[293] The families ended up in various cities in East Texas, including Nacogdoches, Cherino, Camp Ruby, Camp Nancy, and Zavalla where female descendants faced harsh lives in lumber camps. Mary Carlotta Driver Franklin ran a boarding house in Nancy, Texas, to support her family when her husband perished in 1916.[294] Her son died in 1922 from leftover complications of the worldwide Flu Pandemic after contracting the disease at the exact time he was drafted for World War I. Mary Franklin's granddaughter stated that she served meals aboard a railcar, feeding lumber workers from Camp Nancy on the Texas and New Orleans Railroad.[295] The Angelina County Lumber Company operated in the longleaf pine area between Nancy and Manning.[296] Mary Franklin's daughter Mary Alabama Franklin, born in 1909, had lost her father when she was eight years of age. As a teen in 1927, she married lumber camp medical doctor Charles Alexander Chamber's son, Robert E. Chambers, whose namesake was General Robert E. Lee of the Confederacy. The son worked as a forest ranger and was highly thought of in the community and loved by his family.[297] Nevertheless, he strongly directed all the activities of his wife and children. He had wooed her with a special ruby ring. Mary Alabama "Bama" Franklin Chambers, a hazel-eyed, raven-haired beauty ran a store in Zavalla during World War II that her husband had purchased and remodeled. Earlier in the Great Depression, she ran the first telephone company switchboard in the small town. Her husband traveled throughout East Texas and the South, scouting for proper trees to build military barracks during World War II and monitoring German Prisoner of War camps in East Texas. She had dreams of being an artist and expressed that she did not understand why "a woman could not get what a man could get."[298] While a widow in her seventies, she took art lessons at Angelina Junior College and left her artwork to her family on her death in 1998. She had wanted more than the eighth-grade education, which was the norm in Texas at the time. Throughout most of her life, she rose before dawn, "put on her face with powder, rouge, and lipstick," and prepared three meals each day; she picked vegetables, churned butter, shelled peas and beans, shucked bushels of corn, made jams and jellies, fed the poor, cared for eight grandchildren over time in the summers, set "china and crystal stemware" tables in their formal dining room, attended church each time the door was opened, took the census in her area; and yet she could not buy a new dress or a pair of high heels without her husband's visual approval. Moreover, she was only allowed money for one stamp each week to write to one of her three grown children. Into the 1950s, her husband monitored the gas mileage on the family vehicle daily after he arrived home in his work truck. She only had permission to drive to a small store on the highway to pick up the mail. Bama, as she was called, exercised discretion when taking the census in Angelina Country when she faced folks who had no birth certificates. She inquired as to the birthdays of a farmer's three boys. The father looked somewhat puzzled, so she asked what the weather was like when the boys were born. He relayed that one was born when it was hot, one was born when it was hot-hot, and the last one came when it was hot-hot-hot. So, she assigned the boys' birthdays respectively for June, July, and August, each around the middle of the month, while figuring from their heights that they were about two years apart. Chambers, a true woman of substance, could make decisions; however, like so many widows of her time, she outlived her funds while surviving twenty-six years after her husband passed.[299]

West Texas Postmistress

Until 1916, Elizabeth Boyle Smith ran the post office from her ranch home in West Texas, located at Mount Blanco on the only road accessing the Llano Estacado in Crosby County, north of Lubbock.[300] An adventurous soul, Elizabeth had followed her brothers to Texas from Scotland where she met and married rancher and businessman Henry Smith, who became known as "Uncle Hank" while she was affectionately called "Aunt Hank."[301] Her career braided together many skills and in 1988 the National Cowgirl Museum and Hall of Fame inducted Elizabeth Boyle Smith into that institution. With her husband, they opened the first hotel on the plains of West Texas—the Occidental.[302] Hundreds of cattle filled their ranchland, and they enjoyed life in a two-story home of twenty-two-inch-thick Blanco Canyon stone.[303] She fed anyone who crossed her path who needed feeding; she also taught in the first school, and at times acted as a doctor and a nurse until she died in 1925.[304] As a postmistress, she reflected the practice of many smaller communities across the whole state.

In the South, after the Civil War to 1868, the position of postmaster, which is the true term whether male or female, required that no voluntary assistance had been rendered to the Confederacy; therefore, women in Texas filled that job.[305] The trend took hold, with many more females holding those prestigious roles in both East and West Texas. Both world wars solidified the function, as females filled the positions when men fought in various theaters around the world, allowing women opportunities not found in many businesses. By 1958, the United States Post Office employed more women in management than any other entity in the world.[306] During that same year, the Corpus Christi station under female management had over a million dollars in annual receipts. By 2008, females represented sixty-one percent of the 25,089 postmasters in the country.[307] Throughout many rural areas of the state, postmistresses held a starring role in their communities, taking on challenges that improved the lives of those citizens, while earning money as incremental income for their families.

Oil Changes Everything

A single event on one special day changed the direction of Texas and that event was the discovery of oil at Spindletop in Beaumont on January 10, 1901. The recovery of oil from the Texas landscape, both East and

West Texas, represented in every way a male-driven, high testosterone endeavor and was exampled by landmen, roughnecks, and hard-drinking, fist-fighting Wildcatters.[308] Women lived in tents and make-do shacks in the deserts of West Texas. Brothels and gambling places dotted the streets of Beaumont and Port Arthur. Ready-to-wear clothing proved difficult to find in the state. The life of the wife of an oil field worker involved extreme flexibility as the work followed the discovery of new oil fields; therefore, the many moves thwarted the chance for the female to work a steady job.[309] Much like migrant farm workers, Texas families lived migratory lives for over fifty years.[310] In many ways, adjusting to life in the oil fields of the state reinforced the traditional roles of females as homemakers while women brought to those fields as much civilization as humanly possible. Without permanent homes, women rarely had opportunities to fulfill any dreams of working for pay in any normal sense of the word. Oil field settlements, known as "ragtowns," consisted of tents and makeshift shacks.[311] As one oil executive knew when addressing the issue of keeping good "roughnecks," hiring the man meant also hiring the wife.[312] The insular traditional roles typified by the nature of the oil industry prevented changing gender roles in Texas. Men continued as breadwinners, and women accepted new positions in society, as many of their husbands had succeeded in the oil industry. Better living conditions along with discretionary funds allowed for expensive goods such as diamonds and furs. Maybe in an unexpected way, women intensified the motivation for companies that sold all the accoutrements females demanded to live good lives as the state embraced modernity. Both men and women originated some of these future enterprises, however, women instigated the passion to do so. Therefore, women triggered the formation of companies that yielded profits, which increased the state's overall wealth. Strong demand for home goods resonated with females who sought beauty, comfort, and relief from the drudgery of daily living. Men wrote books, fought wars, engineered automobiles, built roads, dammed rivers, drilled for oil, built ships and flying contraptions, negotiated business deals, cut forests, operated companies, ran governments, preached the gospel, and made money; while women desired ready-made clothing, useful furniture, ice boxes, china, drapes, maternity clothes, streamlined food products, sewing machines, better selections of fabric, modern cookware, and a wider assortment of soaps and personal products. The search for a beautiful life that philosophers from Plato to

Aristotle found a necessary component of a life well-lived, kindled, and yielded rewards as enterprising females found circuitous ways to satisfy innate needs. "Beauty itself is but the sensible image of the infinite," said the US historian George Bancroft (1800–1891).[313] While there may not be a single common element in what humans define as beauty, one may surmise that most women know it when they see it or accomplish the concept in numerous ways to bring pleasure to one's life.[314] Women tamed Texas, and Texas produced some quite outrageous women who did so.

Carrie Neiman Dresses the Nouveau Oil-Rich

In 1907, a young Jewish family opened a store in Dallas that would eventually satisfy the wants of newly minted oil millionaires. Carrie Marcus had graduated from high school in 1902, working to become the top salesperson for A. Harris and Company.[315] Carrie Marcus married Abraham Lincoln Neiman in 1905, and with twenty-five thousand dollars, they opened the iconic Neiman Marcus specialty store. Her husband's infidelities drove her to divorce in 1928.[316] Her brother purchased her former husband's interest. [317] Outfitted in her little black dress, she latched her pearls around her neck and went to work showing wealthy women how to dress.[318] She became head of the company in January 1951; however, it was only after the death of her brother. [319] Sales reached twenty-one million dollars that year.[320] Wives of wildcatters, some of whom had once lived in oil shacks and suffered through desert sandstorms while their husbands struck oil in West Texas, frequented the store for designer dresses and fur coats. Carrie Marcus delivered beauty, sophistication, and civilization to newly rich Texans.

A Rebellious Oil Journalist

By 1900, Ada Elliott's family left Arkansas for Waco, Texas.[321] By 1905, as a teen, she traveled the South with a vaudeville cast.[322] After attending Baylor University for a year, she taught school at Bugscuffle near Waco.[323] During her college days, she defended, in an organized protest, for the right of a Socialist to speak on campus. Her ideas may have carried over to her time living in Desdemona, once known as Hogtown, an oil boomtown located in Eastland country near Abilene, Texas. With her mayor husband, they published the Desdemona Oil News after a gusher blew on September 2, 1918. This town, now dissolved, gained the reputation as the worst oil boom town in Texas. "Hogtown, for sheer bad manners, was the worst oil boom town in Texas history, according to those myth-making experts who followed oil booms," A.C. Greene wrote of the town, "Tales of Hogtown during the wicked oil days are too lurid for these pages but we can say that its debauchery might be so well remembered because so much of it supposedly took place in broad daylight and sometimes not in private."[324] The Texas Rangers quelled the outrageous behaviors.[325] The town formed a baseball rivalry between the Desdemona Socialists and the Desdemona Democrats.[326] Socialism, although not thought highly of in most of the state, took some roots here. Their strong rivalry angered the Democrat that owned the field, leading to the Socialists demanding to purchase the playing field.[327] The newspaper assisted with funds to buy the land at the outrageous price of fifty dollars an acre.[328] Fantastically, oil later flowed from that land, resulting in riches for the Socialists![329]

Ada Elliott found herself gambling in a cantina near the Mexican revolutionary, Pancho Villa, in Nogales, Mexico, and in the Great Depression days, Broadway beckoned as she acted in Three Men on a Horse, Blind Alley, and Evening Star.[330] She later ran a Dallas boardinghouse, and while enjoying a corncob pipe, she penned three books.[331] The creative actress, journalist, Socialist, gambler, and woman of multifarious talents also wrote about her medical hypnosis encounters. She rode through the state of Texas on horses, in buggies, and on trains, fighting for female suffrage.[332] Ada proved that a woman could "mix it up" in the oil industry, speak up when her beliefs demanded, write when few women did, operate a business, and live an expansive, well-decorated life while earning a salary.

A Grocery Empire

As of May 24, 2020, Charles Butt and family were worth 10.7 billion dollars.[333] H.E.B. grocery stores number 316 in Texas and another fifty-two stores in Mexico.[334] The person that placed the family among America's richest privately owned companies was his grandmother, Florence Butt, who gambled her sixty dollars of savings when she opened a tiny grocery store in Kerrville, Texas, in 1905, offering credit and home delivery.[335] What forced her into business proved that with necessity came the will to succeed when her husband contracted tuberculosis and could no longer support the family.[336] Before opening her store, she tried her hand at door-to-door selling of A & P groceries that had been sent to her from another state. After having doors slammed in her face because she had been perceived as a peddler, she formulated a plan and executed it with guts and determination.[337] Although many modern business changes have occurred over the last century, the company feeds the hungry and supports many communities through various charities, as Florence Butt herself had done.[338]

From Bread Maker to Bread Empire

Widowhood continued as one of a woman's greatest challenges in the 1900s because many of them depended on their husbands for financial sustenance, as farming usually left little opportunity for any type of independence. Ninnie L. Baird lost her husband but had to feed eight children.[339] Baking bread in her kitchen seemed the natural avenue for her to take care of her family.[340] In 1908, one son assisted her in constructing a small bakery behind her home at 512 Hemphill; each loaf of bread came from a wood-fired stove while three of her children rode their bicycles, delivering fresh bread to local customers.[341] As a flexibility and necessity entrepreneur, it was never her intent to build a large business, but the outcome through her descendants culminated in a large Fort Worth bakery, now computer-driven.[342] Born in 1869, she and her husband had run restaurants and bakeries in two Tennessee towns before he moved the family to Fort Worth in 1901.[343] She had started a baking empire by hard work and great determination to sustain her children regardless of her circumstances. Many Texas widows faced hardships that forced the martialing of untapped talents.

Overall, as the Progressive Era winded down when World War I began, Texas women worked in restaurants, ran boarding houses, nursed the ill, taught the children, laundered clothing, operated switchboards, ran ranches, labored on farms, worked as sales clerks, performed secretarial duties, worked as semi-skilled factory operatives, and ran their households.[344] Other not-so-respectable ways of earning a living included bunco artists, saloon dancers, fortune tellers, and prostitutes.[345] Texas legislators authorized the Girls Industrial College in 1901, located in Denton, Texas, to prepare females for a liberal education with a focus on new industries.[346] By 1904, the first class graduated one student, Beulah Kincaid.[347] By 1910, the United States ranked as the most powerful industrial nation on the planet, with a population of over ninety million.[348] Houston attorney Hortense Ward found success in her campaign for the passage of the 1913 Married Women's Property Act, which allowed more control over both separate and community property.[349] The law stemmed from a national movement erupting from socioeconomic pressures regardless of varied cultural differences between the states.[350] By 1915, fifty percent of all clerical workers in the United States were women. Jobs in business provided more stable employment, and a female with some office training could earn more than a schoolteacher.[351] Average yearly wages for a male were 687 dollars, with the average female earning about half that amount.[352] Fifty-four and one-half years constituted life expectancy if born in 1915, and divorce remained rare, as did single-person households. Overall, the Industrial Age provided amenities that allowed women more freedom outside the home, including easier-to-prepare food choices such as Kellogg's Corn Flakes, tea bags, and Maxwell House Instant coffee; and other helpful home products such as sewing machines, ice boxes, vacuums, telephones, and washing machines.[353] Dry goods stores such as Foley's operated in downtown Houston by 1900 at 507 Main Street.[354] Rural Texans remained in the dark; the cities of Galveston, Houston, Dallas-Fort Worth, Austin, and El Paso lit up every night.[355] Eventually, automobiles would gradually replace horses, and train rides would be possible with new railway systems in the state.

Chapter Six
Women Working in World War I: Caring for the Wounded, Collecting Peach Stones during a Pandemic, Rising Hemlines, and Votes for Women

The years between America's involvement in World War I, beginning April 6, 1917, and the passage of the August 26, 1920, Constitutional Amendment, allowing women to vote, signified a major rite of passage for females that spawned the idea of new-styled women seeking freedom of choice even while some females clung to traditional mores.[356] Two major coinciding events influenced new civil rights for women and those major actions included the United States entrance into World War I, in 1917, and the three devastating waves of the Spanish Flu from 1918 to the spring of 1919. After remaining neutral from the start of the Great War in 1914, the United States entered the conflict under President Woodrow Wilson who commenced the struggle to make the world safe for democracy and to keep the sea lanes open for free trading. Texans had expressed bifurcated views before the war declaration. Several incidents had swayed the state toward war and those included the torpedoing on May 1, 1915, by the Germans of the Gulflight, a tanker owned by Gulf Oil Corporation, in waters near the Scilly Isles with merchant marines aboard from its origination at Port Arthur, Texas.[357] Also, businessmen with Texas connections perished with the sinking of the RMS Lusitania on May 7, 1915.[358] The pro-war stance multiplied after the federal government released the Zimmerman Telegraph on March 1, 1917, which implicated Germany in a secret plot to obtain Mexico's assistance to defeat the European Allies, whereby rewards would have included the return of Texas and other territories to that government.[359] That telegraph passed through the Galveston office of the Mexican Telegraph Office furthering the call to war.[360]

The two-fold catastrophes of war and plague led Texas females to work and nurse the infected when the primary breadwinners were called to serve, and death rates for men soared.[361] Three waves of the Spanish Flu occurred from March of 1918 through part of the summer, during the fall of 1918, and during the spring of 1919, with each wave more virulent than the previous one.[362] Historically, financial data on the economic loss related to the pandemic appears overwhelmed by war costs and little data exists that allowed micro-inspection.[363] Some studies indicated wage growth increased where a lack of employees existed because of the pandemic.[364] Not to be dismissed during these worldwide calamities are the diseases of polio, smallpox, tuberculosis and syphilis, for which no true cures existed at the time. For women, these dual problems brought forth their expected role as healers and caretakers and challenged them in new roles as they replaced working men and became working women out of necessity. Females answered the call to defend the country and support the soldiers as they settled into an acquiescence that this bloody conflict offered no other choices; therefore, women performed "necessity" activities. Approximately 200,000 Texas men joined the various branches of the military, and about 450 Texas women joined as nurses. Twelve thousand women joined the US Navy as Yeomen, non-commissioned officers.[365] New fashion trends percolated before the start of the Great War as hemlines rose even shorter, the shortest in Western fashion history, metaphorically equating to more freedom for women after the conflict. This war, like all wars, both helped and hindered women with future employment struggles.

The Texas National Guard already had experience on the border with Mexico because of Pancho Villa's revolution in that country and his incursions into the US; therefore, when World War I began, Governor James E. Ferguson thought enticing men to sign up would have proved easier, however, his first call to arms proved quite weak and a second call to arms came on July 4, 1917.[366] To motivate the men to enlist, wives and sweethearts encouraged their men to sign up as patriots to the nation, as requested by the governor. Texas Enlistment Week succeeded in new officers and regular enlistees. Women motivated men to fight. While the work Texas women accomplished during war times cannot necessarily be quantified in traditional economic terms, women modified their lives through adjustments that included supplanting men in the workforce while soldiers transitioned to military training and moved onto the war front in Europe. Women had to act as both father and mother to their children, keep their homes, cook their meals, work outside the home in war industries, live through the Spanish Flu, bury their dead, raise their own vegetables, can their own fruit, raise war bond money, and "give impulse and enthusiasm to the men of the land," thereby doing what was stated as fifty percent of the fighting.[367] Posters relayed that every garden equaled a munitions plant communicating the urgency that food represented the most crucial need in the war.[368] America consumed ninety-nine percent of US agricultural produce and now those efforts included feeding the European Allies.[369] Women around the country and in Texas joined the Salvation Army, the YWCA, the Jewish Welfare Board, and the Knights of Columbus to serve the war effort.[370]

Women with registered nurse credentials were encouraged to join the Red Cross. Nurses' Aids helped, and about 7,000 nurses were enrolled in the Red Cross Nursing Service. A branch of the American Red Cross was established in Dallas in 1911 and in Houston in 1916.[371] Duties included assistance with the Spanish Flu of 1918.[372] Women also provided comfort to soldiers on military bases in Texas with dances, parties, and family visitations. As the draft commenced on June 5, 1917, Raymond Fosdick headed the Commission on Training Camp Activities that engaged in opening hostess houses whereby family members and sweethearts visited soldiers. Ladies stepped up to organize and operate these facilities, some volunteering for service in France as canteen hostesses. Adam Janelli, an émigré sea captain from Italy who settled in Dallas as an advertising man, established the Salvation Army in Texas in 1889, under the auspices of the home office in London.[373] From that organization, the famous "Doughnut Lassies" in France cooked pies, cakes, and thousands of these delicious doughnuts for the Doughboys fighting with the American Expeditionary Forces under General John J. Pershing.[374] Although there were only a little over two hundred of these women donning helmets and carrying guns during the war, some came from Michigan, Massachusetts, and Pennsylvania, and is possible that a few came from Texas. On some days, the women turned out 2,500 doughnuts, along with cakes, fudge, and 225 gallons of hot chocolate. [375]

Examples of women's efforts during the war in Texas include those at Camp MacArthur, located in Waco. Construction of the camp began in July 1917, and the Thirty-Seventh Infantry Division of the National Guard joined the American Expeditionary Forces in France in February 1918.[376] After that, new recruits arrived from Texas, New Mexico, Arkansas, and Missouri. The hospital where nurse Loretta Johnson worked in 1918 had a recreational hall that permitted dances and parties with officers on weekends.[377] Texas had numerous training bases and aviation training facilities that enhanced the economies of the various locations, providing various jobs for women, from waitressing to nursing. The war effort in some ways exercised a decentralized but coordinated effort to synchronize women's work during the conflict. The Texas Council of National Defense (TCND) on June 20, 1918, issued a directive to various County Councils and the Women's Committees encouraging the two groups to work closely with one another and to accept and welcome a visit by the Field Secretary, Mrs. Reese Wilson, from the headquarters in San Antonio.[378] Because the Germans used chlorine, phosgene, and mustard gas as chemical weapons, the military prioritized the manufacture of gas masks that included the extraction by fire of charcoal, used as filters to negate damage by Sulphur dioxide and ammonia.[379] The collection of peach stones and the pits of cherries, nuts, plums, and apricots provided the raw material that produced the actual charcoal that filtered the harmful gases.[380] Texas women, through a directive by the TCND, collected these, and two hundred peach stones equaled enough for one mask.

About 22,000 professional nurses served in the war and of those, about 10,000 served on the Western Front.[381] Nurses in the war, whether stateside or on the war front, provided necessary care for wounded soldiers and those suffering from the pandemic; their work was made harder by the lack of antibiotics and treatments for survival. Medical teams from the US began to arrive in May 1917 before the American Doughboys and would stay in Europe until mid-1919.[382] By June 1918, at British hospitals in France, about 3,000 American nurses joined their colleagues in efforts to save wounded soldiers.[383] Nurses qualified for service if they had been formally trained, were between the ages of twenty-five and thirty-five, were Caucasian, and were US citizens; they also had physical exams. A nurse from Texas Roxie Henderson, a graduate of Baylor University class of 1920, served with the Red Cross in France, and as secretary of the Overseas Club, she maintained a correspondence relationship with the university.[384] "My work in the hospitals was rich in experience. The spirit of the men and their appreciation of small services was wonderful. I truly hope these men will not be disappointed in the American girls." [385] Trained Black nurses wanted to serve with the Red Cross or in the military, however, they found themselves barred from either until public pressure allowed service by the time of the Armistice in November 1918; and the Army Nurse Corps granted eighteen the right to join, and of those,[386] locating any specific names of those from Texas proved futile.

Of the over three thousand women who served with the YMCA overseas, four of those were black, and these volunteers provided entertainment, canteen services, sewing, baking, and educational opportunities to both soldiers and sailors overseas.[387]

Five brave Texas women qualified, served, and unfortunately died, earning the status of Gold Star Nurses; those included, Kate Dodson of Casa Blanca, Alma M. Furr of Austin, Myrtle Grant of Hico, Elina Winson Hill of San Antonio, and Mamie Jones of Pontotoc.[388] The cities held the emergency contact information provided by each female as they set sail for France.[389] These female heroes may be buried in France, England, or as far away as Armenia. They perished from various diseases, as no nurse perished from enemy German fire, although some had suffered war injuries such as gas poisoning. These brave ladies may have been US Army nurses, or those working under the auspices of the Red Cross, and all serving without rank or commission.[390] Julia Stimson, who served as both the chief nurse for the Red Cross and director for the Army Nurse Corps, summed up the stamina and strength she observed: Nurses "at the front are having such wonderful times. They are working hard, sleeping with helmets over their faces and enamel basins on their stomachs, washing in the water they had in their hot-water bags because water is so scarce, operating fourteen hours at a stretch, drinking quantities of tea because there is no coffee and nothing else to drink, wearing men's ordnance socks under their stockings, trying to keep their feet warm in the frosty operating rooms at night, and both seeing and doing such surgical work as they never in their wildest days dreamed of, but all the time unafraid and unconcerned with the whistling, banging shells exploding around them. Oh, they are fine! One need never tell me that women can't do as much, stand as much, and be as brave as men."[391]

Texas women entered the US Navy as yeomen and although their first duties constituted clerical work, they soon became trained as electricians, truck drivers, cryptographers, telephone operators, munitions makers, and mechanics.[392] Most yeomen served on naval bases in the country and, astonishingly, received the same pay as their male counterparts, which was $28.75 a month.[393] The last female yeoman left the service in March 1921, as many were needed to process discharge papers for their colleagues.[394] Besides the yeomen in the navy, approximately 223 women served overseas and were nicknamed "Hello Girls." General John J. Pershing, head of the American Expeditionary Forces in France, needed swift communication, and he found that the men could not connect calls quickly or efficiently; therefore, he called for the formation of the Signal Corps Female Operators Unit, requesting females fluent in French as well as English.[395] After serious testing, "Soldiers of the Switchboard" were chosen and sent overseas; these women could connect calls in about ten seconds, whereas the men took about a minute, plus men thought this job was "girl's work."[396] Officers, happy to have them connecting calls, showered them with gifts. The women received medals from General Pershing, however, they failed to win veteran status or benefits, even though they had worn army uniforms.[397] The US Army had not thought highly of women serving in that branch of the military, regardless of General Pershing's approval. Until 1977, when President Jimmy Carter allowed veteran status for the "Hello Girls," the women had been ignored in the history of the war.[398]

Texas produced war matériel and provided training for all branches of the military that occurred at numerous military bases and flight training facilities. Women worked on some of the bases, and two trained pilots. The genesis of man and machine that defined the war clearly described the pivotal role the state played because of Texas oil and its by-products that powered planes, tanks, and ships. Marjorie Stinson, of the famous Stinson aviation family of San Antonio, obtained her pilot's license in August of 1914 at the age of eighteen, with the distinction of being the youngest licensed female pilot.[399] Her older sister, Katherine, flew as an air mail carrier with Marjorie doing the same.[400] However, in 1915, both women started training Canadian pilots, later known as the "Texas Escadrille," at a family-owned training center in San Antonio. Marjorie was tagged with the nickname "The Flying Schoolmarm," and she held the position as the only female in the U. S. Aviation Reserve Corps.[401] Both sisters had stunned the world with their flying skills. Both flew exhibitions for the Liberty Loan Drive.[402] Although the Stinson school closed by 1918, Katherine volunteered as an ambulance driver in Europe with the Red Cross while Marjorie continued barnstorming across the country, becoming a draftswoman for the War Department in 1930.[403] At her death in 1975, a symbolic scattering of her ashes at Stinson Field in San Antonio, Texas memorialized the service to her country and to aviation.[404] Katherine contracted influenza during her service on the war front leaving her with tuberculosis by 1920.[405] After marrying in 1928, a move to New Mexico led her to a new career in home design.[406] Even with her health issues, she lived to the age of eighty-six passing in 1977.[407]

Women, both black and white, also assisted in war industries on Galveston Island. Hispanic women, because of a cultural expectation to remain homemakers, seldom participated in the first world conflict. Adina de Zavala, the granddaughter of Lorenzo de Zavala, who served as the first vice president of the Republic of Texas, participated as the secretary of the Women's Committee of the Council of National Defense.[408] The Emergency Fleet Corporation established by the government shortly after the war began had the primary goal of constructing a fleet of merchant ships.[409] While the natural geography of the Texas coastline prevented massive shipbuilding during the war because of the lack of deepwater ports, the state provided wooden merchant marine shipbuilding in ports of Beaumont, Port Arthur, Orange, Galveston, Houston, and Corpus Christi using the plentiful yellow pine of East Texas.[410] Fort Crockett on the island provided security for the Gulf of Mexico and trained US Marines at the artillery site.[411] During 1917 Black mothers on the island who worked in war industries left their children to be cared for by Albertine Hall Yeager and her husband, Charlie.[412] Black women volunteered and performed well, but almost always in segregated workforces.[413]

The cataclysmic world war became a catalyst for the changes that Texas women and all others in the US would come to know and experience as the new century dawned. The war ended with an Armistice on November 11, 1918, with boundaries redrawn, and new weapons introduced such as planes, tanks, submarines, improved artillery, and poison gas, along with the concept and reality of Trench Warfare. Blood transfusions later would be perfected, and the introduction of new products would make life easier for Americans. Nine million soldiers died, twenty-one million were wounded, some quite seriously, and seven million were left disabled.[414] Overall about ten million civilians had perished.[415] The overall cost reached 588 billion.[416] About 5, 170 Texas military men died either from the war or the pandemic.[417]

Women had remarkedly performed at all jobs and duties assigned to them. Women eagerly expanded war efforts to address the mandatory needs and those that seemed absurd, such as making plans to remove virgins from cities so invading Germans could not rape them.[418] Since 1918 Texas women had voted in primaries and the state reigned as the first Southern state and the ninth state in America to ratify the nineteenth Amendment to the Constitution that allowed women to vote. Suffragettes had finally won their long-term struggle to vote.[419] Women had juggled family life, work obligations, the Spanish Flu, and the war with determination and immense fortitude. Many young women had found the war, however difficult, an exciting part of their youth as some dated officers, made new friendships, learned new skills, and garnered respect from respective communities. However, this war and others had stolen the right to life and the pursuit of happiness for both sexes for the duration of the fighting and the resulting aftermath. But, in some ways, women's lives improved as this epic world event allowed women to work and receive a paycheck higher than ever seen for most females working outside the home at the time. Now they must return home to their domestic chores. Throughout time women have followed men into war, providing necessary chores such as cooking, sewing, nursing, and laundry—in fact, "armies could not have functioned as well, perhaps could not have functioned at all, without the service of women."[420]

Economically, the United States went from a debtor nation to a lender nation, gaining the status of a world power and a military power. Blacks had moved out of the South for war jobs as the North needed employees as immigration slowed during the war. The war represented fifty-two percent of the GDP.[421] Government programs and control of the wartime economy led the way for federal efforts to contain the destruction coming during the Great Depression and the next world war. The pandemic had killed 675,000 Americans, more than had perished in the war.[422] One can more readily understand the pressures, plight, and fear of women living through the combination of war and flu because of the COVID-19 virus that spread across the world from 2019 through much of 2020, and beyond. Fortunately, the latest pandemic of the twenty-first century had not been coupled with a world war. The Spanish flu killed some victims within four to six hours and mostly targeted young men because of the troop movements throughout the war; and while the nature of the current virus and its victims may be different, the deaths affected the psychological health of the country whether in 1918 or 2020. Because of the damages wrought by the COVID-19 pandemic, historians should be more able to understand the events during the time of the Great War; and as a result, they should be more able to expand the explanations for a release of tensions during the Roaring 1920s. The combination of war and plague strained and drained the human soul, but Texas women persevered through the upcoming 1920s, increasing their opportunities for jobs outside the home, even if most of these jobs remained rather static. Education would propel them to greater independence and allow free will, but the journey would be long and tedious regardless of all the "work" accomplished during the War to End All Wars that failed to do so.

Chapter Seven
The 1920s Myth of the New Texas Woman: A Foundation for Working Females

During the 1920s, Texas women remained historically ignored, mired in a male-dominated society that can be categorized as culturally both Southern and Western. Most of them through the Roaring Twenties seldom roared; they "worked capably and quietly through" their husbands and spent their lives nurturing their families, and teaching Sunday School.[423] Avenues for them to effect change included social, charitable, and religious activities. A few left the state creating lives outside the social norms of the time, and they roared raucously and outrageously. Certainly, the Nineteenth Amendment allowing them the right to vote was new and uplifting, but overall, the women of Texas never met the definition of the historically defined "New Woman." However, most importantly, a crucial foundation for the future of working women in Texas planted in the 1920s led to more opportunities after the economic depression of the 1930s and the victory of World War Two in 1945. On June 5, 1920, the administration of President Woodrow Wilson established the Women's Bureau within the Department of Labor with the authority to "formulate standards and policies which shall promote the welfare of wage-earning women, improve their working conditions, increase their efficiently, and advance their opportunities for profitable employment."[424] This landmark legislation by Public Law No. 66-259 represents a functional change that is considered the formal start of female employment in America. Women by 2020 celebrated one hundred years of working outside the home.[425] This chapter highlights a variety of Lone Star women as they worked for wages, bolted from the state to follow their dreams, individually started businesses, or supported their husbands' businesses; and it provides a foundational discussion of the basic accoutrements that women felt necessary to enhance and promote their new status as part of the economic base of the state.

The context within which women began their journey from the home to the office included many other changes occurring in the United States and the world. Without a signature from the United States, the European Allies began the recovery process with the Treaty of Versailles on June 28, 1919. The punishment of Germany proved swift and strong. The United States made a separate peace with the former enemy ratifying a treaty in Berlin on November 11, 1921. Three Republican presidents, Warren G. Harding, Calvin Coolidge, and Herbert Hoover returned the country to a laissez-faire economy that had flourished during the Industrial Revolution years. World governments agreed that war was outlawed; however, nations rearmed at an alarming rate. Overall, the United States eagerly embraced modernism and consumerism with a 1920 population of 106,021,537. Charles Lindbergh made the world's first trans-Atlantic flight, landing in Paris, France on May 21, 1927, while on May 26 the fifteenth million Ford Model-T rolled off the assembly line. Americans enjoyed "The Jazz Singer," the first talking film of 1927. By 1929, Southerner William Faulkner published The Sound and the Fury, although the convoluted and complicated story failed to garner serious attention until 1931, reaching the "Classics" status even later. Prevented by law, the manufacture and sale of "intoxicating liquors," ended at midnight on January 16, 1920.[426] Gangsters smuggling liquor from Canada to Chicago and New York gained the attention of the press and the law. Most of the history of the Roaring Twenties focused on the art and science trends of Europe and the Northeastern US, mostly ignoring the South, apart from noting that the Scopes Trial of 1925 on the teaching of evolution reaffirmed the rejection of science by some of the laggard folks occupying the Bible Belt.[427] While other Southern states did ban the teaching of evolution in schools, Texans debated the issue, but ultimately never passed such formal legislation.

The concept of the "New Woman" rose from the ashes of war. Happy to do so, because of the passage of the Nineteenth Amendment, women voted in large numbers. However, Texas women fit a different definition of the "New Woman" as seen by the elite. The definition of a New Woman can vary in the state as compared to other sections of the country, especially the Northeast and certainly in Europe. How women lived, worked, and improved themselves as the state began the process of urbanization and modernization, depended on the economic base of the state and the creation of an educational system allowing women opportunities for personal liberty. Personal liberty and free will sustain civilization within a construct that benefits all.[428] Therefore, the start of the process in Texas, whereby, over time, women attempted to infiltrate the male-driven workforce proved tedious and sometimes almost impossible. A few women opted to start their own businesses, altogether avoiding male-dominated companies. After the Great War, they had hustled back to their domestic role, however, widows and young urban women found ways to exercise personal liberty because of financial necessity. Most young women were seeking husbands, and a few women with untamed dreams ventured where angels dared to tread and societal norms resulted in ostracization.

American-British author Henry James coined the term "New Woman" and the definition meant a well-to-do female that exercised a strong will and an independent spirit because of her wealth.[429] The term exemplified the rich female expatriates living in Europe, such as Gertrude Stein who helped with the war effort in France, collected art, defined a rose, wrote poems and books, and exclaimed to Earnest Hemingway that the men who fought the war were now "The Lost Generation."[430] Women such as this controlled most aspects of their lives socially and economically and they lived life as they saw fit.[431] The American definition of the New Woman varied as the term referred to educated women of substance able to work and live on their own as professionals without the control of a male and outside their families' parameters.[432] She stands alone, separate from being a social reformer, a good mother, a good wife, or a good daughter.[433] Both avenues to a self-directed life necessitated money and education by elite females. Until educational facilities established degrees for teaching and nursing in the state, not many women had opportunities for fulfillment. Few Texas women lived on their own as many newly trained teachers lived with their parents or other families when attaining their first positions. Many young women went from the farm to marriage at early ages, seldom experiencing an independent life.

Sometimes the definition of the New Woman failed in its intentional meaning, because the concept manifested as a superficial code of dress and behavior for the famous and the rich. However, the importance of fashion and female convenience cannot be excluded because the war necessitated trousers and clothing more adaptable to work.[434] Women embraced the military-styled jackets worn by women in any facet of the war, along with A-line skirts that allowed more freedom of movement.[435] By 1914 at the start of the conflict, trends included the exclusion of corsets.[436]

Shorter hemlines among the Flappers can be understood as a form of rebellion and wearing the short, sassy dresses allowed young women the freedom to move on the dance floor with the new Jazz music in one of the numerous speakeasies of Chicago or New York. However, realistically, shorter hemlines resulted mostly from wool and cotton shortages during the war, when evening gowns were shortened, too.[437] "Mend and make do" reflected reality in much of the US, and certainly in Texas. Of course, wealthier women had more options for fashionable clothing, and some abhorred the idea of wearing trousers after the war.[438] However, some women felt comfort and freedom and continued wearing the new line.[439] Hats, gloves, and modest dresses prevailed in Texas, and since the state forms part of the traditional Bible Belt, women always insisted on special dresses for Sunday worship. Also, from the war came a product that freed women of worry during monthly periods. Because cotton became scarce during the war, Kimberly-Clark created a cellulose-cotton dressing for war wounds that Red Cross nurses serving on the front lines of World War I began to use as sanitary napkins.[440] Kimberly-Clark saw the benefit and worth of a new product that eventually earned the company huge profits. Unable to get drug stores to shelve them, they approached women's magazines to advertise the new Kotex. Ladies Home Journal agreed.[441] Women forced the change that assisted them in caring for themselves. Another interesting change in fashion included the introduction of the trench coat which became standard wear over time.[442] Named after Trench Warfare and designed to repel water, the famous coats were worn only by British military officers.[443] The democratization of the elite trench coat spread from Great Britain to the US military and the general public as a status symbol and later a necessary fashion item for working women.[444] While dress does not explicitly address the topic of "women making money," at this juncture in time, a discussion proved relevant because the needs and desires of women increasingly propelled the economy, adding to the overall GDP of Texas and the country. Women during the age of consumerism drove the decisions as to how the breadwinner's money was spent in many families. Also, the growth of the concept of a professional "work wardrobe" demonstrated the importance many women placed on appearance outside the home. They dressed for church, therefore they dressed for work. As women insisted on dressy suits instead of house dresses, dry goods stores in Texas began with fashion shows from the Northeast. The need promoted economic advantage for businesses in the major cities of the state.

In addition, while historically not often addressed as germane, one cannot dismiss Hollywood's startling changes that had affected women in a totally new, and maybe unexpected way. People went often to the movies, both silent and later to the "talkies." Glamourous Hollywood film stars became role models, regardless of worthiness. Make-up has been part of the human story for thousands of years and, at times, involved men too. Many women who suffered smallpox during Antebellum times wore waxed makeup to hide those scars when entertaining.[445] They held fans at their faces to keep the wax from melting should they find themselves too close to the fireplace.[446] Women who worked during the Great War bought cosmetics. In 1915, Maybelline Mascara was introduced to American women; the scientist named the product after his sister Mabel.[447] Vanity kits were sold that included toothbrushes, and perfume, and Max Factor coined the word "make-up" bringing his business to the United States and creating an empire.[448] From the twenties forward, the desire of women to appear their best drove the market. By 1929, one pound of face powder was sold that year for every woman in the US[449] Approximately 1,500 face creams were on shelves ready to try by the end of the decade.[450] Cosmetics companies began producing various lines of lipsticks, fingernail lacquers, and foundations.[451] Women forced this market as they wanted to emulate Hollywood stars. When the 1920s roared, women desired new hairstyles, and about 25,000 new salons opened in the country; if women could not ask and get the new shorter "bob," they had a barber cut their hair.[452] Hair dryers, bobby pins, perms, and hair color saved women from the now cliched term known as "a bad hair day." Perhaps seen by men as frivolous, many women envision their hair as the "crowning glory" of an overall look. In the business world, women had only one chance to make the first impression when interviewing for employment. Historians should not separate the desire to "present well" in public with the advent of working females who left home and entered a new world of competition with other women. Many hoped to appear more "peacock" than "grey wren," simply to appear pleasing enough to gain the attention of the male that would either hire them or pass them by. For instance, the famous primatologist Dr. Jane Goodall stated, "If it was my legs that helped me get money for what I wanted to do, then thank you, legs."[453] Women, for too many decades, had two strikes against them if they desired employment outside the expected norms, number one they were female, and number two men did the hiring. In past times, one should not be surprised or shocked that many women overtly or covertly obtained jobs supplementing their skills by enhancing their physical attributes and some defended the need to do so to fulfill goals crucial to their success. Not until "Personnel" transitioned to "Human Resource Management" in the 1970s did women become involved in the management hiring decisions necessitated by globalization and the computerized new business world.[454]

The term New Woman in its elite form also exalted all avant-gardists, including Bohemians, aviators, scientists, athletes, and Marxists.[455] Women also could be described as captives of a protected class using caprice to gain money from husbands working to provide for them and the family.[456] The modern woman sought a position as a stakeholder in her future. Many women, though, sought the comfort of being taken care of by the traditional breadwinner during the age of the New Woman. It is doubtful that a woman living in Texas in the 1920s would have realized that she was a New Woman. In fact, "A woman of 1920 would be surprised to know that she would be remembered as a 'new woman'."[457] Most married women at this time did not work outside the home.[458] About fifteen percent of whites held wage-earning jobs if their husbands worked, and most Americans believed that women should not work outside the home if their husbands held jobs.[459] Attitudes controlled societal mores. Black women mostly worked out of necessity, and about thirty percent of black married women worked.[460] As a result of this attitude, wives seldom worked at outside jobs. Overall, in the country, the top jobs in 1920 for women included the following: domestic maid, teacher, stenographer, typist, clerk, farm laborer, laundress, saleswoman, bookkeeper, cashier, cook, and general farmer.[461] While many changes occurred during the decade, it remains the attitudinal adjustments of both men and women that eventually allow women the power to control their lives. The process takes years of evolutionary thinking, along with technological advancements for women to truly compete in the workplace. In Texas, the economic base, the Bible Belt influence, a woman's social status, and the formation of colleges dictated much of what a woman could do outside the home in the business world in the 1920s. The cities in Texas with the most population in 1920 included the following: San Antonio, 161,379; Dallas 158,976; Houston 138,276; and Fort Worth 106,482.[462] Each city offered some jobs for women of all races, however, each city had different economic and environmental factors that influenced the trajectory of each city's economic growth.

San Antonio, as the most populous city in 1920, embraced the fashions of the Roaring Twenties, including Jazz and Art Deco; however, the city advertised itself as a place where life was different.[463] A terrible flood from a decaying hurricane inundated the town in 1921. "Heavy rainfall over a large area in south-central Texas from September 8 to September 10, 1921, produced great floods which caused the loss of at least 224 lives and damage to property amounting to more than $10,000,000."[464] San Antonio was home to a cultural mix of German, Polish, Hispanic, Alsatian, African American,[465] and other smaller ethnic groups, along with a strong US military presence by Fort Sam Houston established in 1876 as the first permanent Army post in the country.[466] Additional facilities such as Brooks and Kelly Army airfields trained pilots.[467] Over time the US military complex launched and sparked the underpinnings of the economic growth of the city, creating a symbiotic relationship that grew every decade from early Texas formation to the future establishment of Joint Base San Antonio in 2010.[468] The relationship promoted and generated oil and gas extraction, construction, trade, transportation, warehousing, retail trade, manufacturing, and utilities. Jobs of various types offered women opportunities in most of these industries which included communications.[469]

Houston, the Magnolia city incorporated in 1837, had been organized under geographic districts early on known as a ward system, including four sections with the addition of two others over time.[470] These "neighborhoods" entailed a heterogeneous makeup that was much later organized into ethnic zones with social stratification, including the elite, a healthy middle class, and a large poverty group.[471] By 1905, the citizens voted to abandon the ward system of short-term elected aldermen and a weak mayor to a political system incorporating the commission form of local government.[472] The result meant a better-run city but led to homogenous neighborhoods that meant minorities had little power. The city operated under laissez-faire attitudes with doing business, free of regulations, seen as paramount.[473] Houston, in the 1920s, introduced air mail service; began the process of air conditioning the semi-tropical climate; voted in money for a library system; opened the first fine art museum in the state; and Henke & Pillot grocers claimed the distinction as the largest grocery distributor under a single roof in all of America.[474] In 1922, eight or nine women worked in the grocery store out of about

245 employees, however, records do not indicate the specific duties.[475] Several new hotels opened that served the city during the hosting of the 1928 Democrat Convention including the Rice Hotel, the Warwick, and the Auditorium.[476] Oil production in Texas grew quickly and a variety of jobs opened for women after World War One, especially in Houston where companies officed. The machines of war had been powered by oil. Texas became a lynchpin that represented the US in the race to acquire more of this precious crude that the rest of Europe raced to acquire from the Middle East. Some of the original oil companies consisted of Gulf Production Company, Southern Crude Oil Purchasing Company, Shell Petroleum Corporation, Magnolia Petroleum Company, J.K. Hughes Oil Company, the Texas Company, Yount-Lee Oil Company, and Mid-Kansas Oil and Gas Company.[477] As the cattle business and the lumber business had been, the oil business followed as the epitome of men's work with women seen as bad luck around an oil rig. Refineries operated along the Houston Ship Channel and proved able to move their product easily and less costly. A variety of staff provided the necessary infrastructure, including females with specific skills. Women fulfilled clerical duties, including dictation, typing, filing, and phone duties; they made the morning coffee and attended to any duties assigned by the boss. Sometimes they ran personal errands, helped decorate offices, and organized social gatherings, among other chores. The position eventually encompassed the title Girl Friday,[478] which became a standard request in future employment ads for companies that required multiple skills. A Girl Friday position morphed over time into a highly coveted job by many women with good secretarial abilities and high-functioning, multi-tasking talents for those easily bored by the monotony of a desk job. Presently, the term offends professional women doing such activities, and the preferential title of Executive Assistant, among other varied titles, remains appropriate. Duties by the late twentieth century and into the twenty-first century remain the same and may include: travel, making travel/vacation arrangements, housesitting, hiring staff, planning large events, and numerous other duties as requested by an executive.

During the 1920s, the city of Dallas completed the trio of major burgeoning cities of the large state and the economy turned on meat processing, leather, cotton, insurance, bank formation, and oil.[479] Harshly segregated, the city had specific areas for blacks that included a string of leftover freedman's towns around an area near rail yards known as

Central Track where businesses, theaters, and clubs created a vibrant community.[480] In one such area known as Ellum, Henry Ford erected a manufacturing plant, while banks and 1920s jazz clubs sprung up around the area that had once hosted a large cotton gin in the 1800s.[481] Cotton remained a huge business foundation for the city and profited as one of the world's largest exchanges. Trains intersected at Central Track, making the area perfect for moving cotton, automobiles, and all other products, produce, and grains that needed transporting in the 1920s. The newly promulgated Federal Reserve System placed a bank in Dallas while Delta Airlines began service to Jackson, Mississippi via stops in Shreveport and Monroe, Louisiana in 1929.[482] Department stores included brands like Sanger-Harris and Neiman Marcus, among others; along with grocers such as Piggly Wiggly, A&P, Long's Helpy-Selfy, Barrel Head, and Clarence Saunders.[483] Neighborhoods formed around Jewish residents from Poland that emerged as Little Mexico grew as people fled the Mexican Revolution in the 1910s and El Fenix restaurant served up Tex-Mex food.[484] Frogtown served as a prostitute haven. La Réunion began as a Utopian group of 200 European settlers that later became business leaders as the land they settled proved not suitable for farming.[485] Scyene housed a few saloons frequented by outlaws.[486] The wealthy moved from Colonial Hill near the Trinity River to the upscale areas of Highland Park and Munger Place.[487] The fifteen-story Praetorian Building on the main street that housed a fraternal insurance company represents one of the first high-rises in the state.[488] People moved through downtown, and the two cable cars were pulled by mules.[489] Several famous hotels served the needs of travelers to the city, including the eloquent Oriental, the stately Adolphus, and the Baker with its lily pond full of swimming ducks.[490] The fashion world embraced Dallas as those in the business traveled to the city to dress the rich.[491] Women held many various positions in these businesses, ranging from maids to cooks and receptionists to typists.

The educational underpinnings for Texas females began with a series of institutions in various Texas towns and cities that mostly addressed the need for teachers, nurses, and home economics specialists. No standardized data about colleges and universities existed from a federal level until the fall of 1968.[492] Modern thinking disrupted the old unfounded prejudices of earlier times that women who used their brain cells interrupted their fertility.[493] Several of the institutions that provided women the needed credentials to succeed consisted of the University of Texas, 1883;[494]

the University of Houston, 1927;[495] Baylor University, 1845;[496] Texas Christian University, 1873;[497] Texas Tech, 1923;[498] Stephen F. Austin State University, 1923;[499] Sam Houston State University, 1879;[500] Lamar University, 1923; [501]the University of North Texas, 1890[502]; and the institution exclusively for females, Texas Woman's University, 1901.[503] Most of these colleges originated with different names and evolved into larger learning universities over the years, however, some originated as teacher preparation institutions. In 1901, the 27th Legislature established the Girls Industrial College, which eventually morphed into Texas Woman's University as a public entity to prepare females with a liberal education and the ability to work in a specialized industry. [504] Even today the university remains the largest of its kind educating women in Texas and the United States.[505] Men as of 1972 entered to halls of Texas Woman's University in Denton, Texas.[506] Texas A&M would not allow women and blacks to enroll until August 23, 1963. The establishment of University Junior College in 1925, and a name change later to San Antonio University occurred, all under the auspices of the University of Texas.[507] Women attended the University of Texas at Austin and enjoyed the benefits of sororities at the time, however many of them married without harvesting rewards from the degrees obtained. Because of segregation, blacks could not attend white universities; therefore, through time, in Austin, two black "normal schools," Huston-Tillotson University, eventually merged, creating one of 107 black institutions of higher learning in the United States.[508] Tillotson provided training exclusively for black females by 1926 and had previously trained teachers since the early 1900s.[509] In Houston, the forerunner of Texas Southern University opened in 1927 as Houston Colored Junior College.[510]

John Sealy Hospital in Galveston offered the first formal training for nurses in 1890.[511] In 1909, the State of Texas formally recognized professional nursing with the passage of the first Nursing Practice Act.[512] By the middle 1920s, the curriculum required a 450-hour regimen. Unlike doctors, nurses dropped out to marry, with some reentering the profession at later times during the home/work lifecycle, which led to an overall average of seventeen years of tenure during the 1920s.[513] Nurses during the 1920s preferred private duty assignments versus hospital floor duty. An example of a major business training organization in East Texas was Tyler Commercial College, formed in 1915 and advertised as the largest business training school in America; it offered the following courses in bookkeeping, shorthand, steno-typewriting, typewriting, cotton classing, telegraphy, business administration, and finance. Twenty teachers taught 2,000 students early on.[514]

Texas women came to undergird so many of the new businesses in the state and understand the transformation required, placing them within the context of the times and in the environment from which they begin the journey from housewives to women who work for pay. The 1920s decade remains a foundational change from which the future of women in the workforce will grow over time to include much of the female adult population, notwithstanding a depression and another world war.

Chapter Eight
Working Texas Trend Setters of the 1920s: Beauty, Boots, Booze, Tomatoes, Tamales, and Wings

This chapter reflects the women who worked to support themselves and the women who labored to support their families out of necessity. Some attained attention because of tremendous success in their respective fields; however, all women, whether cooks, maids, migrant workers, or future business empire builders, deserve attention and thanks from all the women who came after them. Few complained; most forged ahead, determined to earn the money that is vital for living. The combinations of their earnings assisted in the growth of Texas. They consumed goods, provided housing, inspired new products, and agitated for educational opportunities for their children. These women changed the paradigm that eventually allowed women to find their own paths without dependence on the earnings of their husbands.

Cowgirl Actress

Allene Ray expressed the Texas grit necessary for accomplishing her goals and perhaps she does represent a New Woman that could support herself outside of family connections. Allene Ray grew up on a ranch riding, roping, and taming wild horses.[515] The blond Ray made numerous silent action western-styled movies in the 1920s.[516] The athletic star sang, danced, and performed her own stunts, but a weak voice forced her from the business as the silent film industry gave way to talking movies.[517] Cursing on the set offended her, so she insisted on a ban on such words. Her ego, unlike many Hollywood stars, was unassuming and low-key. Born in 1895 in San Antonio, she died of cancer in Temple City, California, in 1979.[518]

Hollywood Actress

Joan Crawford was born Lucille Fay LeSeuer in San Antonio. Crawford overcame a tough childhood, made hundreds of appearances in film and television, and never failed to entertain with her quotes; quotes such as, "If you've earned a position, be proud of it. Don't hide it. I want to be recognized. When I hear people say, "Joan Crawford!" I turn around and say, 'Hi! How are you?'"[519] She won the Best Actress Oscar for the 1945 film Mildred Pierce.[520] As a child in San Antonio, she injured her foot, and a doctor informed her that she would always walk with a limp. However, the tenacious, rambunctious young girl practiced for six months until she danced her way to stardom and a high income.[521] Joan Crawford may not have been the perfect mother as viewed by two of her four adopted children as told in their exposé, Mommie Dearest, but she had strong views she always expressed openly and without reservation, and as any man could say, she did her life her way.[522] As a woman, she most regretted not being able to have children, while the two that shocked the public with the story of their childhood lives with an allegedly abusive mother focused attention on family violence in America.[523] Her friends, however, stood by her, believing the book contained rubbish. When the star died, she left no money to the two children she felt had betrayed her, but she left money to the other two adopted children.[524] Crawford made money and directed her life in a way that proved rare at the time.

Western Star and Speakeasy Owner

"Hello suckers!" a greeting exclaimed by Mary "Texas" Guinan in the center of her 300 Club in New York City, a speakeasy when the 1920s roared, one that mobster Owney Madden insisted that she should be allowed to open.[525] Born in Waco in 1884, she had already made about thirty-six silent western-styled silent movies while slinging a gun and riding bare-back as a cowgirl.[526] On arrival in New York, she was mentored by rum runner Larry Fay as the hostess and entertainer of his infamous Fay's El Fey Club.[527] Anecdotally, she may have saved the Prince of Wales, the future King Edward VIII, from arrest during a raid by having him in the kitchen cooking up some eggs with an apron over his suit.[528] She hobnobbed with the famous, including Clara Bow, Babe Ruth, Charles Lindbergh, Lord Mountbatten, and Gloria Swanson.[529] Arrested in 1927 for violating the Volstead Act, she defied the police and claimed at trial that she operated as only a hostess, and in fact, she was a teetotaler who preferred coffee.[530] A not-guilty verdict was rendered.[531] In the late 1920s, she made more movies, one based on her life where she played club owner "Texas Malone" in Queen of the Nightclubs.[532] Her last act in the play "Too Hot for Paris," a true crowd pleaser, ended in Vancouver on November 4, 1933, when she fell ill and perished on an operating table because of ulcerative colitis.[533] Her service in New York drew a crowd of about 12,000,[534] a true send-off for a bare-back riding cowgirl from Texas. Her life ended about a month before the death of Prohibition.[535] Mary "Texas" Guinan's life represented nonconformism and independence at a time of growing conformism. Although her reputation may have been viewed as scandalous by most Texas women, she earned her way with the wild spirit of an untamed Texas Longhorn. She earned her living based on her talents, all rather irreverently and, most assuredly, illegally at the time of Prohibition!

One of Three Emmas: Prohibition Survivor

Presently, Hotel Emma in San Antonio represents a wonderful place to spend a few days, taking advantage of its 3,700-volume library and sipping a drink called the "Three Emmas" in the lobby bar.[536] The hotel was once housed in the Pearl Brewhouse in 1894, where Otto Koehler secured a formula and produced beer. He managed to acquire real estate around San Antonio and in Mexico, becoming one of the richest men in the Southern United States.[537] A sordid tale of the Three Emmas in Otto Koehler's life could easily entertain as an enticing screenplay. Emma, number one, was Otto's wife, who had suffered injuries in an auto accident.[538] Otto hired Emma, number two, known as Emmi, to provide nursing for his wife. Emmi had a friend, Emma, number three, a tall blonde.[539] Otto set the two additional Emmas up in a home together to conduct his affairs with Emma, number two, and supposedly with Emma, number three.[540] At some point, an argument occurred that provoked the tall, blonde Emma to shoot and kill Otto in 1914.[541] "I had to kill him," she said. [542] Although charged with murder, she fled to the war front as a World War I nurse.[543] Eventually, Emma, number three, the tall, blonde nurse, returned to San Antonio after four years. Arrested and tried for murder, an all-male jury rendered a not-guilty verdict.[544] Free to do so, she married one of the jurors.[545] Emma, number two, married and was not heard from again.[546] Hotel Emma refers to Emma Koehler, the wife and widow of Otto Koehler. She, through some shrewd business practices, managed diversification during Prohibition and became the only area brewery to survive the era by opening a dry-cleaning business and an auto repair shop.[547] Keeping all her employees working, they made ice cream, soda, and a fake beer. She gave the reins to her nephew in 1933, but she remained active in the business until her death in 1947.[548] The business survived ups and downs for about six decades until finally closing in 2001. However, the beer company was revived in 2002 when Silver Ventures created a new Pearl beer.[549] Emma's determination made the Texas tradition possible. She is celebrated with these words, "Gone, but not forgotten. Dia de Los Muertos ofrenda for Emma Koehler."[550] Her life is an affirmation that overcoming physical pain, surviving heartache, and persevering during Prohibition ranks her as a tough Texas businesswoman.

The Chili Queens of San Antonio

Generally, during the 1920s, a variety of jobs existed for women in San Antonio, and those depended on race. During that time, police could stop a female and measure the length of her swimsuit to ensure modesty,[551] and women could not enter St. Mary's University at the new campus in 1923. Joske's department remained an economic backbone of the city's shopping scene, and some white women held sales positions. Frost Brothers opened in 1917 as a high-end department store.[552] During the period from the late 1800s until the 1930s, Chili Queens reigned as the young women who operated food stands around the city, later settling on the location of Haymarket Plaza and Milam Park.[553] They, under the protection of family members, sold an array of tasty, spicy food, including chili con carne, tamales, frijoles, enchiladas, and chili verde to locals and tourists.[554] In truth, these young Chili Queens set the stage for the Tex-Mex industry that grew into nationwide favorites over time. William Gebhardt sold canned chili, canned tamales, and chili powder, along with Elmer Doolin, who prepared a snack that Americans love—Fritos.[555] The men built their companies on the traditions of the Chili Queens that were forced by the 1940s to close because of health concerns.[556] The tradition begun by the ladies culminated in a declaration by the Texas Legislature in 1977 that chili con carne was the state dish.[557]

Newspaper Expatriates

San Antonio in the 1920s represented a cultural milieu, including expatriate Mexicans who sought refuge in San Antonio because of the Mexican Revolution.[558] These were women of great religious conviction, and some would later return to the country of their birth.[559] While in Texas, Beatriz Blanco, a devout Catholic, worked on the editorial board of La Prensa in the 1920s and 1930s.[560] The section of the paper focused on the home and concerns of women.[561] Blanco used her talents to expand her writing skills with short stories and essays, and she sometimes became a literary critic.[562] Like many women of the 1920s, she also participated in female-organized clubs. She led the Club Mexicano de Bellas Artes, which gathered exiled Mexican women and offered support and conversation between friends.[563] While in Texas, she earned money as a productive, temporary Texan.

Young Black Female Earns Wings

Other women from small towns in East Texas had big dreams, especially one young black female who found herself under much duress when no trainer would teach her to fly, yet she sought a path to fulfill her goals. Flying for black pilots during the First Era of American aviation, 1903 to 1939, meant that pilot training schools summarily denied many of them entry simply because of their color. Given those racial restrictions against all blacks, Bessie Coleman heroically refused to allow racism to prevent the fulfillment of her dream to fly. She was born in Atlanta, Texas, in 1892 to George and Susan Coleman, themselves children of slaves.[564] Her father moved the family to Waxahachie near Dallas, where shortly after, he walked out on the family.[565] She cared for younger siblings while her mother worked.[566] After her eighth-grade education, she worked at odd jobs. After attempting and failing to finance a university education, she eventually traveled to Chicago. Finding a sponsor for her flying ambition proved easier than finding a white pilot to instruct her. No pilot would train her. Robert Abbot, owner of the African American weekly Chicago Defender, suggested she go to flight school in a country that did not see color.[567] She became the first black to receive an international pilot's license in France on June 15, 1921.[568] In Europe, she dazzled audiences with what seemed an innate ability to soar in her flying machine.[569] Back in the States, she shined brightly as a barnstorming entertainer who opened a flight school for anyone of any color. One of the lasting consequences of Bessie Coleman's success as an independent woman and role model was inspiring Willa B. Brown to take flying lessons.[570] Coleman also motivated a generation of young blacks to join the new age of flying.[571]

Bessie Coleman's Influence

While Willa B. Brown was not a Texan, she, however, augmented the efforts during World War Two by training black pilots. Brown, by 1934, was taking flying lessons, and by 1937, she received her pilot's license, becoming the first black female to earn a license in America.[572] With her husband, Cornelius Coffey, they established one of the first black aviation associations while operating the Coffey School of Aeronautics in Chicago.[573] She represented the first integrated unit of the Civilian Pilot Training Program and the promotion of black airmen as warriors.[574] Their flight school provided pilots for the Air Corps pilot training program at the Tuskegee Institute.[575] She supervised and trained over 200 pilots who transitioned to attain status as Tuskegee Airmen.[576] These men, trained by a woman inspired by Texas-born Bessie Coleman, helped in the effort to win World War II.

The Lady Bootmaker

Western boot-making reinforced the idea that Texas belonged in the collection of Western states; and in 1925, one strong-willed, hardworking lady re-established her father's business in the town of Nocona—hence the birth of the Nocona Boot company that provided jobs for the small community.[577] Enid Justin, one of seven children, married Julius Stelzer when she was twenty-one years of age in 1915, and they later divorced in 1934 because he left her for another woman. And as she reflected on his leaving, she later realized that she seemed to be the last one to know about his affair.[578] Even on their honeymoon in Galveston, a trip that should have lasted three weeks, she insisted they return home three days into the stay because she loved to keep house and wanted to get started in their newly furnished, rented home in Muenster, Texas.[579] They left on a train at four in the morning, and by later that morning, a category four hurricane swept over the island, destroying the hotel.[580] She felt that God had saved them.[581] The couple had one daughter, Enid's only child, born in 1916 dying in 1918.[582] Her work ethic included long hours and a willingness to open her home to boarders where she cooked, ironed, sold coal and washing machines; and, at the same time, acted as her own shipping clerk and bookkeeper.[583] Justin built her business from the ground up because her brothers moved their father's business, taking all the machinery. She borrowed five thousand dollars and paid it back promptly to obtain the equipment needed to make cowboy boots. Dedication sparked growth, and her business prospered because she manufactured quality boots; some, originally cowboy-lace boots that oil boom workers preferred, and she made military boots, too.[584] Justin remarried in 1940, but the marriage ended in 1945.[585] In 1949, she opened the Nocona Boot Company Western Store. From the 1950s to the 1980s, she increased sales, growing from about one hundred employees to over five hundred employees, while selling boots in every state, and overseas, as well.[586] She opened plants in Vernon and Gainesville.[587] Sales increased from about one million, in 1948, to twenty-seven million by 1981.[588] Known as "Miss Enid" in her community, she also had been described as the lady bootmaker, suffering some discrimination as a female; however, her company reached the status of one of the five best boot companies in America.[589] Fortunately for Justin, her father treated his girls exactly as his boys, where the boot business mattered.[590] "You know, it is not what you know that counts, it is what you do with what you do know that counts." [591] She believed she had been liberated long before the term liberation came about.[592] Miss Enid contributed to her hometown through various charities and organized a 1939 re-enactment of the Pony Express Overland mail route from Nocona to the World's Fair in San Francisco.[593] By 1981, she had merged her company with Justin Boots, a company started by her brothers.[594] Enid Justin's muscular work ethic served her well throughout her life. She succeeded as a businesswoman without questioning if she should; she simply worked and did so efficiently. She also exercised a completely traditional role as a housekeeper and cook. Justin devoted all efforts to her successful, well-lived life. On October 14, 1990, in Nocona, Texas, Miss Enid died, where she had made her life in boots. She had been honored by the National Cowgirl Museum and Hall of Fame in Fort Worth and also by the National Cowboy Hall of Fame in Oklahoma City. A lifetime of honors included, as well, those by business groups, various government entities, and historical societies.[595]

A Teacher and a Business Lady

Mary Eva Dominy Martin, of Trinity Country, obtained her teaching credentials from Sam Houston Teacher's College in Huntsville; however, after teaching only one year, she chose to attend Tyler Commercial College to pursue a business career.[596] She met and married W. A. (Jack) Martin, a returning World War I veteran, and they began their careers at Mayfield Grocery Company in Tyler.[597] Later, her husband and a new partner opened a smoke shop on South Broadway while Mary became a bookkeeper for Jackson's Dodge Motor Company.[598] The couple later bought about a thousand-acre ranch in Flint, where they raised cattle and farmed.[599] She died in 1970. According to her sister Emma Dominy Bolling, Mary "was an ideal sister."[600] Many East Texas women taught school, and some worked with their husbands in various small businesses across the area. All earned salaries and contributed to the fiscal growth of the state.

Not an Ordinary Lady

Carrie Harrison Poe Hensley was born February 9, 1883, most likely in Longview, to John T. Poe, a preacher, and Caroline Haydon Wright.[601] Her siblings had left home, so her father spoiled the young child. During the holiday, each enjoyed finding special little gifts in their Christmas stockings and spending days opening each one until emptied.[602] While at her aunt's home in Longview, she heard the shots fired when the Dalton Brothers robbed the bank.[603] She played under her father's chess table when he and her uncle engaged each other in a game.[604] Carrie actively advanced the cause of women's rights because, after high school, she left home to become a secretary at a railway office in St. Louis, Missouri.[605] Males filled most professional secretarial positions in the 1800s and early 1900s. She bravely took the job. The date of her graduation was unclear. However, she most likely could have been in her late teens. Her family noted that "No one ever doubted the least bit that Carrie was not a genuine lady," and she lived all ninety-six years in that mode.[606] Flamboyant and independent at a time when acting demurely defined womanhood, she definitely colored "outside the lines."

Agricultural Extension Demonstrators

While not often mentioned in Texas history books, a program originated from the US Department of Agriculture in the early twentieth century engaged women in rural areas of the country as educators to enhance the benefits of efficiency farming.[607] The Cooperative Extension Service originated through an act of Congress with the Smith-Lever Act of 1914, a brainchild of Seaman K. Knapp.[608] His son, Dr. Bradford Knapp, chose Edna Westbrook Trigg of Milam County to head up the new program, and she came with excellent qualifications as a wife, mother, teacher, and principal.[609] Paid a salary of one hundred dollars a month, Trigg was expected to cover her expenses from her pay. Dr. Knapp later became president of Texas Technological College, which eventually became Texas Tech University.[610] Trigg traveled alone on country roads, visiting farms and ranches, teaching common sense farming techniques and skills. Agents gathered to teach at Girl's Home Demonstration Clubs across the state in the 1920s, often meeting at the Texas State Fair in

Dallas.[611] Trigg formed and supervised Girls' Tomato Clubs around the county, along with the Boys' Corn Clubs. These organizations eventually underpinned the concept of the 4-H Clubs, which are so presently popular in the state.[612] Trigg, as a teacher, encouraged younger agents to save for college education and saw that her daughters understood the value of an education.[613] One daughter followed her mother's footsteps, becoming a twenty-year agent in Eastland County.[614] Another example of a member of the Women's Home Demonstration team included Mary Wheat Kee from East Texas, whose great-grandfather helped originate the city of Woodville in Tyler County.[615] Kee married James Taylor Kee, a teacher, sawmill worker, and a trustee of several school boards, while Mary worked in their church, reared six children, assisted a local doctor with the births of local babies, and nursed the sick in her community.[616] Like Trigg, Kee insisted that her children obtained educations, and five of her offspring attained teaching certificates and taught in area Trinity County schools.[617] Two earned Master's degrees, and one became a lawyer in Angleton.[618] Skills taught by agents throughout the state included canning, sewing, cooking, household management, family health, poultry raising, and vegetable gardening.[619] Education led to home-based businesses with women and young girls selling canned tomatoes and peaches, along with the selling of poultry.[620] The program changed to address the needs of the times, performing exceptionally well during the Great Depression to ensure proper nutrition for rural children.[621] During World War II, agents executed plans to increase food production for America, for the military, and the Allies.[622] By the 1960s, the agents concentrated on senior citizens and diseases such as Diabetes.[623] The federally sanctioned and state-run agency safeguarded the stability of rural families while improving their lives and assisting their move into the middle class. These resilient and determined women made the most of their talents and insisted on passing a strong work ethic to their offspring, creating a wealthier Texas, whether measured in money or backbone.

Answering the Call

A fire alarm located near where the operator's connected calls warned the fire department with a loudly piercing sound triggered by the turning of an electrical switch in the community of Trinity beginning in 1926.[624] Mrs. J.B. Wooten and her co-workers answered a switchboard for the Trinity Telephone Exchange owned by Mr. W. A. Bell.[625] Three hundred separate numbers and a large number of party lines, along with seven long-distance lines, made up the telephone company. All operators were female, with three working during peak times, two covering a swing shift, and one a married lady, connecting nighttime calls.[626] The company shared space in downtown Trinity with the bank, the drug store, and a general merchandise store. W. A. Bell sold his company to Mid-Continental Telephone Company in 1928, and as compared with modern times when companies dramatically altered personnel and business plans, no operators lost their jobs, and the procedures remained the same.[627] Many telephone companies in the late 1800s had originally hired male teenage employees; however, they proved rude and uncontrollable in many cases.[628] While many exchanges may have been larger than Bell's company at the time, the overall direction in Texas and America trended toward female operators. By 1920, thirty-five percent of all Americans had a telephone, and by 1930, about forty-one percent enjoyed service in their homes. These ladies sat for long hours, and sometimes, their weight and height were figured into those selected for positions, along with how they spoke. Many of these women performed technical duties that kept the board operating. In small towns, women operators knew about the community, reported the weather, informed people as to the time, tended to be fashionably dressed, remained calm in emergencies, and did some local gossiping, too.[629] The position became more formalized over time with restrictions as to conversations allowed with customers. Many operators worked for corporations and hotels during the 1920s and 1930s. Communications proved vital for a state as large as Texas, which needed companies to be connected promptly, whereby crucial decisions could facilitate doing business and creating profit. And the ladies provided those needed connections at a time when the state was expanding and modernizing.

Roping, Riding, and Winning

Jewel Frost Duncan rode and roped as a young girl on a West Texas ranch.[630] During the 1920s, women had little opportunity to compete in roping contests.[631] That changed when Duncan became the first female in 1929 at the Pecos Rodeo to rope in a competition with men.[632] Her friend Isora DeRacy Young joined her, competing at rodeos, and by 1935, Duncan won the title of Rodeo Queen.[633] Born in 1902, Duncan died in 1984.[634] Inducted into the National Cowgirl Museum and Hall of Fame in 1976, she had broken the traditional rodeo rules by proving she had the talent needed to win.[635] Many West Texas females performed chores on cattle ranches just as their male siblings had, and most were quite driven and independent.

Necessity Tamales

In 1926, Adelaida Cuellar found herself needing to support and feed twelve children.[636] Although she was born in Mexico in 1871, she married in 1892 in Laredo, Texas, where the couple started their lives.[637] Both engaged in sharecropping and worked as migrant farmers. At the Kaufman County fair, she sold her tamales, which proved so appealing that she repeated the effort the next year. While she cooked, her sons ran a local Mexican restaurant in Kaufman; however, the Great Depression overwhelmed the business and the community.[638] Her legacy included four East Texas restaurants, along with one each in Oklahoma and Louisiana, operated by her sons.[639] Although these closed by the close of the 1930s, her sons relocated to Dallas, opening El Charro.[640] The place proved popular with a profit within three years.[641] El Charro became El Chico, and El Chico Corporation grew across the state of Texas with twenty varied business ventures.[642] Her sons, known as "Mama's boys," had made Mama proud.[643] She died in 1969, leaving a successful, profitable business that promoted the growth of Texas.

Hotel Keeper

Mattie Eliza Horn Swinney Hatcher's family arrived in Texas in 1849. Hatcher was born November 28, 1862, at Magnolia Springs.[644] After schooling in the town of her birth, she attended a college in Jasper known as the South East Texas Male and Female College, later known as Jasper Collegiate Institute.[645] Self-reliance and self-direction identified the young woman.[646] She married medical doctor Samuel H. Swinney on April 10, 1884.[647] While living in Coryell County, their first child, a son, died.[648] By 1887, the couple resided in Nogalus Prairie, moving on to Centralia in Trinity County.[649] By the time they relocated to Groveton in 1900, they had three sons.[650] The hotel business seemed appropriate for them, and after a fire that destroyed one building, they purchased the Holley House, raised it, and built the Swinney Hotel. However, in 1908, on a trip to Houston, Samuel died. She ran the hotel, and in 1912, she and John B Hatcher married. He had served in the Spanish-American War and earned his living as a printer for the Trinity County News.[651] Mattie Hatcher's three sons died during her lifetime: one in 1910, another in 1917, from an automobile accident, and one in 1926 in Tucson, Arizona.[652] Daughters Mattie May and Fannie May married and had children.[653] Grandchildren visited the hotelier, enjoying summers with her.[654] Mattie Swinney Hatcher served excellent meals in her hotel restaurant to Groveton workers and she had pride in a productive pecan tree that she had planted when the hotel was first opened. She resided in a small home that she had built next door to her hotel. Dying at 98 years of age on October 15, 1961, she is buried with her family members and her two husbands at the Groveton Glenwood Cemetery. Mattie Swinney Hatcher—tenacious female role model and survivor of tragedies.

A Dollar a Day

A dollar-a-day pay in East Texas, in the 1920s, supported widow Mattie Rosalie Terry Hood Hearn and her four children.[655] She supplemented her earnings by renting out two of the five rooms of her house on Ellis Avenue in Burke.[656] Mattie Terry, daughter of Sanford Warren Terry and Eliza Cornelia Cockerham, spent her childhood in Crecy, where her father farmed and taught school.[657] She married John Shelby Hood in 1906, a carpenter and prolific home builder in both Trinity and Angelina counties.[658] He also served as a mill foreman for the Trinity County Lumber Company, among other mills in East Texas.[659] Shelby and Mattie cared for his brother's two children for a while, after both he and his wife and two of their children, succumbed to the flu epidemic of 1918.[660] In 1920, Mattie and Shelby moved to Lufkin and later moved to Burke, a small town just south of Lufkin.[661] While Shelby worked on a new school building in Tallulah, Louisiana, a drunk 75 year old man shot him in the back, killing him.[662] No reason for his murder surfaced and the men did not know each other.[663] Mattie Hood, with no means of support, moved in with her sister.[664] Her parents lived next door. She searched and searched for employment, becoming depressed over her situation.[665] At last, she gained a part-time position with W.M. Glenn Furniture Store.[666] Later, a full-time position at Davis Grocery Store paid her a dollar a day.[667] With this income, she moved a block away from her parents and sister, renting out two rooms for Travis and Zelda Hearn and their newborn child.[668] Travis Hearn's father visited the young couple to engage with his first grandchild.[669] Ben D. Hearn met widow Mattie Hood, falling in love with her and marrying her in 1927.[670] Both enjoyed farming, and they immediately moved to the country to raise crops and game.[671] Ben D. Hearn lived until 1955, and Mattie died at her daughter's home in 1961.[672] She is an example of many widows during the 1920s who suffered tragedy, worked hard to overcome setbacks, labored to feed their children, and eventually were fortunate to find love again. She wanted to farm and did so in a grand manner.

A Variety of Texas Women in an Assortment of Jobs in the 1920s

Beaumont: Althea Chessman worked as a bookkeeper for Flanagan and Sons, a stevedore firm, in the San Jacinto Building.[673]

Beaumont: Florence Stratton, an off-and-on writer for the Beaumont Journal and the Beaumont Enterprise, produced a book chronicling the history of the city in 1925 titled The Story of Beaumont.[674] Her weekly article, "Susie's Spindletop's Weekly Letter," provided the community with information on the city's activities.[675] She designed the home she had built, located at 1929 McFaddin, using bricks from the 1892 Beaumont Courthouse and those from her grandfather's plantation home.[676] Stratton, who never married, died in 1938, leaving her property to her niece.[677]

Beaumont: In 1927, Margaret Richardson cooked for George T. Adams, Sr., and his wife, Stella, at their 2205 North Street home.[678] Mr. Adams was the president of S. L. Adams & Co. Hardware and Marine Supplies store.[679]

Lubbock: Mrs. Lottie Pinkston, with her husband, had a general store in the city that catered to an incipient black community.[680] She voluntarily granted credit to families in the neighborhood and hired blacks to work in her store.[681] Besides groceries, the store sold kerosene, ice, and coal.[682] At the time, Pinkston's cordiality toward blacks was rare among the general population.[683] Most of the black females worked as maids for the more prominent in the area.[684]

El Paso: While not an individual woman doing business in the 1920s, a group of women that formed The Woman's Club of El Paso achieved many social and educational accomplishments such as the teaching of music in schools, the introduction of kindergarten, the promotion of food safety, the necessity for city sanitation, and the ladies paid for the first physical education teacher in the city.[685] In 1924, Mrs. Percy McGhee lobbied for a Woman's Division of the Chamber of Commerce, and Kate Moore Brown served as chairman/director for the first two years.[686] The women knew the importance of business and commerce as crucial to sustaining the population of El Paso within a liberal mindset necessary for a strong middle class and the uplifting of those with little means.

Chapter Nine
Grace Under Pressure: The Great Depression Years, 1929-1941

"Control your destiny or someone else will," stated the late American business giant Jack Welch.[687] During the time from the crash of the US Stock Market on October 29, 1929, until the start of World War II, the United States and the Western industrialized world suffered the greatest economic downturn in history.[688] For women in Texas, controlling their destinies after a decade of promise became more challenging; however, they resolved to persevere with grace under pressure. The major causes of the tragic economic downfall can be described by the acronym FLOOD, which included rampant fraud, uncontrolled laissez-faire, massive overproduction, brazen over-speculation, and a downward spiral in foreign trade. Most Texans still farmed as independent owners, tenants, or migrant workers at the start of the troubles, and the state remained mostly rural. At first, Texans thought that the disaster in the Northeast would only affect that segment of the country because the state produced cotton, lumber, oil, wool, and food from farms that would sustain the population. However, the depression proved a contagion stronger than anything the state produced could overcome, and most Texans faced hard and tragic times for a decade. For example, a migrant farmer in Bryan earned eight cents a day for hoeing cotton.[689] In conjunction with the financial disaster, four hurricanes, two tropical storms, and a gigantic drought coupled with blowing sandstorms ravaged parts of the state.[690] Women ran farms with their husbands, and those looking for work in the cities faced shame for doing so because jobs should be given to male breadwinners. Only one in every four workers was female, and in a survey in 1936, eighty-two percent of Americans believed jobs should go to men.[691] Yet, some new businesses would open, and some women would flourish, taking chances during times of duress to control their destinies.

The total population of the state by 1930 was 5,824,715. Houston, where "seventeen railroads meet the sea,"[692] and Dallas will overtake San Antonio as two of the largest urban communities at the start of the new decade. The four largest urban areas in Texas included Houston, population 292,352; Dallas, population 260,475; San Antonio, population 231,547; and Fort Worth, population 163,447.[693] The top ten positions that engaged women in the working world in 1930 included the following: operatives (manufacturing), domestics, teachers, stenographers and typists, clerks, saleswomen, bookkeepers and cashiers, farm laborers, cooks, and laundresses.[694] While the railroads and Model-Ts transported goods and people, the radio connected Texans to the world and abolished cultural differences by connecting both rural and city folks with information and entertainment through the dark days of the Depression. About twelve million Americans had radios, and toward the start of World War II, approximately twenty-eight million enjoyed the radio.[695] Again, Texas women worked to support their families, whether on farms, ranches, or in urban areas. Various government programs and experiments that came to fruition in the state included decision-making made by women of Texas.

What women wore provided some psychic comfort because how one presented themselves provided a measure of control in one's life at a time of stress and uncertainty during the Swing Era of the Great Depression. The new Swing Era was a dilution of jazz by big bands with multi-instruments and multi-musicians.[696] Fashions for women in America reflected the financial downturn as women remade dresses until mending could no longer sustain the garment, and then they purchased a new frock, if able, or bought material to sew a new pattern that reflected the 1930s styles.[697] Texas urban working women wore tightly fitted coats and suits that had feminine pleating and now emphasized the waist.[698] Gone were the more frivolous dresses of the freewheeling 1920s. The suits copied men's wear, however, blouses had ruffles and skirts ended mid-calf. The purpose of dressing in a business suit showed bosses that the female took work responsibilities seriously. Paris fashions, while still influential, had less and less importance because Hollywood exercised more influence over women's clothing and hairstyles in America. While dress lengths grew longer, necklines plunged a bit, perhaps due to new methods of making bras that now reflected cup size.[699] Hair tended to be shoulder length with waves or soft curls, and make-up finished the pale look that was highlighted with rouge and lipstick, as having a tan indicated outdoor physical labor.

"Although both men and women downsize consumer spending in response to recession cues there is an exception to this and this is beauty products," said Sarah E. Hill, an assistant professor of social psychology at Texas Christian University in Fort Worth.[700] As Lady Bird Johnson, former US First Lady, stated, "Flowers in the city are like lipstick on a woman—it just makes you look better to have a little color."[701] The sales of make-up and various cosmetics doubled during the economic disaster, even as industrial output plummeted.[702] Farming women and ranching women dressed according to their chores and duties. Many housedresses for rural women were sometimes constructed from flour sacks that came in a variety of pretty prints.[703] Women made curtains, tea towels, underwear, shirts, and quilts from various farm supply sacks.[704] As always, in Texas's past, women wanted special dresses for church. The hats and gloves continued, but wide-brims and pillboxes replaced the Cloche-styled covers of the 1920s. While women could not change the decade of hardships, they managed to endure, adapting when possible.

Some changes in the maintenance of the household occurred during the depression that made the chores easier for urban women, as changes slowly trickled to rural areas. Women faced the challenge of how to feed their families within serious budget restrictions and to provide entertainment that lessened the pain of living in economically turbulent times. Technological advances assisted some women during the time, including electric washers, coffee pots, and water heaters, along with lighting and running water.[705] Still, many rural areas did not have such amenities; however, New Deal projects introduced such advances to farmers and ranchers in both East and West Texas. Cities enjoyed deliveries of blocks of ice to sustain ice boxes, while farmers and ranchers seldom enjoyed iced beverages.[706] However, the Servel brand produced a gas refrigerator during the 1930s that those without electricity could purchase, and it produced ice in a small freezer portion of the eight- to ten-cubic-foot machine.[707] Iced tea enjoyed at Sunday dinners with fried chicken and an occasional banana pudding in summertime provided comfort in rural East Texas.[708] The General Electric Monitor became available as a right-priced electric refrigerator in 1935 as the result of the New Deal loan program.[709] Entertainment included such iconic movies as "The Wizard of Oz" and "Snow White and the Seven Dwarves."[710] The epic Civil War romance film, set in the American South, "Gone with the Wind," based on a popular novel by Margaret Mitchell, arrived at movie theatres in 1939.[711]

Radio Queen

Claudia Alta Taylor, born December 22, 1912, in Karnack, had all the privileges afforded to those of wealth in Texas; however, she knew pain because her mother died in 1918 when she was quite young.[712] An aunt and nursemaid reared the young girl who preferred nature and books to the company of other children.[713] Her father's money presented educational opportunities many could not afford. She excelled in her studies and entered the University of Texas in 1930 during the throes of the Great Depression.[714] Unlike many students, she had an automobile and access to a charge account. But unlike some of the well-to-do, she seemed naturally frugal. Later in life, when shopping for clothing at Neiman Marcus, she set a limit as to spending on clothing for either herself or her two daughters, refusing to let desire overwhelm her sense of fiscal responsibility at a time when her wealth proved sufficient enough to purchase more.[715] Graduating with a history degree in 1933, followed by a degree in journalism in 1934, she did not formally work in the private sector until World War Two. By the 1930s, women with college degrees had entered universities hoping to graduate with skills that enabled employment, however, women had also obtained degrees to attract suitable husbands.[716] Fewer than 100,000 women attended college in 1900; however, by the 1940s, about 600,000 were attending.[717] Like many women of that period, marriage was a natural progression of life, and she married on November 17, 1934, during the Great Depression at Saint Mark's Episcopal Church in San Antonio; they honeymooned in Monterrey, Mexico, and her husband spent much of the time discussing business and his life goals, while she wanted to enjoy the architecture and foreign culture.[718]

Claudia Taylor's life became intertwined with her husband's ambitions, and she would, over time, be lauded as an author, advisor, and activist, but she exercised strong business acumen with her ownership of KTBC, an Austin radio station that had a weak signal and operated from a dirty office.[719] While historians tended to focus on her lack of business experience, she used her degree in journalism as any man would have, and she purchased the station in her name. While it is true that she inherited money from her father that provided funds for the control of the station, the business was in the red by about six hundred dollars a month.[720] Her dedication and commitment were reflected in her own words, "I spent one day myself with a bucket full of soap and rags and whatever suitable things there were, washing the windows, while some of [the employees] just stood around there with their mouths open thinking, What kind of person have we got here?" [721] They truly had a businesswoman who used her education to fulfill a personal goal. The FCC had approved her purchase of the radio station in February 1943 and she came armed with knowledge of programming, promotions, advertising, regulations, and management.[722] Moving the radio station to a new location, she quickly dispensed with owed invoices and hired new management.[723] By August of 1943, after the station became a CBS affiliate and the power of the station doubled and operated around the clock, a profit of eighteen dollars was realized.[724] She worked hard in Austin while her husband, Lyndon Baines Johnson, served in the United States Congress in Washington, D.C.[725] They represented a double-income family at a time when that proved quite atypical.[726] During the war years, she hired female staff, including Nellie Connally—future first lady of Texas—as well as Anne Eastland and Louise Vine.[727] By 1945, the station had realized a profit of 40,000 dollars after taxes.[728]

With two young children and a husband making the move to the US Senate, Lady Bird, as she had been called since childhood, built a television station KTBC-TV in Austin; and in 1952, on Thanksgiving day, the station delivered the University of Texas versus Texas A & M football game.[729] Lady Bird Johnson bought interests in other Texas television stations in the Austin area.[730] By 1959, the company reached a value of about two million dollars, and in 1960, Lady Bird continued to expand by adding an FM radio station because she saw the value in new technology.[731] With the new call letters KLBJ-FM, the station became the longest-broadcasting FM radio station in Austin by 1973.[732] The legacy of Lady Bird Johnson's business life included her innate ability to hire truly excellent broadcasters and to venture into new technology with open eyes.[733] In 1988, the Texas Association of Broadcasters (TAB) and the Texas Broadcast Education Foundation set up a scholarship for a deserving University of Texas broadcast student.[734] TAB bestowed Lady Bird with the Pioneer Broadcaster of the Year award in 2007 for outstanding service to her community.[735] Lady Bird carved her career outside the realm of her what-would-be husband, who became the thirty-sixth president of the United States. Like other women of her time, she had learned shorthand and typing and made the statement that doing so would get a woman through the door.[736] Her shrewd business decisions finally overwhelmed the need for her to know how to type. Little did she know that typing tests would become the litmus test for working women well into the 1990s, whether degreed or not. Her duties as First Lady, along with her environmental efforts to beautify America, were much lauded; however, she stands as a prototype for women doing business in Texas.

Rodeo Queen

Ruth Roach Salmon ran a ranch in Nocona with her husband in 1938 Texas.[737] However, she mastered roping and riding in the early 1920s and rode in Buffalo Bill's Wild West Show that traveled around the world.[738] During her twenty-four-year career, her favorite event was bronc riding.[739] Roach's rodeo victories included titles of World Champion All Around Cowgirl, World's Champion Girl Bronc Rider, and World's Champion Trick Rider.[740] Rodeo became profitable in 1930 when investors would sponsor events. Roach exhibited freedom and rebellion as she road while standing with her arms raised, performing at rodeos. Elizabeth Atwood Lawrence wrote about the rodeo, stating that

> "The bronc, central symbol of rodeo, seems to represent an outlaw, a force of resistance to conventional society. Rodeo people believe that its rebelliousness is genetic and cannot be taught. Something within a particular animal causes this behavior, and makes it incorrigible, even though the horse may appear docile at times and go through stages of its life when it appears to have been tamed . . . The unpredictability of a bronc is a key quality, and one which expresses the essence of rodeo itself."[741]

Ruth Roach Salmon lived a thrilling, far-from-conventional life "working" at something she found rewarding and fulfilling. She earned money doing what came naturally.

A Well-Connected Lady

An example of a government experiment at communal farming came about during Franklin Roosevelt's New Deal, beginning in 1932 when Mrs. John Martin Thompson reached out to a powerful friend for relief from the financial misery in her East Texas community. Woodlake had housed a mill operation, starting in 1882, when John Martin Thompson and Henry Tucker began their sawmill operation on 12,000 acres.[742] Kerosene lamps were used in the early 1900s and no paved roads existed, along with a four-room school building by 1925.[743] After the economic crash money proved scarce and Mrs. Thompson sold forty-acre plots to workers that had been with her for many years.[744] She called on Jesse H. Jones,[745] the man later known as "Mr. Houston" for his financial expertise and his service to the country under three presidents, Wilson,

Hoover, and Roosevelt.[746] At the time Jones headed a powerful arm of the New Deal, the Reconstruction Finance Corporation and he had saved all banks in the city of Houston from collapse.[747] A definite powerhouse, he dispersed billions of dollars to farmers, industries, and citizens.[748] Through the Texas Rural Communities Program, homes on 2,000 acres at Woodlake housed unemployed people from various Texas cities.[749] An almost perfect community of farms located within the area of a trading post and a high school, all built for communal life, was completed in 1935.[750] The experimental 1800-acre area included a blacksmith shop and a large dairy with about 200 cows for milk.[751] The homes constructed came equipped with a modern bathroom, a deep water well, and an individual septic system.[752] The city folk who moved to these special homes were to produce food and to share the bounty.[753] The flaw in the plan included a lack of farming know-how and a major lack of incentive.[754] The farm manager became exasperated and abandoned his duties.[755] The winds of war blew in Europe by 1938 and as jobs became available in war industries, these ne'er-do-well farmers abandoned their homes for jobs in urban areas.[756] Mrs. Thompson exercised her best discretion to prevent hunger and desperation during times of duress.

Clerking for an Oil Company as a Widow

Gertie Pool Bell became a widow in 1932.[757] However, she fortunately found work during the depression as an office clerk in Beaumont for Magnolia Refinery (now Mobil Oil).[758] Bell had graduated from Groveton High School in 1920 and took advantage of an educational opportunity to study business in Beaumont before she married an Englishman trained in Scotland as a pharmacist.[759] Casper Bell found his way to Canada and later came to Texas, marrying Gertie Pool on June 1, 1924. Sadly, her marriage lasted only about eight years; however, her job at the oil company endured for thirty years.[760] During those times, she traveled, cooked, and enjoyed reading.[761] She lived seventy-eight years and was buried in Forest Lawn Cemetery in Beaumont.[762] Gertie Bell supported herself, enjoyed church activities, and represented a woman working during the Great Depression.

Cotton Picker and Wild Grape Scout

Isicetta Nicholds James' parents combined the names of family members to bestow on their daughter, born March 20, 1915, in Trinity County.[763] Much later in life, sometime before her sixty-second birthday, she traveled to the Groveton courthouse to obtain a birth certificate.[764] With no name on the birth certificate and no sex of the baby given, she guessed the old doctor simply forgot to record those necessities onto the legal document.[765] One assumes that the date, March 20, 1915, was correct, along with her parents' names, Herman Nicholds and wife, Nellie Nicholds.[766] Isicetta enjoyed life on the farm with her three brothers and two sisters.[767] As the oldest, she babysat and enjoyed farming. Her ancestry carried Indian bloodlines on both sides of the family. [768] Isaac Ross Shinn, her great-grandfather's mother, was one-quarter Indian.[769] His great-grandfather became chief of one tribe, either the Crow or the Shoshone in North Carolina. Great-grandpa Shinn married Grandmama Sarah Shinn in Mississippi in 1850.[770] By 1858, the family was living in Trinity County Texas, later purchasing 400 acres in Walker County across the Trinity River.[771] Courthouse microfilm records at Huntsville, Texas indicate that the land was bartered with a saddle, a gun, some boots, a dog, and a horse.[772] Great-grandpa Shinn belonged to the Masonic Lodge formed by Sam Houston at Huntsville and they shared a friendship.[773] The elder Shinn later returned to Trinity County, buying land in White Rock Bottom, near what is now known as Shinn Branch on some deed maps.[774] As a child, along with her brother Woodrow, they roamed the land crawfishing as a small branch provided ample of what Isicetta thought were nasty little creatures that she refused to eat when the family enjoyed crawfish tails.[775] She hunted rocks, swam in the old fishing hole, thinned corn, chopped cotton, and picked cotton.[776] Isicetta believed in hard work and that cotton picking provided great exercise that produced healthy people who were "not too overweight."[777] The farm had cattle, chickens, and hogs as most did during this time in East Texas.[778] She and her brother scouted for blackberries and wild grapes that provided fruit, and the family grew peanuts and canned vegetables for the winter season. Things were harder during the Great Depression. She, at nineteen years of age, married Elder Lee James sometime in 1934.[779] Her family survived the depression with little money, and she picked cotton for one cent a pound. Isicetta could pick a hundred pounds a day and earned one dollar or more if she managed to gather over a hundred. [780] Cloth at Ben Gates Store cost fifteen cents a yard whereby her mother sewed her a new dress every week while the season lasted.[781] She recalled that she wore a new dress to church every week for quite a while.[782] Isicetta Nicholds James and her husband had one son born January 10, 1947, in Trinity, Texas and her marriage had lasted forty-seven years when her husband passed on February 14, 1981.[783] She loved living and exploring on the farm, but most of all, she represented many young Texas women giving life all that they could during trying times.

Maternity Clothes by Page Boy

During the Great Depression in Texas, many women suffered through the times by sewing their own clothing and washing clothes in the drought-plagued ponds and rivers where water levels had fallen greatly. For example, parts of East Texas received no rain for three years.[784] Many women struggled as New Deal projects attempted to ameliorate the pain of the depression. However, in 1939, two sisters from Dallas, Elsie Frankfurt and Edna Ravkind formed Page Boy Maternity clothing by raising five hundred dollars to launch their innovative company.[785] Edna was pregnant at the time and her sister who had graduated from Southern Methodist University after studying mathematics created an outfit for her that they later obtained a patent for the design.[786] The company extended from coast to coast.[787] An extraordinary woman, Frankfurt, before her marriage to industrialist Franklin Pollock, traveled to Tunisia with several businessmen as emissaries for the Small Business Administration and served on President Reagan's National Advisory Council on Continuing Education in 1982.[788] Both she and her sister carved a special niche that served the needs of women in a trying time.

Texas Cattle Breeder

Dr. Wyatt S. Miles of Pennington, Texas lost his wife Mary Lee Bradley Miles on October 8, 1912, marrying her sister Claire Bradley on June 6, 1915.[789] Claire's birthday was October 21, 1882.[790] Attending the Steele Academy she studied Latin and spoke it as well.[791] The Miles moved to Crockett near the start of the Great Depression where Clair truly enjoyed raising and breeding cattle for the next forty-two years, and she managed her husband's estate, which included registered horses from Kentucky, after his death in October 1941.[792] Claire crossed Red Brahma with Hereford cattle. She also reared their three children. Claire lived a long life, dying at 98 and she is buried in Evergreen Memorial Cemetery, Crockett, Texas.[793] She, like many widows managed farms and ranches during the Great Depression and beyond.

Miss Annie's Eggs and Butter

During the Great Depression, both before and after, Annie Spinn Neumann grew chickens and raised cattle outside of Brenham, Texas. Blue Bell Ice Cream, a Texas favorite since 1907, used the finest ingredients including Miss Annie's superior cream.[794] Miss Annie gathered her eggs and cream, driving her horse and buggy from her farm located about four miles from town into Brenham delivering her products from her cart.[795] Most of the community knew her and they tolerated her horse and buggy in town. She yelled out to customers as she never left her perch on the buggy, insisting that customers and the Blue Bell employees come to her to unload their purchases.[796] Even when she bought supplies, the store sent a clerk to take her order.[797] Her supplies, she insisted, were top of the line.[798] By the 1950s, she still insisted on her horse and buggy delivery method which caused more than a few traffic jams in the city.[799] Although a bit eccentric, Miss Annie worked for fifty years as a perfectionist businesswoman delivering the best products to locals and her sweet cream enabled Blue Bell to create a delicious dessert loved by most Texans lucky enough to have it sold in their communities.

Chapter Ten
War, Betrayal, and Red Lipstick: Texas Women at Work, 1941-1949

No one wanted World War II except the dictators of Germany, Italy, and Japan—certainly not the Brits, most assuredly not the Americans, and absolutely not the women. Those who sought such hostilities were both mad and bad by exercising such menacing masculinity. Women reacted through a silent code of adaptability and acquiescence that reflected their overall status as non-decision makers but as necessary participants in a concerted effort to defeat the Axis powers. Women learned to accommodate adversity during the bifurcated decade of war and peace by bridging the gap between their private life roles and public life responsibilities as a civil-military fusion emerged during wartime. The combatants entered another world conflict with Germany's blitzkrieg into Poland which precipitated a cascading number of countries into vicious combat between totalitarianism and freedom. The United States entered World War Two shortly after the Empire of Japan attacked Pearl Harbor on December 7, 1941, a little after eight in the morning. America had put the pain of the Great Depression aside and quickly scaled up against the jackals of war. The European Allies had been defending themselves since the early hours of September 1, 1939, after Adolph Hitler's German army rolled into Poland when the ground was hard and firm enough to sustain his tanks and the Luftwaffe softened the targets from the air.[800] The Blitzkrieg Principle of war worked and would until the Battle of the Bulge on January 25, 1945.[801] Finally, the Germans surrendered at Reims, France on May 7, 1945; and the Japanese faced defeat that same year by August 15th with a formal ceremony on September 2nd after the United States dropped two atomic bombs at strategic locations in Japan. War betrays and destroys the essential foundations of civilized society—security and the right to life. Texans heeded the call to war and the women adapted by modifying their personal goals, melding into a wartime economy, assisting good men who fought to restore world order from the chaos of Hitler's vanity, Mussolini's insanity, and the false pride of the Japanese.

In 1939, France when some thought another invasion possible, Lucien Lelong, the head of the couturiers' association, said, "The more elegant French women are...the more our country will show people abroad that it does not fear the future."[802] The future that perhaps should have been feared looked horribly bleak in the early 1940s. Men from hostile countries had mismanaged the world, leaving women and families unmoored, living in gales of circumstances beyond their control. American women heard another clarion call to arms, as their European sisters had earlier, and they left their homes to provide sustenance and war matériel while the men went to fight the good fight to erase totalitarian Nazism by defeating Hitler, Mussolini, Tojo, and Yamamoto. From the home front to the war front, the labor of Texas women working as Rosie and her sister Riveters provided the war matériel to defeat the enemy. As their British counterparts were doing, the war-women of Texas painted their lips, dabbed on perfume, and repaired ships on the coastline wearing trousers and work boots. Some would work as spotters of enemy aircraft, others would keep the children of working women, some would feed the workers, some sold war bonds, some joined the various military branches; some flew airplanes, some repaired trucks, some worked at the numerous military installations around the state, and some worked as maids and cooks in boarding homes at the coastal ports where women repaired naval ships. During the war years and the aftermath of the conflict, some women faced the aftermaths of eight hurricanes that hit the Texas Gulf Coast, three of them blasting Galveston Island, one struck at Freeport, two at Matagorda Bay, and two east of Sabine Pass.[803] Along with these disasters, eight tornadoes struck around the state, causing deaths, many injuries, and massive loss of property.[804] Rationing of various foods, including sugar and necessities such as gasoline, forced women to modify lifestyles and recipes to feed their families and sustain good health.[805]

At the start of the 1940s, the following represented the top ten occupations of women and the number one position included "operatives," meaning jobs in manufacturing. The other occupations ranked from two to ten, respectively, are private household workers, stenographers, typists, secretaries, teachers, clerks, and saleswomen; bookkeepers, accountants, cashiers, waitresses, proprietors, managers, officials, and housekeepers to private families.[806] These jobs, modified because of the war, include

350,000 US women as non-combat female pilots, photographers, mail clerks, nurses, intelligence clerks, drivers, translators, government office workers, and nurses.[807] On the home front, women gardened, took over family finances, drove taxis, and worked in the construction, lumber, steel, and munitions industries.[808] The population of Texas reached 6,414,824 in 1940.[809] The US unemployment rate in 1940 was 14.6 percent with an 8.8 GDP, and as the war progressed the rate dropped continually in 1941 to 9.9 with the rate in 1942 reaching 4.7, while in 1943 the rate reached a low of 1.9 percent.[810] GDP during the war years ranged from 17 to 18.9 for the country. The state remained mainly agrarian at the start of hostilities, but that quickly changed when oil became a war requirement. Texas beef provided food, and the state became the training grounds for well over a million-armed forces personnel. The War Manpower Commission had nineteen million women working for the war effort, but by 1942, six million more were needed.[811] Bulletins encouraged women to work outside the home, to find childcare if possible, and to defend the country should Hitler come to the US shores. But, if women provided the necessary labor, that horrible thought would never come to fruition and Hitler would never arrive on US shores. The notice stated that women should defend the country with guns, knives, or bare fingers.[812] Additional women answered, taking war jobs, and earning money that later would help with down payments on future homes when the men returned victorious.[813] The saved funds helped jumpstart the postwar economy based on a peacetime environment.

"Use it up, wear it out, make it do," became a necessity during the conflict and although the US did not have the Limitation Order on clothing as Great Britain had imposed, the Roosevelt administration emphasized restrictions with order L-85 issued on March 8, 1942, from the War Production Board (WPB) that limited textiles for female clothing by fifteen percent.[814] Therefore, the ruffles, pockets, full skirts, and pleats disappeared in women's clothing.[815] Uniforms for the military had taken precedence. Clothing and textiles signal female identity during conflicts and this war reflected the idea that women will adapt, create, and adjust to restrictive measures. Hem lengths and the widths of pants became regulated.[816] The natural transition to military-styled clothing for women seemed appropriate. The WPB chose not to regulate wedding dresses and maternity clothing, and some women shared wedding dresses to conserve fabric and as acts of patriotism.[817] Civilian clothing became expensive during the war, therefore women worked to remake men's suits into women's suits and to mend where possible.[818] Sewing represented a patriotic duty and silk stockings disappeared while women scrambled to obtain nylon hose.[819] While presently younger generations may not appreciate the efforts by women to wear hose, at this time, it was unthinkable for women to appear in public with unadorned legs. Hose had back seams and women painted seams on the backs of their legs should they not have real ones. Pants or trousers became the work clothing for many women in factories and hair needed a covering to prevent industrial accidents; snoods, turbans, bandanas, and headscarves met that challenge.[820]

Makeup and painted nails, along with perfume, all available in the US during the war, ranked as important to the War Production Board and to working women.[821] The WPB had not confiscated the ingredients that proved necessary to produce makeup and lipstick, however, they prevented new lines of beauty products.[822] Elizabeth Arden created, at the request of the federal government, a special makeup kit for the Marine Corps Women's Reserve that matched their uniforms in colors designated Victory Red or Montezuma Red.[823] Also, for females wearing makeup, it represented an act of defiance against the enemy because Hitler preferred German women without adornments of any kind, including perfume.[824] The British employed red lipstick in their war effort to intimidate and psychologically attack the German Führer's concept of a proper Nazi woman whose place was creating progeny for the Fatherland.[825] Red lipstick also showcased femininity in war, thereby keeping women somewhat moored in their respective gender roles while they worked in male-driven jobs. Women were encouraged to buy makeup products in bulk and many women supported various companies in the states, creating profits for these entities.

A Texas Lady Heads the Women's Army Corps

The Women's Auxiliary Army Corps (WAAC), created in May 1942, allowed women to serve under the direction of Texan Oveta Culp Hobby, who eventually attained the rank of colonel.[826] Culp assisted in gaining Congressional support for women to support the whole war effort within the military. She convinced Congress and the public that women had a place in the war "for the purpose of making available to the national defense the knowledge, skill, and special training of the women of the nation."[827] The WAACs worked and served in the Ordnance Department, Transportation Corps, the Chemical Warfare Service, the Quartermaster Corps, the Signal Corps, the Army Medical Department, and the Corps of Engineers.[828] While the women she led did not receive comparable paychecks as the men, they still worked with high levels of dedication. The entity she led later integrated into the army with a name change, Women's Army Corps (WAC).[829] Culp possessed an astute understanding of Washington's mechanisms within the War Department and, therefore, was the right choice for the position.[830] A retrospection of her dynamic life included interests in politics, journalism, and a dedication to civil service.[831] Born in Killeen, Texas on January 19, 1905, she emulated her father's dedication to civil service and his love of the law; he served in the Texas legislature and practiced law.[832] As a student for two years at Mary-Hardin Baylor, as now known, Oveta Culpa Hobby worked as a Texas legislative parliamentarian during part of the Great Depression, while taking law classes at the University of Texas.[833] While she never obtained degrees from either institution, and her career included a failed run for a position in the state legislature, she strove for excellence in her many accomplishments.[834] In 1945, Hobby received the Distinguished Service Medal for outstanding service by the army.[835] She married former state governor, William P. Hobby, working at the newspaper he owned in Houston—the Post—both before and after her military service. [836]

Peg Makes Binoculars

In the World War II years of the 1940s, women repaired warships as welders in Beaumont-Port Arthur-Orange, a geographic area known as the Golden Triangle because of oil and port capabilities. Frightened about Hitler's vicious war, Houstonian Peg Gordon worked as a Rosie the Riveter at the National Instrument Corporation handling parts and inventory for this company that provided binoculars to the Navy. [837] By the post-World War II era, men took their warrior ethic back to work and to the boardroom while women returned home, living in what was praised as the Cult of Domesticity. However, Gordon continued to work in a clerical position at Black Brothers Furniture Company.[838] Most women working in the 1950s found themselves directed and corralled by male personnel managers toward clerical, secretarial, and Girl Friday positions. These positions were generally low-paying without benefits and were overwhelmingly talent-limiting.

Annie Get Your Binoculars

In Huntington, Texas on June 6, 1908, Annie Lee Jones was born, and she married George Russell on August 31, 1931.[839] Before she married, Annie Jones obtained teaching credentials at Stephen F. Austin State College and taught for a while at Huntington.[840] She later resigned with a move to Groveton because the road between Lufkin and Groveton had not been completely paved, creating a commuter nightmare for the young teacher.[841] Her husband's employment with Brookshire Brothers had taught him about the grocery business and the couple opened their own store, George Russel's Grocery and Feed.[842] As World War II began for the Americans, her husband volunteered but health issues prevented his service, however, that did not deter him from doing his best to assist in the war effort.[843] Annie Lee wrote about local servicemen for the Groveton News and her husband kept the store open late because soldiers arrived in town with no place to stay the night.[844] He drove those who needed rides to various communities in the area because he knew the time was short before the soldiers returned to war.[845] Annie Lee picked up her binoculars serving as an airplane observer during the war.[846] She was one of many women serving with the Aircraft Warning Service that reported air traffic stateside. For her diligence, she obtained a commendation and earned wings as the observer with the most hours at the task in her geographic area.[847] Unfortunately for the family, their store burned to the ground in 1953, however, always industrious, the husband and wife team worked with a motor club, NAA selling to businesses and professionals in nine counties in East Texas.[848] A move to Freeport and a career in retail for her husband led Annie back to her teaching roots. After about fifteen years as an elementary teacher, she retired in 1973 when her husband became gravely ill.[849] After his death in 1974, Annie Lee married retired Colonel James D. Nutt in 1980.[850] The couple resided in Carthage at first, later moving to Lufkin in 1987 where he died December 1, 1992.[851] Annie passed away in 1995 and she and her second husband are buried in the Glenwood Cemetery, Groveton, Trinity County.[852] Annie Lee Jones Russell Nutt expressed many of her natural talents during her long life. She taught school, helped run a store, wrote for the local newspaper during the war, and looked to the skies for enemy aircraft with her binoculars.

Iva Marie's Wartime Texas Chili

Iva Marie Jones married George William Bayless of Oklahoma when she was fourteen years of age at the Poteau Courthouse on February 18, 1926.[853] A child of Jim and Carrie Victoria Fox Jones of Wister, Oklahoma, she was born May 18, in either 1910 or 1911.[854] Iva Marie Jones Bayless lived with her husband, a Teamster and boss, in a boarding house at a logging camp run by the Bushall Lumber Company in southeast Oklahoma.[855] Iva Marie, apparently a quite charming young woman, was well-liked by the boarding house owners because they refused to charge rates for a party of two.[856] Relocating to the Pineywoods of East Texas in 1929, they settled in Trinity, where her husband owned several businesses over time, and the couple were blessed with four children, one son and three daughters.[857] During the latter part of 1939, he opened a grocery store and gas station and during the war, Bayless opened on main street the Confectionary.[858] A photo of Iva Marie and her young daughter, Georgia Ann, and her husband at their gas station taken with a gasoline deliveryman may indicate she also helped with the running of the station. Iva Marie, with the assistance of her friend Rodie Batton, cooked together, and Iva Marie's chili became known as the best in the area by the locals and the military police from the prisoner of war camp located between Riverside and Huntsville.[859] Teenagers gathered at the main street sweet spot to consume malts, ice cream, hamburgers, and fountain drinks while enjoying music on the jukebox that probably included such songs as "Tangerine" by Jimmy Dorsey, "As Time Goes By," by Rudy Vallée, or "I'll be Seeing You" by Bing Crosby.[860] The Bayless family attended the Church of Christ in Trinity.[861] George Bayless passed at the age of seventy-four on March 1, 1978.[862] The couple lost their only son in an automobile accident in 1949.[863] The daughters married and lived in various Texas cities.[864] After the death of her husband, she remained in Trinity, where one daughter, Georgia Ann, and her spouse, Dr. Stephen Montgomery, resided.[865] Iva Marie Jones Bayless died in Crockett, Texas, on January 16, 2001, she was a true, hardworking Texas lady apparently known and well-liked by her community. Her husband "lovingly cared for his family," and she no doubt returned the love and kindness.[866] Her wartime chili offered comfort during stressful times.

Ladies Fly the Skies of Texas

British historian, Sir Denis Brogan, once said, "To Americans, war is a business, not an art." Word War II sent all the airlines to war.[867] The US government formed the Air Transport Command, and it claimed 200 of the 360 commercial aircraft in America's fleet. World War II "made America lord of the air."[868] In 1940, a young pilot, Richard Earl McKaughan, Sr., who attended high school in Houston with his friend and idol, the iconic Howard Hughes, organized Aviation Enterprises, Incorporated to facilitate the sales and service of aircraft.[869] His operation entailed the use of an inspected and approved hangar at Houston's Municipal Airport to overhaul aircraft, train pilots, and originate flight programs. His company won a contract from the government to train female pilots for the Women Air Force Service Pilots at Avenger Field in Sweetwater, Texas. [870] The first group of female pilots arrived in Texas on November 16, 1942, and from that date, Aviation Enterprises' ace pilot and future vice president of McKaughan's company, Henry E. Erdmann, directed the training of 1,074 brave pilots.[871] Erdmann believed in the abilities of women pilots.[872] The women noted in their bimonthly newsletter, "The Fifinella Gazette," which was underwritten by Aviation Enterprises, that Erdmann lacked the usual attitude of male pilots toward his female counterparts and certainly for that vote of confidence the women were grateful.[873] The women came from all over the US, however, they trained in Texas, first in Houston and then at Avenger Field located near Sweetwater. While in Houston, the community embraced these young women who had already trained as pilots. The ladies tended to stay out late being entertained by locals, and some enjoyed several libations, therefore training became better served at the bare barracks in the isolated dry climate of West Texas.[874] Grits and meatloaf fed them; exercise sustained them while the classroom trained them. They delivered aircraft to numerous bases where male pilots took them to war in both the Pacific Theater and the European Theater.

Flying High and Buzzing Skinny-dipping Soldiers

A college graduate by 1940 at nineteen years of age Texan Nell S. Stevenson Bright learned to fly in Amarillo, joining the WASP in Sweetwater in the seventh class.[875] Her schedule after graduation included a seven-day flying week.[876] Like the male pilots, about one-half of her class had washed out.[877] Flying enticed her at six years old in West Texas, when she rode with a barnstormer.[878] When her young brother, a member of the Army Air Corps, arrived home on leave during the war, his sister pulled a "Doolittle takeoff" and buzzed their hometown.[879] Stevenson Bright flew a variety of aircraft when stationed in El Paso.[880] The WASP flew missions releasing poison gas over trainees to test gas masks, however, one pilot on the mission thought that her release of gas proved successful when it failed.[881] While returning to base, she buzzed some skinny-dipping troops but when she pulled up the poisonous gas spread over the troops.[882] Fortunately, no harm came to anyone, but she thought some were killed and she believed herself responsible.[883] Overall, at the deactivation of the WASP, Stevenson Bright felt pride as a pioneer, revered by female pilots in today's military.[884] She married at the close of the war and wanted to serve in the Reserves but lost her position after she had a child.[885]

They Gave Their Lives Working for the Nation

Thirty-eight female pilots died in the service of America during the war. Two WASP members with Texas ties died in the service of their country— Betty Pauline Stine, and Lea Ola McDonald. The great niece of famous humorist, Will Rogers, Betty Pauline Stine, from Fort Worth, flew as one of Erdmann's trainees.[886] Growing up in California, she attended a state college for two years, however, she later transferred to the University of Arizona.[887] Betty Pauline returned to Fort Worth Municipal Airport where she trained to fly before qualifying for the WASP.[888] Betty crashed into a mountain.[889] A review of the disaster indicated a fire in the tail of the aircraft sparked by engine exhaust caused the disaster.[890] She parachuted, however, when several people finally reached the spot where Stine came to rest her life was in jeopardy because her body had taken a severe beating as the wind dragged her across the mountainous terrain.[891] She died at the base hospital at Blythe Army Air Field, California on February 25, 1944.[892] Lea Ola McDonald graduated from basic training on April 15, 1944.[893] She received orders that based her at Biggs Army Air Field located in El Paso, Texas. McDonald had worked for a Douglas aircraft factory in California when she learned about the WASP; she applied and was accepted.[894] McDonald hailed from Arkansas but grew up in Seagraves, Texas with her brother.[895] After about two years at Wayland Baptist College where she learned to fly, she relocated to Canyon, Texas, attending West Texas State College for an unspecified time.[896] Lea McDonald crashed on landing an A-24 during a practice flight on June 21, 1944.[897] No doubt both women loved flying and considered education as necessary. Hard work and determination made it possible for them to succeed at her goals. Both gave their lives for their beliefs and Stine's death prompted enhanced parachute training needed by the lady pilots.[898]

Eighteen Months in the Philippines

Maria Sally Salazar of Laredo, Texas obtained her sister's birth certificate to join the Army's WACS.[899] She needed to have attained twenty-one years of age and she was only nineteen.[900] Salazar was one of the many Latinas who wanted to serve their country and did so either in the military or in industrial jobs. After her training, she found herself stationed in the Philippine jungle in mostly an administrative position, however, her duties expanded to tending the wounded.[901]

The Ladies of the 6888 Mail Battalion: "No Mail, Low Morale"

These are the African American Texas Ladies who served by routing the mail to soldiers in World War II:

> Allen, Hazel PFC; Booker, Bessie PVT; Boyd, Erma Pauline PVT; Brown, Ruth Verjil T5; Chinn, Freddie William PFC; Cole, Florence Marie T5; Ellis, Marguerite J PFC; Goodloe, Juanita SSG; Harris, Ira Mae PVT; Hill, Mary Louise PFC; Hooper, Mildred Lois PFC; Hopkins, Pauline Lewis PFC; Howard, Dorothy Lee CPL; Hughes, Ernestine Elizabeth T5; Jackson, Ella Mae PFC; Lawrence, Jerrell SSG; Lee, Catherine PFC; Lewis, Lucille SGT; McClung, Ruby Lee SGT; McKnight, Martha Anna PVT; Mills, Ophelia PFC; Minor, Helen Beatrice PFC; Nelson, Catherine Louise SGT; O'Brien, Ruby M SGT; O'Riley, Essie Oralea PFC; Ortiz, Mablyne T5; Pate, Kate PFC; Penn, Essie Lee PVT; Peterson, Mildred Elizabeth PVT; Powell, Calonia V 2LT; Rettig, Jewell T5; Revernal, Minerva Loraine PVT; Ricards, Eddie T PVY; Richardson, Winnie B PFC; Roberts, Onnie Lois PFC; Robey, Florida Elizabeth T4; Smith, Erma L PFC; Smith, Lucille PFC; Stuart, Rose T4; Taylor, Millie Mary PVT; Walton, Johnnie Mae CPL; Wright, Myrtle Elizabeth PFC; Zenon, Mable Jeannette PVT.[902]

About seven million military personnel in the European Theater had not received mail from home in about two years, as letters and packages clogged warehouses in Great Britain and France. [903] By 1944, the War Department finally allowed black women the opportunity to serve overseas under the 6888 Central Postal Directory.[904] The 855 African

American WACS, including those above from the state of Texas, would sort, decipher names, locate personnel, and forward much-needed mail to the front lines between February 1945 to March 1946.[905] The ladies received training at Fort Oglethorpe, Georgia, arriving in Birmingham, England in February 1945.[906] The ladies found themselves in a damp, barely lit warehouse crammed with backlogged mail working in three eight-hour shifts using seven million identification cards to help identify those hopeful recipients.[907] Duplicate names proved difficult as did the many nicknames on envelopes.[908] Each clerk processed about 65,000 pieces of mail each shift.[909] Rodents scrambled through packages containing the remains of home-baked goods.[910] The locals invited the women to tea, while they remained segregated from any nearby Red Cross facilities.[911] In June of 1945, the ladies transferred to Rouen, France where they worked in performed their mail distribution duties until October of 1945 when another transfer took them to Paris until their mission concluded in March 1946.[912] Blacks had been limited to ten percent of the total of the WACS, but those who served found some economic security as well as pride in jobs extremely well done.[913] The WACS offered alternatives to civilian jobs that went to whites first in many cases.[914]

Aircraft Riveting in Fort Worth

Ona B. Reed found herself drilling holes into two pieces of metal forcing them together, working with another lady called a bucker.[915] She worked on B-24 bombers and C-87 cargo planes in Fort Worth for Consolidated Aircraft.[916] She put the rivet in with the gun pressing against the rivet while the bucker, who could not be seen, "held a bar up against the other side of the rivet."[917] The bucker knocked once for a good take or twice for a bad take that resulted in removal of the rivet.[918] Ona Reed remembered the importance of preciseness and perfection as weighing heavily on her mind was the security of the male pilots in combat.[919] Even a simple vibration could affect the integrity of the aircraft. Her male cousins flew in the war, and she later married a war pilot.[920]

Chapter Eleven
1950s Recalibration: Women Return Home, Some Chose Work

No woman can be free unless she is financially stable; the post-war economic landscape conferred on women a cultural expectation that accepting the status quo of a male-driven path to security best represented the route to a fiscal sanctuary for married women. Working women now faced a sliding scale of diminished power, however, they had learned skills to accommodate adversity. War widows and traditional widows continued to face less than optimal financial security. Texas warriors had returned from World War II, having to adjust to families, fiancés, and finances. Texas lost 22,000 men and women in World War II, leaving many families shattered and without breadwinners.[921] For the men who returned, the women who made decisions as to how to manage the family, the finances, and the war-time jobs, needed to reverse roles with their spouses. Men needed jobs to support their families; therefore, society emphasized and promoted the traditional domestic role for women as the Baby Boom began. However, thirty percent of women in the country and twenty-eight percent of Texas women worked outside the home in the 1950s; and census data emphasized a rising new paradigm that revealed a startling fact that the economy would suffer greatly if every single woman did not show up for work.[922] Alice K. Leopold, Director of the Women's Bureau, wrote in her report, "Changes in Women's Occupation 1940-1950," the following: "Picture the situation in an individual office, store, factory, restaurant, schoolroom, hospital, telephone exchange, bank, if every woman employee remained away even for a single day. Then multiply this by thousands of establishments and by the workdays of a week or month. In such an exercise the imagination can to some extent envision the basic importance of women's contribution in modern industrial life." [923]

An old saying in Texas, "If mama ain't happy, ain't nobody happy," resonated in the state and many Southern homes as well. The Baby Boom era and the so-called Culture of Domesticity kept some women trapped in an artificially created world not to their liking; however, some women enjoyed the time while nourishing their children, making after-school cookies with milk, and creating a special Christmas for their families. Most discord resulted from a lack of choices for women who preferred earning a paycheck. Then, unexpectedly, another conflict, the Korean War, took the country by surprise on June 25, 1950. Texans had just begun to settle into what may be styled as another "return to normalcy." But, that concept of normal had been shaken so many times that one wondered if any time could have been described as "normal." The economy, shattered from years at war and while finally rebounding, had to sustain wartime jobs. Once more, many women will again assume the role of keeping the national economy going while producing needed war matériel. The necessity generated by war gave some women the impetus to continue working after hostilities subsided.

Texas-style feminism began in earnest after the Korean War that ended in 1953, however, the impetus remained within the milieu of both social and religious expectations of the status quo until the new century. Women of the 1950s focused on obtaining husbands to ensure financial security. On a national level, Jaqueline Bouvier married future president John F. Kennedy in Rhode Island on September 12, 1953; she was twenty-four and he was thirty-six. He had reigned as an eligible bachelor and she was approaching old-maid status.[924] Bouvier graduated from college, traveled to Europe, and worked as the Washington Times-Herald "Inquiring Camara Girl." The term "girl" reflects attitudes toward working women in the 1950s. Texas women were reticent to verbalize their frustrations unless among themselves, or to even ponder picketing or protesting in the land of cotton, cattle, and oil. Mothers and grandmothers in the state fed their families new recipes using Jell-O molds and made the intricate recipe for the Post-War Japanese fruitcake for the holidays. Happy to have coconuts and pineapples, along with spices unavailable during wartime, women pleased families and neighbors at parties and picnics with their prize cooking. Metaphorically, the use of fruits and spices from islands and Asia celebrated the victory in the Pacific won by their husbands and sons. After the war, the stress on femininity encouraged women to dress demurely and the common, popular description of women included words such as "every inch a lady."[925] One did not shop or arrive in public without proper attire. Women who worked wore polka dot dresses, poodle skirts, and suits supported by girdles and newly styled brassieres, but nothing too alluring or tight. Housewives wore shirtwaist dresses that could be purchased from Sears's catalog for about ten dollars; and most women preferred short, curled, and permed hairstyles.[926] Pedal pushers and clam diggers with modest bathing suits became accepted for recreational events, not for shopping. These cultural preferences complemented the Cult of Domesticity, reinforcing the traditional role of women in society. Within these parameters, some women would work in paid jobs and a few would establish themselves as businesswomen in every sense of the word.

Data in the 1950s indicated that about 26.8 percent of Texas women worked in paid jobs.[927] The population of the state reached 7,711,194.[928] The top ten occupations for women began with operatives not elsewhere classified, that term usually referred to manufacturing jobs.[929] The other occupations included stenographers, typists, and secretaries; clerks; sales clerks; private household workers; teachers; nurses; bookkeepers; waitresses; and managers, officials, and proprietors.[930] Minimum wage would advance to one dollar from seventy-five cents during the 1950s.[931] In the 1950s, the divorce rate in the United States rose and a decline in the rate of marriage occurred.[932] In 1950, eighty-two percent of the female population chose the state of marriage and women generally spent eighty-eight percent of their lives married.[933]

Using Houston, Harris County as an example of potential employment for women in support roles seems apropos because the area with its population of 802,000 was the largest in the South with a strong economy, especially during the Korean War days[934] In the early 1950s, Houston's port led the world in the export of petroleum, petroleum products, rice, cotton, and carbon black with six major railroads leading to the industrial area. Iron and steel fabricating, cement production, flour milling, shipbuilding and repair, and chemical production remained strong industries, and in 1952, 82,500 persons worked in these fields.[935] The single largest industry was machinery producers which employed 15,000 workers.[936] Another 11,000 workers produced oil products.[937] Food and like products employed 10,500 persons. While the above data was impressive, about 64,000 worked in the retail sector with 20,500 in the wholesale trade.[938]

Dusty Roads and Dry Creeks

Women ranchers with their husbands or independently lived through seven terrible years without water in one of the worst recorded droughts in Texas history. West Texas can be dry with low humidity, however, between 1950 and 1957 rain refused to fall and this massive drought forced about 100,000 farms and ranches out of business by 1960 with owners looking for other ways to make ends meet.[939] Reflection has shown this time proved worse than the Great Depression drought.[940] Ranchers living on the Edwards Plateau had seen hailstorms kill 300 lambs but knew what they called the "drough" measured one hundred times worse than previous droughts.[941] Nancy Nunns of Junction, a retired certified public accountant in 2012 recalled that she received a raincoat she never wore.[942] "For Christmas in probably 1951, my great-aunt gave me a raincoat. It was bottle green and trimmed in white, buttoned up the front. It was quite a raincoat," Nunns says. "And, of course, it just never rained. And I grew and grew, and the raincoat didn't. That was the start of the drouth, and we just outgrew it before it started raining."[943] "Drouth" was commonly used at the time as a synonym for drought.

Executive secretary for the Texas Sheep and Goat Raisers Association in 2012, Sandy Whittley lived through the drought in San Angelo and she relayed that the first year was a little dry, but she realized by the third year a rough and tough life lay ahead for ranchers.[944] She recalled that President Dwight Eisenhower visited San Angelo in late February 1957 to inspect the area and the rains came for the first time in seven years.[945] The consensus on the grapevine was that these ranchers and farmers switched from voting Democrat to Republican.[946] Texans danced in the rain enjoying the drops on their faces.[947] However, the rain that started in February never stopped through the spring and summer, leading to massive river flooding that damaged bridges and destroyed homes.[948] Damages reached 120 million and the lasting outcome initiated a move from rural to urban communities by many farmers and ranchers. Women adjusted their lives by working in different urban jobs. Willing adaptability facilitated changes that produced new lifestyles necessary when mother nature had interrupted primary dreams.

Texas Female Oil Landman and Financial Planner

Another conflict, The Korean War of the 1950s took men across the globe to fight Communism, therefore many women returned to work, and some enjoyed the paycheck and made decisions whereby the "mama at home" role no longer sustained their dreams. At this juncture, a young, determined Texas lady, Sue Birdwell-Alves, worked in a trucking company in San Francisco during the conflict while her husband served in the war.[949] Excitement abounded when she received her paycheck. Earning money felt powerful. She later made a decision that changed her life and set an example for women forging their futures in the 1980s and beyond. Sue Birdwell Alves represented a self-starting opportunity entrepreneur who broke the chains of domesticity. Her journey included a male mentor and more education. She pinned her butterfly broach onto the left side of her yellow suit as she prepared to take on the male-dominated oil business. Her 1951 degree in home economics from Southwestern University in Georgetown, Texas, provided her some management skills, but no recognition that she had qualifications that would result in a corporate position. She forged herself into a forward-thinking Texas businesswoman of substance, character, and determination during a time when she felt that the women's liberation movement thwarted her efforts, and many oil men articulated an Antebellum sclerotic agenda that prevented the advancement of women in the workplace. Landmen in the oil business conducted the business side of the oil, gas, and mineral exploration industry and they negotiated and drafted contracts and leases. By 1974, she divorced her controlling oilman husband whose credentials included a degree from Texas A & M as a member of the corps and service in the Korean War. She struck out on her own, reared her two children, and by forty-five years of age she could claim the title of the first independent female landman. She disrupted the traditionally male-driven oil business through her persistence, but as she believed, mostly through her powerful work ethic. She suggested several avenues for success and these included education, continuing education, and male mentors where possible; and she, at the end of her life, stated that women simply must work harder, smarter, and longer hours to obtain what she had accomplished. Birdwell Alves laid a foundation worthy of duplication. While true that she came from a well-educated family of means, she drove herself fearlessly forward and represented a positive disrupter of the status quo, shaking off the usual business paradigm dictated by men. Notwithstanding changes in laws, she broke the barriers necessary to join traditionally all-male clubs.[950]

Helen Corbitt: Texas Caviar and Heavenly Peanut Butter & Jelly

Helen L. Corbitt produced five lifestyle-changing cookbooks during her career while "civilizing" the Texas palate with her creative cooking skills that caught the attention of Stanley Marcus of the famous Neiman Marcus up-scale clothing store in Dallas.[951] After some time spent enticing her to provide the chef services at the store's Zodiac Room, she left the famous Driskell Hotel in Austin and moved to Dallas in 1955.[952] The Irish Catholic chef, born on January 26, 1906, was not a Texan, but she transformed herself into a disruptive, adopted Texan where she lived the balance of her life.[953] Born in upstate New York, she traced her maternal family from her English heritage to the Mayflower settlers.[954] Through her career in the state, Corbitt taught discerning Texans that chicken fried steak and black-eyed peas may be great when hot and paired with cornbread; however, the peas, seasoned well and served cold, could be enjoyed as Texas Caviar.[955] She never married but mentioned three proposals, and her life in the Great Depression greatly affected her decision to relocate from the Northeast to Texas in 1940.[956]

As a child, Corbitt cooked macaroni and cheese and a pound-like cake in her mom's coal stove.[957] After graduating from a boarding school in Watertown, New York she enrolled in Skidmore College where she received a Bachelor of Science degree. Her dreams of medical school proved difficult because the Great Depression decimated the family finances of her attorney father.[958] With the family home lost, Corbitt knew the agony of life without enough funds and she always remembered to include inexpensive recipes in her cookbooks along with the most expensive ones.[959] She made available recipes that assisted beginning cooks and highly seasoned ones with enough income to include real caviar. She found employment in troubled times at the Presbyterian Hospital in Newark, New Jersey working as a dietitian and menu planner.[960] During this time, a custom to welcome newcomers included a "throw a buffalo" party.[961] Held outdoors in a park where a large fire was reduced to embers and large cuts of buffalo steaks were thrown on the coals, seared, dunked into melted butter, and eaten with fingers.[962] She thought the steak was superb.[963] Offered a better-paying job at the Cornell Medical Center in New York City, she embraced the varied cuisine available in the metropolis.[964] She made extra money baking rich chocolate cakes.[965] However, at thirty-four years old in 1940 she wanted more money.[966] After sending out inquiries and applications, she left New York arriving in Austin after accepting a teaching position in the Home

Economics Department at the University of Texas (UT).[967] Managing the University Tea Room she gained quite a reputation in town as people ate her delicious fare on Sundays.[968] Dismayed at the typical Texas fare, she found a unique way to serve black-eyed peas for this Southern staple. Pickling them in garlic, onion, and vinegar with oil her new variation became Texas caviar.[969] One of her students noted that Corbitt demanded excellence from her students, while she gave more than anyone.

Corbitt's reputation in Austin at the university aroused the interest of the Houston Country Club. Money became the prevailing issue.[970] Houston offered thirty dollars more than the university. UT refused to match the salary, so Corbitt packed and left for Houston where she stayed during the war years. [971] Thinking that one day she would return to New York, she slowly unpacked her suitcases and finally, her trunk when she realized Texas was now home.[972] Creating a special eggnog for lady golfers during food rationing, she miraculously saved butter and sugar for the male golfers who enjoyed her coconut pie.[973] With her club duties, she managed for twelve years to write a newspaper column each week on food for the Houston Post, the Arkansas Democrat, and the Dallas Time-Herald.[974] She had a knack for serving incredibly good food to large groups of people and spread this knowledge around the country for the next thirty years.

Corbitt fielded the questions about her single status. Never choosing to marry, she noted that three proposals had come her way, but work was her cause, and she said, "I couldn't see myself being limited to any one man."[975] No doubt, this proved a brave statement for the times. She wore a large diamond on her right hand, the story surrounding it was never revealed.[976] Corbitt left to work for the Garden Room restaurant located and owned by Joske's department store in Houston, however, she later faced a "firing" by the Garden Room because she and the executives had differing goals.[977] A Driskill Hotel offering led her back to Austin and the political world of Texas.[978] As 1952 dawned, she became known as the "Hashed Brown Potatoes with Sour Cream Girl." [979] The use of "girl" at the time failed to ignite discussion in the 1950s oil state. She made Canadian Cheese Soup and served Orange Chiffon Pie with Prune Whip Top.[980] To enhance tapioca pudding, she decorated it with candied violets and served this to Lyndon Johnson, as it was his favorite dessert.[981]

Corbitt seemed happy at the Driskill, but Stanley Marcus had opened the Zodiac Room at his Neiman Marcus store in Dallas and he needed

Corbitt to perfect his creation.[982] She thrived creating fabulous menus for the restaurant and Marcus better understood her "uncontrollability."[983] Style shows combined with brunch, lunch, and tea created by the innovative chef made the experience exceptional. Marcus created a marketing bonanza titled "Fortnights" that occurred in October to connect his business with the various cultural charities and foreign guests in Dallas.[984] The two-week event allowed Corbitt to shine as the chef of the event. After the festivities, Corbitt toured Europe, connecting French food creations with her special touch.[985] Each year, the focus for Fortnights changed countries, including Italy, Switzerland, Denmark, and Austria, among other themes. She worked hard, demanding the same of her staff.[986] After fourteen years at the Zodiac Room, Marcus, in 1969, asked her to consult on the food production at the Greenhouse, a fancy spa in Arlington.[987]

During her long career, some workers relayed that when she lost her patience, she also threatened to go to "Ireland and never come back!"[988] So it was not a surprise when she was awarded a ticket to Ireland at her retirement celebration, a round-trip ticket.[989] She wrote many cookbooks, entertained guests at her Dallas apartment, conducted cooking classes at the Zodiac Room, and in 1961, she received accolades as the first woman to earn the Golden Plate Award.[990] Corbitt introduced the dinner party that happened around the kitchen instead of a formal dining room. The Confrerie de la Chaine des Rotisseurs awarded her the Escoffier Gold Plaque in 1968 and she served a three-year term on the Board of Governors of the Culinary Institute of America.[991] In Texas, she served on the Agricultural Board.[992] The dream that a transplanted Texan could "civilize" the wild state was fulfilled by such women as Helen Corbitt. Women pioneers of earlier times who forged their lives in the rough days of the state would be proud of her accomplishments. During the last year of her life Father Don Fischer, a chaplain at the University of Dallas, (later monsignor) visited her, and she offered him a delicious peanut butter sandwich loaded with butter, a generous spread of peanut butter, topped with fine preserves instead of usual jelly.[993] "I went away thinking that if that was what peanut butter and jelly was supposed to taste like, I had been a very deprived child."[994] In 1978 Helen Corbitt died of cancer.[995]

Pearls and Pink Oil Tools

Women of Texas have the same true grit and strong wills as the frontier ladies who preceded them. Texas' foundation was shaped by those women who had married ranchers, lived in shanty oil camps, endured wars, picked cotton, grew peanuts, made clothes from flour sacks, and somehow managed their survival during widowhood. Another post-Korean War woman, Irene Wisher, of San Antonio, stepped out into the Texas sun from the secretarial desk to the oil field in the 1950s.[996] She owned and operated Pinto Well Servicing Company by 1973 through low-key hard work.[997] She noted that women of the time could never rise above a job that was mid-management level in a large oil company.[998] Later, she would have her oil rigs painted pink when men believed it was "bad mojo" for a female to step into the oilfield.[999] But they eventually painted their own oil tools pink.[1000] She believed women could be feminine, wear dresses and pearls to the oil field, and be successful too.[1001] Wisher believed that men in the oil and gas industries had firm opinions and attitudes that women were not welcome at the tops of their male-driven businesses.[1002] Another business anomaly, Wisher laid a predicate for future women entering the traditionally male-driven oil industry.

Nine to Five Rejected by Airline Stewardesses in Texas

During the incipient stages of the jet age in the 1950s, Earl McKaughan—the owner of Trans-Texas Airlines—made a conscious decision to hire young women as stewardesses who had not been trained as nurses.[1003] McKaughan advertised his airline as one that flew the Empire of Texas.[1004] His airline structure, format, and all business forms duplicated military procedures. He had trained the Women Airforce Service Pilots during World War Two.[1005] Because oil men ranchers, and other businessmen who needed to travel for business within the large state had shown some reticence to do so because flying was new and perceived as dangerous, McKaughan believed if men saw youthful females dressed in western-styled outfits reflecting the tough cowboy image, they would be embarrassed because if a female could fly confidently, how could they not board the aircraft.[1006] His ploy worked. The position of stewardess in Texas in the early days gave women a chance at freedom in many ways, however, men ran all aspects of the industry and set up rigid rules for these young women. But, as schoolteachers on the frontier, these women could not marry and had to have nice smiles and soft hands. Stewardess training emphasized the position of captain resembled that of a semi-god. It was mandated stewardesses have telephones, so the airline could reach them twenty-four hours every day. However, Southwestern Bell Telephone, in many cases, required a signature from a father for young females to have accounts.[1007] As the aviation industry grew, a serious and long-term fight for rights and equality ensued for these young women of the skies who had preferred seeing the world rather than answering a telephone from nine to five behind a desk. The paycheck provided them the freedom to exercise their dreams even when affording an apartment proved difficult; thus, the rise of "stew zoos" where many shared rents and two to four women lived together. Fortunately, flight schedules kept them gone much of the time. More important to them was the freedom to travel the state, the United States, and the world because reciprocal travel agreements on other carriers that included only a small fee made that possible.

Supper with Passengers and Photos in Life

One of the original stewardesses hired by Trans-Texas Airways (TTA) included Paula Rogers who was informally accepted because she truly looked exactly like the photograph that accompanied her application.[1008] The company originally had not seen the benefit of hiring stewardesses and the first cabin attendant was future captain, Kelly Steel. He hurried from plane to plane, greeting and attending to passengers during the carrier's first year of operation.[1009] By 1952, cabin attendants were required on all US commercial aircraft for passenger safety by the Civil Aeronautics Board and were federally mandated to attend recurrent training every six months.[1010] By 1958, with the formation of the Federal Aviation Agency, procedures were specified by the Federal Air Regulations that continue to be updated. In May 1958, Ruby McGee represented TTA in New York City for a multiple-interline stewardess layout and article in Life Magazine that sought to "glorify the rather delightful phase of air travel." But, as Paula Rogers said,

> When I started flying for TTA on DC-3s in 1956, my day began in Houston at seven o'clock in the morning. By the time we got to our final destination at three o'clock that afternoon, we had stopped in Lufkin, Longview, Tyler, Dallas, Brownwood, San Angelo, Pecos, Marfa, and El Paso. We would have a twenty-four-hour layover in El Paso, and then make the same stops on the way back to Houston arriving around midnight. We didn't carry that many passengers on the DC-3 and most of them were repeat

> passengers, mainly ranchers from the surrounding rural communities. Flying the same route for seven years, I got to know many of them so well that they would invite me to have dinner with their families.[1011]

Stewardesses in the 1950s provided excellent service and received many complimentary letters from passengers; and they flew some celebrities and political figures such as Mrs. Franklin D. Roosevelt.[1012] The airline expanded service in 1958 to include routes to Little Rock, Arkansas; and Memphis, Tennessee; along with Pine Bluff, Hot Springs; and El Dorado, all three of which are in Arkansas. The stewardesses knew their regular oil-related passengers, especially those from Lion Petroleum.[1013] Many more young ladies from small towns and large cities would be hired during the start of TTA's jet age during the 1960s.[1014]

Annie Get Your Gun

Gail Davis flew as a passenger on TTA and although not a native of Texas, she attended the University of Texas at Austin, studying drama.[1015] She married in Austin and after the war in 1945, the couple moved to Hollywood where she worked as a hatcheck girl. An agent discovered the young lady who knew how to rope, ride, and shoot along with showcasing her singing and dancing talents. Gene Autry cast her in the Annie Oakley television show that featured her as a "charming heroine" who could shoot guns out of bad men's hands. As the first female to star in a traditionally male role, she influenced young female viewers that possibilities existed beyond traditional roles. Davis, whose real name was Betty Jeanne Grayson, starred in thirty-two movies and as a guest in many Westerns after her show ended. Born in 1925, she died in California of cancer in 1997. She was honored with membership in the National Cowgirl Museum and Hall of Fame. According to Gene Autry, Oakley was "the perfect Western actress."[1016]

Elizabeth Clair McMurray Nesmith Graham: No Typos Allowed

A secretary operated with rules and those included possessing good typing skills, a pleasant voice, a good demeanor, and the ability to know where the boss is in every single minute so she can tell the right people the wrong place," as secretaries in Waco, Texas joked.[1017] Most secretaries in the 1950s could expect to remain secretaries by the 1960s and beyond. A young man could start in the mail room and work hard to receive promotions that could lead to the boardroom. A female may begin as a receptionist and become a secretary, however, no transitions to higher positions were considered or expected; mostly her job led to the "bored" room. Bette Graham provided a refreshingly different route to success from secretary to entrepreneur. Graham, an amateur artist, mixed water-based tempera paint with various concoctions that eventually surfaced as something she called Mistake Out that corrected typing errors.[1018] Divorced in 1946 with a son, she earned 350 dollars a month and used some of those funds to purchase needed ingredients and the bottles to hold her special formula.[1019] Other office secretaries asked for the wonderful solution to typos that occurred with newly obtained electric typewriters.[1020] During the late 1950s, she and her son operated a home business producing her magical white liquid eraser that most secretaries needed and kept close by their typewriters.[1021] Michael Nesmith, her son, later joined the popular band, The Monkees. By 1958, Graham applied for a trademark and patent, naming her entity Liquid Paper Corporation (LPC). She married Robert Graham in 1962, and they jointly worked on marketing the product; however, the marriage ended in divorce. LPC grew from the home office of Dallas, spanning the world to include plants in Belgium, England, Canada, and Australia.[1022] Graham operated as a trendsetter because she sought an ethical work environment that not only relished her customers but focused on her employees by providing a company-owned credit union, accompanied by on-site childcare centers.[1023] Moreover, she created a retirement fund whereby employees could match the company contribution of fifteen percent.[1024] Graham also reimbursed employees' education fees at seventy-five percent.[1025] Soaring sales led to a production company and millions of unit sales by 1975. In October of 1979, she sold her creation to the Gillette Company for 47.5 million dollars.[1026]

Bette Clair McMurray Nesmith Graham, a Dallas native, was born in 1924.[1027] Her parents were Christine Duval McMurray and Jesse McMurray.[1028] She did not finish high school but attended secretarial school instead.[1029] She took her office duties seriously, working her way up to the position of executive secretary for the chairman of the board of Texas Bank and Trust in the early 1950s. Anxiety and frustration with the soft-touch electric typewriter led her to solve the problem of unintended strokes. Her advice to women included cautions such as, "women must learn to fight, but to fight with love. They must become more, and by that, I mean more confident of their abilities." She long believed that men in business operated within a "brutish" Darwinian swamp that made decisions that if legal, may not have passed ethical standards.[1030] Graham viewed money only as a conduit to problem-solving. [1031] She set up two foundations to assist women, including unwed mothers and battered women. Near the later days of her life, she had hoped to establish a gallery for the artwork of female artists such as Georgia O'Keeffe. Graham died on May 12, 1980, at the age of fifty-six, leaving a great legacy for women inventors.[1032] She always insisted that workers had a place on rotating committees whereby corporate decisions could be made by all those involved in the success of her company.

Chapter Twelve
Working Women of the 1960s & 1970s: A Bifurcated Transitional Social Economic Construct

In Texas, during those heady cultural revolutionary days, women could still obtain college degrees in home economics, and many did. However, the winds of a cultural war blew out old expectations and ushered in new dynamic lifeways for women aspiring to have it all. How women defined "having it all" remained somewhat illusive and not truly yet defined. While dreams of a Texas Ranger swooping one up and off to a supposedly safe life were long past, young women still hungered for and half-expected the unrealistic Prince on a White Horse. The Cinderella myth theoretically reached its last dying days with the advent of the 1968 Cultural Revolution which saw an upheaval of social constructs within the mix of an unpopular Vietnam War that manifested like no other at that time in the history of the United States. For black females in Texas, work life and true civil rights remained in flux. Lower-paying jobs plagued black women and Hispanic females. Life for blacks remained unsettled until the Civil Rights Act of 1964 and beyond. The women in Texas were not risk-averse, however, they found themselves in a rapidly changing social earthquake with the advent of the birth control pill and an increase in the divorce rate; and life for a married couple with children became more expensive prompting mothers to look for work outside the home. Many women chose marriage and children over potential career paths while some wanted both; and yet a few sought freedom from all constraints that prevented their development in the business world where rewards included monetary recompense worthy of their talents.

While most of the history of working women has addressed the issues of balancing family life within the context of the business world, a less discussed reason that women faced when attempting to exploit their talents in the state spotlights a Texas-style second wave of feminism that flourished differently than traditionally examined case studies of those generated by Betty Friedan's seminal post-WWII Feminist Movement. Friedan's ideas originally centered around college-educated peers who expressed boredom with their lives in traditional marriages. Texas women had little time to contemplate such situations. The characteristics and roots of the Texas-styled movement, resulted from a Southern culture that emphasized exaggerated feminine nurturing patterns and an extraordinarily embedded cultural worldview that promoted male dominance resulting from a warrior ethic tied to the historical significance of the Alamo and the presence of multi-military installations supporting US military efforts in large and small world conflicts within the large state that amplified perceptions by men that women possessed little, if any, business or organizational acumen. Coupling that underlying attitude with a male-driven economy based on cotton, cattle, and oil, the bloody history of Texas produced euphoric feelings of overall superiority by men that permeated workplace attitudes for many years. However, the state encouraged the growth of corporations giving women an open door to begin the process of working outside the home.[1033]

Until the Cultural Revolution of the 1960s, many Texas men dressed in Western-cut suits with cowboy hats on their heads when the Seven Sisters oil companies dominated the economic foundation of the state.[1034] An evolving economic base and various educational opportunities proved consequential for women, as they meandered an antiquated male-controlled business system in search of optimum ways to maximize their talents and realize their dreams. Women in the state by the 1960s Feminist Movement realized their lives still revolved around gender constructs and social mores that placed "girdles" on and metaphorically around their bodies and their dreams. Women realized that education underpinned the key essential element of undercutting the dominance of men who through centuries had subjugated them as mere sex objects and laborers.[1035] A decade of potential promise erupted into social discord and life in America disrupted the basic tenets of the traditional 1950s. Houston became the seventh largest city in the country and, in 1960, John F. Kennedy became president, asking what you could do for your country instead of the reverse. The top ten jobs for women in America changed some when manufacturing jobs dropped from the top position falling to number four, replaced by clerical jobs at the top. The other opportunities for women included sales/sales clerks; secretaries; private household staff; teachers;

nurses; bookkeepers; waitresses, and managers, officials, and proprietors. The 1960s jobs included ownership of companies for the first time since records were kept. By 1970, the top five jobs in order of rank for women included: secretaries, teachers, salesclerks or retail, bookkeepers, and nurses.[1036] The last five in order of rank included: waiters, typists, sewers and stitchers, cashiers, and maids; private households with 78,607,961 employed women in the US The US GNP for 1962 was $612.18 B. and, by 1970, the amount was 1,073.11 B.[1037] Per capita in 1962 was $3,280 and, by 1970, the amount was 5,230.[1038]

These following realities reflected the cultural dregs of dominant backcountry men who promoted and perpetuated female dependence. In the post-war era of urbanization, men marginalized women entering the workplace. In Texas, running for office, serving on juries, joining private clubs, establishing bank accounts, buying real estate, renting apartments, and opening brokerage accounts represented continuing battles that were not realized until the 1960s and 1970s Feminist Movement. The differences in the cultures of the Northeast and the South most likely accounted for the anomalies in the approach women took to obtain rights. Mothers taught Texas women to use polite language, to dress as ladies, and to act in public in such a way as not to attract attention. While Texas women may have known that there were no more bears for their men to kill, they challenged the status quo less stridently. These reticent feminists never proved as clamorously active as Betty Friedan-styled feminists of the Northeast, especially those women graduating from Texas high schools in the middle 1960s that represented a cultural gap between generations of women from the stay-at-home mothers of the 1950s to the somewhat misplaced or a lost generation of Texas Belles coming of age during the 1968 Cultural Revolution. These females represented a transitional group of young women some of whom crossed over to the new paradigm of Women's Rights, while others genuinely wanted to marry, have children, and serve them cookies and milk after school.[1039] Many traditional women in the state worked with their husbands in building small and large businesses; some continued operating long after the death of a spouse.

The new expectations for women who wanted a career drew all the attention, while those who wanted to remain in traditional roles were less inclined to speak out for fear of being chastised as old-fashioned and out-of-date. Transitional daughters suddenly found themselves in the middle of an unexpected whirlwind, a freewheeling era of drugs, rock 'n' roll, communes, and Bohemian-styled dress where peace signs adorned torn blue jeans. Women raised to be thoughtful and courteous were told they were fragile, and they faced a new world during the 1968 Cultural Revolution with little preparation. These young women had learned to wear slips with skirts and dresses, hose with seams and garter belts. They had sung "Rock of Ages" at church on Sunday and were told to burn their bras on Monday. These transitional females helped cook Sunday dinner and knew how to sew, mend, and entertain properly as a Texas woman should. Suddenly the pretty white gloves they wore to church were put away for weddings only, grandma's broach now left in the jewelry box. There was not much comfort that an advertisement of the time offered that women could not only buy the bacon, they could fry it up in the pan because they first needed a seat at the table.[1040] They often majored in home economics to perform their household duties with great expertise. These degrees rarely helped them transition to a corporate career.[1041]

For example, Houston Lighting & Power, a company of about 6000 employees during the 1970s, exercised power as a male-driven entity that hired women both with and without degrees who were all placed in clerical/secretarial positions.[1042] After a degreed employee returned from having a baby, she found herself without a job because of an outdated and palpably corrosive work environment. She filed an Equal Employment Opportunity complaint that roiled upper management but also resulted in a major revamping of both corporate hiring practices and promotion criteria. Women with college educations finally moved into better positions by the late 1970s.[1043] However, many companies relegated women to the typing pool regardless of educational level, and during interviews, women had to reveal their age, marital status, and intent to have a family, and some were asked if they were on the magical birth control pill. The trust in the pill that became popular in the 1960s, with about 6.5 million patients, suffered a backlash in the 1970s because of health concerns and issues of patriarchal control.[1044]

Texas men continued to control the lives of women during the Vietnam War years from 1965 when on March 8, 1965, the 9th Marine Expeditionary Brigade put boots on the ground in Vietnam. By the end of the conflict, jetsam from a war that divided the nation, in some ways divided the perceptions women had about the men who fought and the men who chose to avoid service. Perhaps this contentious, discordant conflict represented a major change in how masculinity would be defined in the future. Wars were now protested and questioned by a population no longer united behind a Texas president who had fought for the Civil Rights Act of 1964 but had left office defeated by an unpopular war. At the time and perhaps unconsciously, the Vietnam War began the changing of minds concerning the warrior ethos of previous conflicts. The direction of the military changed dramatically when President Richard Nixon in 1971 introduced Project VOLAR, "volunteer Army" leading to a professional defense apparatus that no longer involved those who had been conscripted.[1045]

"You're Going to Make It After All"

The transformation from the turbulent 1960s into the 1970s metaphorically represented another "moving frontier" such as promoted by Frederick Jackson Tuner's "Frontier Thesis that emphasized only males."[1046] Women now moved this frontier forward. Texas men had forged the state, along with the Texas pioneer woman. Texas females now entered the workforce as new members of the next economic frontier in great numbers. The Mary Tyler Moore Show debuted on September 19, 1970, ushering in a new work dynamic placing a spotlight on a single professional woman living in an apartment on her own; and the accompanying song, "Love is All Around" that opened the show ended with the star throwing her beret up in the air indicating that she was "going to make it after all."[1047] Young single women enjoyed the show from their apartments, munching on popcorn and nachos, either asking, "Why can't that be me? Some answered, "That is me." A new day was hatched from years of repression. Women wanted promotions and better salaries. The women of the 1950s and 1960s adjusted somewhat as their age and upbringing underpinned the life they had already lived while a new generation demanded more independence and more choices. Bridging the gap proved tedious and a dichotomy existed. By 1978, working women in the US passed fifty percent and their efforts assisted in adding to the GDP of large cities.[1048]

Working for "Something to Do"

During the 1960s, some married women with husbands of means saw opportunities to run small businesses. Margaret Purswell was one of those females who desired a life outside the traditional homemaker role. Teenagers and hamburgers go together and one drive-in that bridged the gap between the chaos generated in the 1960s by the hippies provided Cleveland high schoolers a Friday-Saturday night respite was Darks Drive-In. Dan Purswell's wife, Margaret, "wanted something to do."[1049] Certainly one can conclude that Margaret Purswell had plenty to do when operating the popular drive-in, located next to present-day Moore's Furniture, just north on Washington Street in a community north of Houston, off Highway 59. While fortunate that her husband had the means and opportunity to provide Margaret with "something to do," it was Margaret who diligently worked to succeed in giving teens a place to gather and stay safe on weekends. Her work generated family income and apparently satisfied a longing to have meaningful work to do that did not encompass homemaking skills.

Cecile Bell Neal Young Creates Businesses in Houston

Cecile Bell Neal Young exemplified the Texas female who worked jointly with her spouse to create several businesses, and they also held part ownership of others. She met Clyde Edward Young while both worked for Armco Steel in Houston and they married on April 13, 1946.[1050] He had fought in World War II in the Pacific Theater and was honored with three bronze stars, among other medals. Before the war, Clyde Young engaged in sawmill work in Trinity County where Bonnie and Clyde stole his father's car that Clyde drove to work. He had trained at Ellington Field in January 1943 before his war service training as an airplane mechanic and welder. Cecile Young came from San Augustine, was born on February 1, 1916, and she graduated from San Augustine High School in 1935. After attending the Elliott Business College in Houston, she worked at Armco Steel. The couple had two children in the 1950s. The couple actively participated in businesses in Houston with total or part ownership of a welding shop, a beauty salon, a restaurant, and an automotive body repair shop during the 1950s and 1960s. Clyde also worked at Ellington Air Force Base, retiring in 1969. He died in 1977. The couple's daughter, Shirley Ann Young, born in 1953, became a computer science instructor at San Jacinto College, South Campus, in Houston, as a Baby Boomer who entered the new economic information age as part of the transitional era in Texas.

Bloom Where You Are Planted: 35,000 Feet Above the Ground

Carole Marie Bloomquist was born in Houston on January 22, 1946, at St. Joseph's Hospital to Charles Thor Bloomquist and Ethel Marie Bloomquist. She came from spirited, adventurous people on her paternal side as her grandfather John Bloomquist had traveled from Stockholm, Sweden to work on the Panama Canal and was honored with his name on the plaque at the museum. While working on the canal, he met Texan John Stehr. Bloomquist ended up in Palestine, Texas with his friend and they worked on the East Texas railroads. Stehr's wife Beatrice had a sister Marion and John married her. He later died of a heart attack in 1938. His granddaughter Carole Bloomquist followed in his footsteps as an adventurer and risk-taker.[1051]

The young Bloomquist had one older sibling Elizabeth Anne Bloomquist Martin. The two struggled through a sometimes-difficult childhood because their mother suffered from Multiple Sclerosis and cancer that eventually took her life. Her maternal grandparents were of little help, and both daughters sealed a strong relationship with their father, as stated by her, "Father! Our 'rock;' most wonderful man I've ever encountered." Bloomquist also looked to her sister as a mentor. "We were nurses, cooks, students, and achievers. We became survivors." As a Baby Boomer, she became a Transitional Woman at a time when the feminist movement erupted, causing women to take stock of their positions on life in Texas as a female. She questioned most of what the movement espoused and was never what she stated, a "woman libber." An adult at an early age, Bloomquist paved her life her way, given even more difficult times, however, she persevered with a true-grit personality and a witty, bold, and engaging sense of humor. She attended J.P Henderson Elementary School, Stonewall Jackson Junior High, and Stephen F. Austin High School, all in Houston. The family moved to Beaumont and she graduated from French High School after her father married Cora Vernell (Nell) Marshall Wall Bloomquist. Her father worked for Glidden Paint Company and her stepmother worked in the mortgage business. The new family forged a good relationship and they enjoyed being together, cooking together, and visiting their new relatives on their stepmother's side.[1052] Bloomquist's father embraced his second wife's family as some gathered on Friday or Saturday evenings to play dominos. A generous man, he arranged for a teenage step-niece to take art lessons at the offices of Glidden Paint on Saturdays, driving her there and picking her up while engaging in conversation about various art techniques.

Bloomquist enrolled in Lamar State College of Technology

(now Lamar University) in Beaumont in 1963, working in college as a telephone operator for one year.[1053] She had a combined major in biology and marketing. Bloomquist was shaken and heartbroken when her traditional college life with boyfriend Kerry Gene Cohn, twenty years of age, ended as he and three other Lamar students died of carbon monoxide poisoning most likely from an improperly vented stove at Crystal Beach, near Galveston, Texas on January 20, 1964.[1054] She suffered great loss for the second time in her life. Resilient, she went forward.

After two years as a student, her life changed abruptly and dramatically during the summer of 1965 when her father suffered a debilitating stroke whereby, he eventually entered a nursing facility, dying on October 30, 1976. Caring for her father and supporting the financial efforts of her stepmother became paramount, therefore, she sought employment to supplement the overall efforts to sustain him while in a nursing home for many years. Her father had strongly believed in education for his daughters; therefore, it almost seemed a given that she would graduate since she was smart and determined. When deciding to work, she knew the jobs popular for females in Texas at the time included jobs as teachers, nurses, court reporters; secretaries, or flight hostesses/stewardesses. Knowing that she could not technically meet the height requirement as an air hostess, Bloomquist convinced Dorothea Kenney at Trans-Texas Airways in October 1965 to hire her based on a personal promise that she would "grow" to meet the height standard. She was hired! She piled her hair on top, always perfectly coifed, to attain the height she had promised to grow. Not shy, and a good conversationist who proved meticulous about her dress and demeanor, she fit the "personality" of an inflight hostess. Many of her colleagues did not have as much college as she had when she began flying. Domiciled in Houston after two weeks of intensive training under Jan Guillory, she flew out of Hobby Airport until 1969, when the new airport opened north of Houston. All hostesses were required to attend recurrent training each year She expressed that she truly had a "more than normal fear of flying—scared." But the reasoning had to do more with control handed over to others than an actual fear of flying. Many of the pilots during those days had been veterans of World War II and or the Korean War, giving solace to many who flew. Even during hard times in her life, she felt she directed her destiny.[1055]

Feeling lucky to have a non-traditional job, Bloomquist embraced most of the restrictions and rules for these young women of flight. Rules included those dictating the wearing of a girdle, restrictions on nail color and hose color, types of jewelry worn, staying single, keeping weight at specific levels according to body type and height, and mandatory retirement at 32 years of age. During her long career in the air, she wore different uniforms that ranged from Texas-themed outfits that eventually evolved over the years to reflect cultural changes and the varied international destinations of Continental Airlines. Examples included the original Trans-Texas cowgirl outfit that was modified with a grey skirt, white blouse, and black pumps while keeping the original red tie and cowboy hat with the airline emblem. This outfit morphed into blue pencil skirts and red bandana trim with pillbox hats. Chanel, during the late 1960s, created basic dresses with jackets that included color choices of bright orange, Robin's egg blue, lime green, and sedate gold, along with one of the first overcoats. As the new livery rolled out with purple as the Texas International Airline color, the stewardesses dressed in hot pink, grey, and purple stripes with choices of pants, dresses, a semi-double-breasted jacket, along with a grey cape, and matching gloves. Next, a gaucho outfit with a Spanish flare included, brown, black, burgundy, and beige pants, dresses, and gauchos, worn with boots, all topped with an optional wide-brimmed hat. Bloomquist's favorite uniform came in red, white, and blue denim with Texas International "star buttons" and included hot pants, dress pants, and a skirt. After Texas International acquired Continental Airlines, the newly merged airline introduced various ensembles in navy, beige, and peach. These changes came as another cultural fashion evolution that left the Mod fashion trend that gave way to a professional, softer style of dressing. Reverting to older traditions in aviation, the middle 1980s brought a modern version of the basic navy uniforms.

Bloomquist's attitude at seventy-four-years of age in 2020 was that some of the original rules should be reinstated. She believed the abandonment of many of the expectations and rules began a devolution of the whole travel experience that led to passengers showing up in flip-flops, and other fashion faux pas. And she stated unequivocally that union membership proved no benefit to her. She married Galveston banker Emmitt F. Hutchins in 1971; however, they divorced within two years. "Lord, no!" she had not flown to find a husband, and, moreover, she did not care what others wrote or thought about stewardesses. The position was respected at the time and she exhibited pride in her career.

Bloomquist, also known as "Bloom" by colleagues and friends, enjoyed flying US Southwest destinations most of all. She flew from 1965 to 1985, working as a flight attendant supervisor from 1982 through 1985. The airline transitioned from Trans-Texas Airways to Texas International Airlines in 1968, and by the 1980s the airlines absorbed the bankrupt Continental Airlines, Inc. into the family of Texas Air Corporation and airline management decided to retain the Continental name because it was more widely recognized. Bloomquist thought highly of her passengers until the 1980s; her charges before had dressed well and behaved respectfully. While deregulation in the middle 1970s democratized aviation allowing competitive ticket prices, passengers no longer "dressed up" to fly creating a less-than-optimal flying experience for those who did. The trend reflected the cultural changes at the time, and it continued to evolve, or maybe devolve according to various viewpoints as society transitioned to a more casual environment.

When President Jimmy Carter took office in 1977 Bloomquist had no idea that an event would occur whereby she would meet someone who had lived through a horrific experience. In 1978 President Carter commented that Iran was "an island of stability in one of the most troubled areas of the world," [1056] In reality, the country soon erupted in revolution.[1057] Students that subscribed to the "Line of the Imam" (Shia Muslims) seized control of the US Embassy in Tehran on November 4, 1979, taking sixty-six Americans as hostages.[1058] As a result, a 444-day diplomatic hostage nightmare began.[1059] The remaining fifty-two hostages were freed on January 21, 1981, just hours after President Ronald Reagan's inaugural address.[1060] Former hostage William B. Royer, Jr. worked as the assistant director of the Iran-America Society.[1061] The goal had been to foster cultural understanding between Iran and the US[1062] His most treasured item was some dental floss, and he lived in the same pants for the whole time that he said could stand on their own when finally removed.[1063] In the 1980s Royer will work in the English Teaching Division of the International Communication Agency.[1064] The attention and notoriety received when coming home proved uncomfortable for him.[1065] But he said, "But I feel it served a worthwhile purpose—it brought Americanism back to the country."[1066] Bloomquist flew his mother and sister to meet Royer in Washington, D.C. at BWI (Baltimore Washington International Airport) in 1981. Then, she flew the three of them home to Houston; what she described as a truly memorable and wonderful experience for her. [1067]

During her flying career, Bloomquist flew the University of Houston football team, among other college teams; many National Basketball Association teams; and the Houston Astros a couple of times. She also enjoyed the opportunity to meet some powerful people. On May 1, 1976, Ronald Reagan sang the words to "The Eyes of Texas Are Upon You" via telephone from his hotel room hotel in Indiana. Hundreds of Reagan followers in Houston listened, bursting into applause.[1068] By the 1980 general election, in a 40-state sweep, Reagan trounced Democratic President Jimmy Carter in Texas, 55 percent to 41 percent.[1069] Continental Airlines contracted with the Reagan campaign in Texas to fly the candidate and his team across the state. The airline chose Bloomquist as one of the flight attendants who flew these flights. She had already flown domestic military charters during the Vietnam War, meeting many different US armed forces personnel; and felt comfortable hearing their experiences; and now she had the opportunity to meet the future president, a man she described as "one of the most gracious passengers ever; couldn't believe how nice he was."[1070] She remembered making about four stops and one where she attended the rally. Bloomquist later flew him back to California after the events were completed.[1071]

Overall, Bloomquist described her time flying as the "best job for a woman—glamorous, adventurous," and what she thought was a well-paid career for the time. A true female pioneer, she never felt like she should be described as such. As a human being and not simply as a working, single female, she described herself as independent, financially responsible, with honesty and loyalty as her best traits and greatest accomplishments. By 1987, Bloomquist left her beloved profession for the real estate business after obtaining proper licenses. She always continued to educate herself by attending numerous seminars over time. Bloomquist has worked with friends and family to buy and sell homes. Her dedication, honesty, and loyalty remained paramount; therefore, many customers contracted with her more than once. Overall, she represents the spirit and concept of rugged Texan individualism whereby pioneers "pulled themselves up by the bootstraps." Texas women simply put on their high heels and walked gracefully into the new business frontier. Even with friends and a few mentors, she "made it after all." Bloomquist viewed her airline colleagues as "family." The original Trans-Texas Airways owner, Richard Earl McKaughan, Sr., in 1948, established the airline as a group of family-like members that ran an airline serving the needs of Texans.[1072] When the century turned and beyond, many of her friends were part of her airline history.

Many flight attendants have traveled the world, as Bloomquist had when visiting Australia, Canada, Mexico, Nicaragua, the Caribbean, Ecuador, Bermuda, Portugal, Spain, France, Italy, Croatia, Turkey, Greece, Austria, Switzerland, Lichtenstein, Germany, Russia, Great Britain, Finland, Sweden, Denmark, Estonia, and Belgium. She knew, the opportunity would never have been there for her had she not worked in the aviation industry.[1073] Continental Airlines in the late 1980s and early 1990s promoted and sold in the company store a Tee-shirt with the slogan, "Marry Me and Fly Free," although this seemed a bit silly to many women who flew or worked in other departments for a living the words meant that many of these women experienced travel that enhanced and promoted an understanding of the world beyond provincial neighborhoods and US shores. These adventurous ladies of the sky drank French wine, sailed the Rhine, smiled back at the Mona Lisa, and broke bread with many other people from varied cultures. They learned history, geography, and other languages—all educational. To Bloomquist, one of her most urgent, long-term goals became amplified when family tragedies occurred—that of becoming financially independent. She won the battle women have to prepare for, to retire, using a dedicated work ethic. "The Government Accountability Office (GAO) presented highlights from their 2012 report, Retirement Security: Older Women at Risk, which showed that over the past decade, the median household incomes of women over age 65 were 25 percent lower than their male counterparts."[1074] Bloomquist ensured her financial security, but the issue remained a constant concern for many Baby Boom women working during the 1960s and beyond. By 2008, there were 154,700 flight attendants working for commercial airlines.[1075] The job of stewardess evolved into title changes and became a career for many that have lasted thirty to forty years or more. While her life had serious challenges, as most humans do, Bloomquist forged ahead in trying times, and as much as possible, she has lived her life her way.

From Tortillas to Lil' Lamas: "Mama Ninfa"

Widowhood remained congealed around a well-woven theme throughout the history of working women in Texas. What women accomplished as they faced major decisions when left to feed, clothe, and educate their children on their own has produced some great stories of perseverance. In Harlingen, Texas, to farming parents on May 11, 1924, Ninfa Rodriguez Laurenzo was born into a family as one of twelve brothers and sisters. While attending a business college in her hometown, she married Domenic Thomas Laurenzo. After a move to Houston, the newlyweds opened the Rio Grande Tortilla factory on Navigation Street. Because of her husband's Italian heritage, they created and sold tortillas and pizza dough, when pizza restaurants in Houston were basically non-existent until the 1960s with the entrance of Shakey's Pizza Parlor, a California franchise.[1076] Laurenzo's husband unexpectedly died in 1969, and she knew that her five children needed her financial support. This need meant mortgaging her home to open a small taqueria at the location of the factory. In 1973, a ten-table restaurant followed where she promoted her family recipes; and with funds from a friend, a second dining room was added.[1077] Known as "Mama Ninfa," she circulated her dining rooms, greeting her customers with warm words, always speaking as a friendly neighbor, and, of course, inviting patrons to return.[1078]

Within ten years, Laurenzo built and operated nine restaurants in Houston and one in Dallas turning her delicious Mexican food empire into a multi-million-dollar enterprise employing 800-1000 people, serving approximately two million customers per year.[1079] She served on many various charitable boards, and in 1984, Vice President George H. W. Bush chose her as a goodwill ambassador to greet Pope John Paul II in Puerto Rico. She also won an award from the US Hispanic Chamber of Commerce along with her induction into the Women's Hall of Fame in 1998. In 2001, Mama Ninfa passed away leaving a strong legacy that gave hope to other women to create businesses that make a difference in communities. Mama Ninfa believed that children must have a strong and early educational foundation and that belief led to the development of the Ninfa Laurenzo Early Childhood Center, Home of the Lil' Llamas, that catered to prekindergarten students that opened in 2004 by the Houston Independent School District at 205 North Delmar within the same location as her original restaurant.[1080]

From Maid and Dressmaker to Dallas Civil Rights Icon

On January 7, 1967, Juanita Craft reached a status awarded to ten women that year as she was named one of Dallas' 10 Most Outstanding Women.[1081] She stated, "I had no children, so I adopted the world."[1082] While her civil rights legacy remains paramount, there is also another way to measure her accomplishments. Craft's long-term fight for civil rights resulted in added financial strength to businesses in the state of

Texas through her dogged efforts to open lunch counters, restaurants, the 1954 Texas State Fair, and theaters to blacks.[1083] She fought to integrate two Texas universities allowing black students to attain degrees after the Brown v. the Board of Education, Topeka, Kansas Supreme Court decision of May 17, 1954.[1084] While she was not, per se, a businesswoman, her efforts allowed businesses to increase revenues with the addition of more customers which made more profits for more companies. Blacks staged a sit-in at Sangers Tea Room Lunch Counter in May 1960.[1085] They were barred from eating at Piccadilly cafeterias and not allowed entry until the Civil Rights Act of 1964.[1086] However, before that time, forty Dallas businesses had removed discriminatory signage and let people of all races become customers.[1087] Craft worked tirelessly for civil rights and no doubt her efforts for freedom prompted a larger base of customers for these businesses. Born in Round Rock, Texas on February 9, 1902, she was the only child of two schoolteachers, David Slyvestus and Eliza Balfour Shanks.[1088] Her mother took care of her until she died in 1918 of tuberculosis after a race-based refusal of treatment at a San Angelo sanitarium.[1089] The teen went to be with her father in Columbus, Texas. In 1919, Craft graduated from high school and became a student at Prairie View A&M University where she studied sewing and millinery for two years.[1090] A move to Austin led her to Samuel Houston College where she earned her teaching certificate.[1091] She worked as a maid at the famous Adolphus Hotel in 1925, gaining employment as a seamstress later.[1092] Craft voted in Dallas County in 1944 becoming the first black woman to exercise that right.[1093] By 1975, she would serve two terms on the Dallas City Council, after a long career establishing 182 rural NAACP organizations.[1094] Craft supported improved conditions for Hispanics and American Indians, along with her service on the Governor's Human Relations Committee.[1095] She hosted two famous visitors for discussions concerning the civil rights movement, Lyndon B. Johnson and Dr. Martin Luther King, Jr., at her home located at 2618 Warren Avenue where she lived for fifty years.[1096] Craft died in 1985 and was honored with the Juanita Jewel Craft Recreation Center along with a Dallas city park.[1097] Her home on Warren Street is on the National Register of Historic Places.[1098] Peripherally, this passionate civil rights paragon made possible the growth of companies because the customer base for Texas businesses increased with integration.

First Black Female Pilot at the Controls of a Commercial Airline

The first black female airline pilot found employment in 1978 at twenty-eight years old with Texas International Airlines (TIA) which was based in Houston, Texas from its origination in 1944 by Richard Earl McKaughan, Sr. [1099] The airline had emerged from several iterations ranging from Aviation Enterprises to Trans-Texas Airways. McKaughan believed in women pilots as his company had trained the Women Airforce Service Pilots in World War II.[1100] Jill Elaine Brown-Hiltz, was born in 1950 in Baltimore, Maryland to Gilbert and Elaine Brown. Gilbert Brown owned and operated a construction company while her mother taught art. By the age of nine, Brown-Hiltz drove a tractor and performed physical labor at the farm the family owned in West Virginia.[1101] Brown-Hiltz received a Bachelor of Science in home economics from the University of Maryland. Her family possessed a great sense of adventure. She stated, "Daddy was tired of getting speeding tickets," so the family flew as a hobby. For a while, after college, she worked as a teacher, however, she wanted more so after a short stint in the United States Naval flight training program, she logged more hours and obtained her commercial license.[1102] She worked for a black-owned Wheeler Airlines before being hired in Texas. At the time of the hiring of Brown-Hiltz, aviation entrepreneur Francisco "Frank" Lorenzo had taken control of TIA. By 2008, there were 8,083 female pilots working for commercial airlines in America.[1103] She earned her way and opened the skies for female pilots of all races, but later focused on increasing the number of black female pilots.

Chapter 13
Texas Women Breakaway, 1980s and Beyond the New Century

Women bypassed the male-dominated business paradigm by launching innovative business strategies that created and enhanced their own vision of success. As 2021 dawned, Texas ranked the ninth largest economy in the world by GDP.[1104] US GDP was 21.4 trillion with the state of Texas at 1.9 trillion, a little less than Italy at 2 trillion.[1105] Texas cities transformed themselves into dynamic economic geographical areas that emphasized growth in information technology, biotechnology, life sciences, aerospace, aviation, defense, and expansion of the already-established energy industry.[1106] Ninety-seven Fortune 1000 companies called Texas home with fifty having status in the Fortune 500, with an additional 2.7 million small businesses.[1107] By 2010, Houston, San Antonio, and Dallas ranked among the top ten urban US places—number four, number seven, and number nine, respectively.[1108] Houston has morphed into an international city where up to 145 languages are spoken, indicating an immensely diverse population.[1109] As a transportation hub, Dallas is home to the Dallas-Ft. Worth International Airport, which ranked in 2016 as the fourth largest airport by passenger count in the country, along with the original Dallas Love Field. Houston's Bush International Airport allows travel to much of the world while Hobby Airport permits domestic destinations. Dallas is now known as the Silicon Prairie for its new high tech companies. Texas has seven airports in the top U.S; in 2017, over one hundred and eighty million passengers crisscrossed Texas. Safely moving and connecting person-to-person in places where business ideas flourish and families gather remains the goal of the industry, and international travel has increased greatly during this expansion.[1110]

Women travel, conduct business, make deals, expand their companies, and ensure success. While discrimination still existed, the old work rules that applied to females crumbled as educated young women entered the business world. Texas women increasingly started businesses across the Lone Star State. The period from the 1980s to the first few decades of the new century proved robust and strategic for women of the state. Also, the period underscores an awakening that women had options to start businesses; to become side-entrepreneurs, meaning part-time business operators working less than twenty hours per week on their business adventures;[1111] to crash the glass ceiling; or to become lawyers, doctors, architects in various firms; or to venture into space technology. An all-encompassing approach to business possibilities created an environment that pushed the Transitional Woman toward the Texas "Breakaway" Woman.

Changes occurred that allowed women in the state to "breakaway" from past business practices, and these included a surge in female college attendance; the fact women demanded businesses that catered to their specific needs; the option for women to join a more inclusive military; and a somewhat better chance that women could crash the glass ceiling, reaching the boardroom. Women created ways that motherhood, making money, and becoming successful proved possible in ways that were never truly encouraged or pursued. Of the 122 million women in the US in 2009, 59.2 percent participated in the labor force and the rate has grown steadily despite the economic downturn of 2008 and the earlier major stock market loss on "Black Monday," October 19, 1987. [1112] Overall, occupations for women only gradually changed over the decades, as the following information indicates, with teaching and nursing remaining as mainstays for how women earn their living. By 2018, the position of a manager ranked number ten of the top ten positions that women hold.

The following represent the top ten jobs for women in 1980:[1113]

1. Secretaries
2. Teachers
3. Bookkeepers, accounting, auditing clerks
4. Nurses
5. Cashiers
6. Managers, administrators
7. General Office Clerks
8. Waiters/Waitresses
9. Salespersons
10. Nurse Aides, orderlies, attendants

The following represent the top ten jobs for women in 1990:[1114]

1. Secretaries
2. Teachers
3. Nurses
4. Cashiers

5. Bookkeeping, accounting, auditing clerks
6. Managers, administrators
7. Nurse Aides, orderlies, attendants
8. General Office Clerks
9. Supervisors, proprietors
10. Sales workers

The following represent the top ten jobs for women in 2000:[1115]

1. Secretaries
2. Teachers
3. Nurses
4. Cashiers
5. Retail Sales
6. Bookkeeping, accounting, auditing
7. Nursing, psychiatric, home health care
8. Customer service representatives
9. Childcare workers
10. Waiters, waitresses

The following represent the top ten jobs for women in 2010:[1116]

1. Teachers
2. Secretaries
3. Nurses
4. Cashiers
5. Nursing, psychiatric, home health care
6. Retail sales
7. Customer service representatives
8. Waiters, waitresses
9. First-line supervisors of retail sales workers
10. Maids and housekeeping cleaners

The following represent the top ten jobs for women in 2018:[1117]

1. Teachers
2. Nurses
3. Nurses, psychiatric, home health care
4. Secretaries
5. Cashiers
6. Customer service representatives
7. Retail sales
8. Waiters, waitresses
9. First-line supervisors of retail sales workers
10. Managers

This government data does not reflect some of the dramatic occupational changes occurring for Texas women. In the United States, forty percent of businesses are presently female owned.[1118] In Texas, 27.8 percent of executive positions were held by women in 2017.[1119] Overall, six million Texas women worked, providing security for their families and adding to the GDP of the state.[1120] Three types of entrepreneurial enterprises include: those where women must work for survival and necessity; those where women demand a flexible schedule for family reasons; and those who have professional degrees and desire an autonomous practice.[1121] The necessity entrepreneur represents women who have sought quality employment without success and, out of necessity, start their own companies that provide services such as hair or nail salons.[1122] The flexibility entrepreneur tends to start businesses that may include childcare or other health care and social assistance entities.[1123] These women require flexible working hours that larger companies may not offer. They tend to have small children and/or elder parents that require care, necessitating control over their work hours. Opportunity entrepreneurs include "lawyers, bookkeepers, architects, public relations firms and consultants."[1124] Approximately one-half of female-owned businesses are focused on these efforts. More profits are realized by the other half of women-owned entities that include the following: "utilities, other services, construction, accommodations and food services, and administrative, support and waste management services."[1125]

By 2017, women had obtained 51.3 percent of bachelor's degrees or higher in the state of Texas.[1126] Education amplified a woman's chance of success and five top-tier universities such as: the University of Texas at Austin, Texas A&M at College Station, Texas Tech at Lubbock, the University of Houston at Houston, and Rice University at Houston delivered and secured the credentials women needed for success. Among the top business schools in the state include: Rawls at Texas Tech, Mays at Texas A&M, University of Texas at Dallas, Cox at Southern Methodist University, Hankamer at Baylor University, Bauer at the University of Houston, McCombs at the University of Texas at Austin, Neeley at Texas Christian University, and Jones at Rice University. Along with those institutions, numerous four-year universities and junior colleges located all over the state allowed women the opportunity to pursue various degrees that propelled them in their journeys toward economic independence. Various institutions allow both in-person and online training for nurses and the state has a minimum of ten medical schools for doctors.

Furniture from Home & Help from Children

By the 1980s, Texas women flocked to the department stores to purchase the new career clothes required or expected in the offices, in hopes of garnering a promotion since many had acquired degrees and work skills. Texas women either gladly or reluctantly bought button-down oxford blouses in the colors of men's shirts, choosing from a variety of bow ties or male-like ties to accompany their business gray, blue, or black suits. Unfortunately for many women, the "dressing like a man" idea, in hopes of being taken more seriously, failed to gain much traction. The power business outfit came with massive shoulder pads, pencil skirts, and blouses with ties, all topped with puffed, curled hair that accentuated femininity, while overall suggesting seriousness. Many women dressed in all black as a statement of determination, while human resource advisors suggested navy blue suits because the color suggested truthfulness. However, many women had little reason to embrace the current fad emphasized by women's magazines. For example, women such as Houstonian Irma Gonzalez Galvan was widowed when her husband was murdered in 1982.[1127] What she would have worn seemed quite irrelevant, considering her circumstances. She found herself with no insurance, no income, no backup plan, and certainly with little chance of finding a job substantial enough to support her four children. Through her journey, she was at first a necessity and flexibility entrepreneur, but later became an opportunity entrepreneur. Galvan found a little place in downtown and filled it with her home furnishings.[1128] Her children came to work with her as she sold sandwiches.[1129] She later introduced Mexican food that was widely received as delicious and enjoyable.[1130] Galvan hired her children, later inspiring other women to create their own businesses. She taught that dedication, hard work, and love helped her realize her dreams. Her talent and tenaciousness sustained her in the early years and underpinned her great success.

Linda Dean Richmond Schele: The Maya Speak

Numerous descriptions and accolades defined Professor Linda Schele of the University of Texas at Austin, especially her codebreaking of the Maya glyphs. While much has been written about her astonishing contributions to the study of the Mesoamerican past, one must add to Schele's contributions another accomplishment, that of stimulating the state's economy by including the positive financial repercussions of her groundbreaking studies. With a personality as big as the state, sometimes offering an "Oh shit," from the stage, she made Austin the hub and center of Mesoamerican conferences and gatherings because scholars and non-scholars came to the Maya guru to hear her ideas and theories.[1131] Extraordinarily, she yielded a massive number of drawings, exhibitions, articles, and books during her fifty-five years of life. Philosophically, the gregarious Schele believed in open access to her discoveries, and she encouraged non-academics to offer opinions and ideas that she included in her talks and writings. Her life exemplified a determined, creative genius that sought an inclusiveness to education seldom realized in the esoteric world of academia.

Schele came about her life's work quite by accident. In 1970, she and her husband David, an architect, spent Christmas vacation in the Yucatan for the purpose of photographing Maya ruins for the University of South Alabama where Schele taught art.[1132] She had gained her credentials in education and art from the University of Cincinnati.[1133] Fascinated by the ruins, the couple toured the ancient city of Palenque where she met important artist, Merle Green Robertson and he led her into the ancient world of the Maya.[1134] The first Mesa Redonda de Palenque organized by Robertson occurred in 1973, and during the small conference, Schele and Peter Matthews deciphered a large portion of the Palenque king list.[1135] This opened the academic door to great breakthroughs and discoveries for Schele.[1136] In 1975–76, while a fellow at Dumbarton Oaks in Washington, D.C., Schele focused on pre-Columbian studies with various scholars that furthered the interpretation of Maya hieroglyphics.[1137] By 1977, she organized the Maya Meetings in Texas where all who were interested were welcome to attend.[1138] She achieved a Ph.D. in Latin American Studies in 1980, with her dissertation published in 1982 and titled, "Maya Glyphs: the Verbs;" it was awarded "The Most Creative and Innovative Project in Professional and Scholarly Publication."[1139]

Schele expanded her body of work after 1988 to include today's Maya culture. Along with Frederico Fahsen[1140] and Nikolai Grube, she held thirteen workshops on her study of hieroglyphic writing to citizens of both Guatemala and Mexico.[1141] Presently, today's modern Maya scholars are translating the writing system of their antecedents. The government of Guatemala, the Universidad Francisco Marroquin, and the Museo Popul Vuh honored Schele with two Diplomas of Recognition. "Schele published four major books on the Maya and their Civilization: 1990, A Forest of Kings, co-authored with David Freidel; 1993, Maya Cosmos: Three Thousand Years on the Shamans Path, co-authored with David Freidel and Joy Parker; 1997, Hidden Faces of the Maya; and 1998 The Code of Kings: The Sacred Landscape of Seven Maya Temples and Tombs, co-authored with Peter Matthews."[1142] Schele passed away in 1998 of pancreatic cancer, but her legacy lives, expanded within her students and with those novices that came to know the Maya and the implications thereof—that our planet is fragile and past societies have wrought havoc on their environment, that is often replicated in our modern world. Schele's final resting place is among the ancient Maya on a hill-top facing Lake Atitlan in Guatemala. Schele generated curiosity with her love and dedication to her cause. The Maya Meeting at Austin, Texas continued after her death; and in 1999, brought together about 600 participants from around the world for the conference that lasted from March 11–20.[1143] While not born in Texas, she came from Tennessee, like so many pioneers of the past have, and she created a business of the Maya that enriched the state financially and intellectually. Her efforts proved as important as the Rosetta Stone had been to the interpretation of Egyptian hieroglyphics. Perhaps she extended the definition of a new Texas frontier beyond its original scope—into an understanding of the future through the ancient past.

Texas Women Serving Their Country

Opportunities for women serving in the military provided alternative routes to careers. Although women have served in the military for many years, varied positions offered more opportunities. Benefits included the same wages for women as for men, and if women served long-term, they were more likely to move up the ranks than if they attempted to infiltrate the boardroom of a major corporation.[1144] Sadly, many women do not remain in service long enough to reap the rewards of promotions.[1145] Women joined the various military branches to gain educational opportunities and to travel, along with desires to improve their communities as they serve and earn livings. As of 2019, 2.5 million females served in the US Military, many of them from Texas.[1146] For example, Texan Janine White felt called to serve as early as high school when she joined the JROTC.[1147] She began her service in the US Army in 1994, retiring in the winter of 2020 at the rank of Colonel.[1148] Major Melissa Downs, US Air Force retiree, joined in 1998 as Security Police.[1149] Deployed several times, she later attended Officer Training School, became commissioned as Personnel Officer, serving as Force Support that encompassed Manpower, Personnel, and Services until her retirement in 2015.[1150]

Sergeant Lateisha Broomfield, a US Army member who served from 2001–2008 stated, "I'm proud of my military service because it makes me a part of an elite group of strong, determined, fearless women who had the courage to serve their country while often balancing being a mother."[1151] Another example of a career-minded Texas female included Keeli Jarrard Darst, who served in the US Coast Guard from 1989–2009, retiring as a Lieutenant Commander.[1152] Through her career, she advanced to enlisted rank of E-6, first Class Health Services technician and Laboratory Technician.[1153] Darst performed numerous laboratory procedures and served as a chair-side dental technician, in addition to dispensing pharmaceuticals. She then worked in a branch of the Coast Guard that monitored the health of personnel working in areas that presented high health risks because of exposure to chemical or physical agents.[1154] Overall, her job included marine environmental protection, along with safety and security.[1155] As a team member, she responded to oil spills, marine transportation events, and events both natural and terrorist instigated.[1156]

Mary Kay Ash Mentors Royalyn Reid

While improvements gradually took hold, Texas women still faced discrimination when applying for positions at human resources departments of many companies, both large and small. Women continued to work in gender-specific jobs, where human resources directed them to clerical positions that left them in stagnant occupations with salaries that failed to allow them financial independence, much less any opportunities to save for retirement. However, as a new century was near, African American Royalyn Reid, in 1998, founded her own Dallas-based company, Consumer & Market Insights (CMI), and focused on hiring stay-at-home moms who had left powerful corporate careers to embrace family life.[1157] As a start-up, she knew the pitfalls of high overhead costs, however, she came equipped because Reid had worked as a scientist for the iconic Mary Kay Cosmetics. After ten years at Mary Kay, she decided to be a mom, but she was hesitant to give up her career goals. The primary business focused on marketing research but has expanded to training and conference management. A multi-million-dollar company resulted. Reid's success has merged all three types of female entrepreneurs. She bridged the gap between those women who, as was said in the 1960s, "wanted to have it all." Mary Kay had planted the seeds and Reid grew the business. Mary Kay Ash, the Estée Lauder of Texas, founded her company in 1963; she had three children and needed the flexibility of selling and marketing cosmetics directly to customers.[1158] Both women no longer had to confront men, they simply carved out a needed niche and employed qualified women who no longer had to type a certain speed, take dictation, or make the morning coffee. Ash incentivized women who reached $100,000 in sales with the reward of a pink Cadillac.[1159] She did not choose navy blue or black, but chose a soft feminine color while earning millions. Reid, of CMI, presently plants new seeds, and, on that foundation, more women of all ethnic backgrounds will follow. Women did not have to emulate men, nor did they require permission from a man. They created a woman's world.

Do Let your Babies Grow Up to be Cowgirls

Iconic Texas country singer, Tanya Tucker, needed all the necessary fashionable outfits for the Grammy Music Awards. Enter two Western apparel experts who happened to be sisters—Audrey Franz, CEO and Cheryl McMullen, Creative Director of the Double D Ranch enterprise. They dressed the award-winning singer/writer, a native of Seminole, Texas who started her stellar career at age thirteen, singing "Delta Dawn" in 1972.[1160] The ranching sisters enjoyed a grand time with Tucker as they dressed her and reminisced about their trip in her tour bus traveling from the Staples Center of Los Angeles to Nashville. Franz and McMullen surprised themselves when they serendipitously created a business after a skiing trip to Taos, New Mexico.[1161]

The launching of their business began with an Indian blanket coat and an over-heard conversation. McMullen recalled seeing a blanket coat in a grocery store aisle. While at a local restaurant, she discussed her find and a man from another table told her where she could buy such a coat. She brought one back to Texas. With encouragement and mentoring from their father and mother, the sisters took their idea to the fashion market in Dallas, creating a business that has endured and grown for thirty years. Creativity sparked a variety of clothing, inspired by the history of the state that embraces all the free-spirited women who forged Texas overtime, including American Indian and Hispanic influences. The sisters admitted that any lack of fashion training did not deter them because passion and belief in the dream propelled them. Women drop by their place of business in Yoakum to visit and to buy unique Western clothing that underscores the history of ranching and its importance to the development of the state. Currently, the business partners embrace working with family members and are exploring methods to expand licensing agreements that include branching out with boots, hats, and jewelry. By the end of 2020, the sisters functioned as mentors to women, kindling fresh ideas of entrepreneurship by placing experienced business ladies with younger novices. They remain hopeful for positive results. Charitable endeavors enhance the sisters' community involvement. The sisters define their customers as strong and daring, certainly "not wallflowers." They embrace social media, using it wisely to connect to customers that sometimes become friends. With each Western clothing collection, they remain true to their South Texas ranching history, perpetuating the cowgirl image that is deeply connected to the state's origins.[1162]

Linda Jordens Galayda: New York Fashion and Texas Brangus

Linda Jordens Galayda ran a family ranch in Katy, Texas with the help of her husband that bred Brangus cattle.[1163] Later, she will own and run a ranch in East Texas. She has an international following online that seeks her advice on best ranching practices; Galayda sought out many resources to enhance her knowledge of ranching.[1164] Growing up on a ranch instilled these values—stressed and inculcated in the children of ranchers: your word was your bond, your family is God-fearing, and it takes a team to engender success.[1165] Galayda worked hard as part of her family, as she stated, "no silver spoon here;" Galayda commuted from her New York fashion career to the working ranch for thirty years.[1166] She mesmerized her colleagues with stories of her duties on the land in Texas.[1167] While she traveled the world to exotic locations, such as Paris and Cairo, meeting celebrities and enjoying Continental cuisine in fancy restaurants, Galayda knew that chuck-wagon food under the Texas stars suited her just as well. Her dad, never impressed with her world travels or rides in limousines, expected her to drive a pick-up truck and work the cattle when home, and help with the fence mending.[1168] She noted that many people living and working in New York City had little knowledge of the origins of their food.

By 1997, with her dad's health failing, he decided to invest in the Brangus breed because he saw that line as forward thinking.[1169] Galayda later realized when she made decisions for the ranch, she understood how consequential those were because each could make a great difference in the overall success of the ranch.[1170] She sought knowledge from ranching experts, other breeders, and she took advantage of various Texas A&M programs.[1171] She began a blog on all aspects of ranching and exercised her marketing background when selling cattle. Her blog has links to all subjects concerning every aspect of cattle ranching.[1172]

After the Katy, Texas ranch was sold, the Galayda family faced one of their most challenging times during the drought of 2011 at their new ranch in Elkhart, Texas. Although the severe drought from 1950–1957 represented the worst time in the state, the 2011 event entailed the most critical single-year event.[1173] June to August recorded the driest summer on record.[1174] Livestock ranchers suffered along with cotton producers. Texas is the largest producer of cattle in the U.S, therefore, the loss was enormous at $3.32 billion, according to the US Department of Agriculture figures.[1175] Galayda simply described the horrible conditions on her 2500-acre ranch as, "awful."[1176] The family dipped into savings to buy hay after they culled the herd of weak cattle, selling them to save the balance of the herd.[1177] Cattle grazed at night because of the intense Texas heat.[1178] Wild fires proliferated in the area, leaving her anxious and worried.[1179] Hay costs rose and she flagged trucks down to check where the hay originated, as Texas had no hay.[1180] She orchestrated the best plan possible, drawing on all of the experience in the fashion world, applying the same business principles to save her bovine stock.[1181] About $140,000 dollars of their cash reserves helped save the ranch.[1182] Heifers were sold at bargain prices while cattle were moved to smaller pastures, attempting to keep them closer to water that they had hauled in themselves.[1183] The workday began at 4:30 a.m. because by 10:30 a.m., the heat prevented hard outdoor work.[1184] The drought year of 2011 ended with the new year when rain fell, filling the ponds and creeks.[1185] Eventually, the grass grew and the cattle once more thrived, however, some cattle suffered health issues from the harsh drought as her herd had dwindled to 370 from 500 head.[1186] Galayda needed to heal from the stress of the year. She survived and continued to maintain her ranching business while blogging and engaging in the sharing of her daily duties with her "girls"—the cows she loved so much, a herd that her father had begun back in the 1990s. She combined her fashion dreams with her ranching duties, using her business savvy in productive ways when surviving trying times.

Linda Elane Barras Whiteley: Solutions With No Boundaries

"Women think differently than men. There is not a right or wrong way of thinking, it is just different. The difference led me to problem-solving in a different manner."[1187] Linda Elane Barras Whiteley, born on July 22, 1965—the start of what is now defined as Generation X—grew up in Port Arthur, Texas, known at the time as the "City that Oiled the World." Her parents, Bobby Donald Barras and Patricia Smith Barras greatly influenced her early life up to her entrance to Texas A&M; she majored in Industrial Engineering at a time when Science, Technology, Engineering, and Math (STEM) classes mostly consisted of males. Whiteley remained consistently determined to compete in a man's world, understanding the hard-fought battle for acceptance in that world had been a lengthy predicate orchestrated by tough Texas women insistent on opportunities to run businesses and to succeed. Generation X represents about sixty-six million people and many presently are the movers and shakers in both business and politics.[1188] Whiteley's goals and her career direction did not reflect realities for women in 1987, when she graduated from college and obtained her first job. Many women in the workforce, in a time of rising divorce rates, continued in the fields of teaching and nursing while managing a home with children.[1189] Both her grandmother and mother offered the advice that Whiteley could do whatever she set her mind to do. Whiteley had influential female family members and a strong educational background, proving that these basics are crucial to success; if one possessed the will power to gain the knowledge necessary for success in the business world, including being able to financially support oneself.[1190]

Whiteley grew up in a supportive household with her two brothers, one sister, and parents that never allowed her to quit anything she started. She took advantage of learning from her female relatives which included a variety of personalities with varied careers, including a teacher, an accountant, a nurse, a landlord that traveled the world, a butcher shop owner, and a pre-K school owner. Her mother, a professional artist whose thinking and ideas proliferated outside of conventional thought, inspired Whiteley to always look beyond standard answers when creativity proved necessary for future business solutions. Her father, a tall man that played football at Rice University, challenged his daughter when playing catch. He threw a strong ball that often knocked her to the ground, and she later realized that "getting up when down," was the intended lesson—one she learned well.[1191] A prolific reader, she frequented the Gates Memorial Library, hoping to read every book. During summer, her mom sometimes offered the curious child a subject to research; however, the requirement was that she stand on a box and present to the family her findings, thereby teaching her invaluable speaking skills. Her father taught her the value of a dollar by having her justify in writing the cost of any new thing she wanted. And he would later suggest, as she approached college-age, her life should include being financially independent, and that meant that she earned the money to support herself.[1192]

Whiteley's education in Port Arthur schools incorporated new teaching methods introduced in the 1970s by the state of Texas. Those included transformational ideas such as allowing students to progress individually at their own speed. Audiovisual aids, team teaching, nongraded approaches and accelerated classes transformed the teaching-learning processes.[1193] She attended Sam Houston Elementary, where the nongraded approach flourished and ability ranked more important than age. Learning resulted from hands-on demonstrations. Foreign language instruction began in the first grade and Whiteley embraced French, enjoying the processes necessary for proficiency. The evolution of foreign language education came from a multitude of political and social changes from the 1960s to the 1980s; these included: the aftermath of WWII, the launching of Sputnik by the Russians in 1957, the Civil Rights Movement of the 1960s, the change in Immigration laws in 1965, and President Johnson's Great Society programs which included the Bilingual Education Act of 1968.[1194] The introduction of foreign languages during elementary school assisted those such as Whiteley, whose career would take her to foreign countries where an understanding of other cultures and languages enhanced her ability to do business. While in junior high at Thomas Edison and in high school at Thomas Jefferson (presently renamed Memorial High School), she competed in tennis and participated in Student Council activities.[1195] While training with the boys, she learned that women used different strategies and that her determination should not be described as aggressiveness, but assertiveness. Playing a competitive sport prepared Whiteley for working in a traditionally male-dominated industry. At the time of her high school graduation, Ronald Reagan occupied the White House with a goal of jumpstarting a stagnant economy. Republican Bill Clements remained the governor of Texas until his defeat in the 1982 election that brought Democrat Mark White, Jr. to Austin. The state suffered from falling oil prices and a weak economy.

Whiteley entered Texas A&M University in 1983 and unlike many Texas women of the past, she had a "directed" career path and set goals in mind. She executed her plan, and while the college courses challenged her, she had a strong background in math and science, accelerated by an incredibly strong work ethic. "Look to your left and right, two of you won't make it," warned the orientation guide.[1191] Whiteley noted that professors treated females the same as the male students. A serious student, she had the intelligence and tenacity to complete the degree, and those two criteria rang true for males and females. A humorous part of her education occurred while she was enrolled in a welding class. The necessary helmets, gloves, and apron were all designed for males, therefore the helmet window fit too low on her head and she could not see her work! She welded her piece to a table. Asking for help, the instructor guided her hand and she kept saying, "I do not see anything."[11961197] He laughed and told her, "You don't see anything because your helmet is too big, and the window is at your chin!"[1198] Improvisation resulted in a helmet that permitted her to succeed. She became proficient by coming in early and staying late. While never wanting to weld for a career, Whiteley thought she could possibly be in a position of a supervisor at some point in her career, so it was important to understand the craft. Also, one summer, she received a Westinghouse grant and helped develop robotics for the insertion of microchips. While this experience was not enjoyed or relished at the time, she later realized how challenges engendered a desire for more of them. Whiteley is included in the approximately twenty-eight percent of female STEM workers in an industry segment that employs nearly three times as many men as women.[1199] Unfortunately, data shows that women with STEM degrees do not pursue careers in the field, and many more leave their job than men.[1200]

With her credentials from Texas A&M, she sought employment in a newly formed technology entity, Compaq Computers. Because she had no true work experience, she had to sell herself as an employee who could do the job. Whiteley convinced the Human Resources Manager to hire her because of her willingness to save the company money. During this time, in 1986, the Space Shuttle Challenger exploded in January, killing all aboard; people tuned in to watch Cagney and Lacey, Dynasty, and Cheers; Oprah Winfrey's show began; Intel introduced the 386 series of microprocessors; and Internet Mail Access Protocol was defined for email transfer.[1201] This new idea that became Compaq had been originated by three senior engineers from Texas Instruments who met for dinner at the landmark House of Pies in 1982, on Westheimer Road in Houston, and plotted on a paper placemat.[1202] Each of the men—Rod Canion, James Harris, and William Murto—invested one thousand dollars each to begin their new adventure.[1203] She wisely chose this startup company to gather skills in cutting edge technology.[1204] As the companies first college-hire, she redesigned their service center for the introduction of a new product in 1998—the company's first laptop. This laptop PC with VGA graphics was the Compaq SLT/286.[1205]

Whiteley changed her life after one year at Compaq with her marriage to husband James (Jim), whom she described as "wonderful, talented, and brilliant." Linda and Jim were married thirty-two years as of April of 2021 and share their lives with two cats and three hunting dogs.[1206] A PhD in engineering, he graduated from the Air Force Academy, later working as a test flight engineer for the Air Force, flying and testing the new models of stealth military aircraft. He supported her in all of her endeavors and felt strongly successful men are not intimidated by strong women. The world shook on October 19, 1987, from a 508-point crash on Wall Street.[1207] "Tango in the Night" by Fleetwood Mac entertained the young generation, along with the movie and music from "Dirty Dancing." Robin Williams re-visited a tumultuous time in America with his movie, "Good Morning Vietnam."[1208] The newlywed couple transferred to the Wright-Patterson Air Force Base in Dayton, Ohio where she remembers being the only female industrial engineer on classified stealth aircraft and missile programs, working as a civilian employee.[1209] "Stealth, also known as "low observable," technology, still conveys an overwhelming combat advantage. It reduces exposure by a full range of signatures—electromagnetic, infrared, visual, and acoustic—but the main one is radar," that allowed for combat and attack superiority.[1210] She had a security clearance and worked on several different classified programs with team members of fifty to one hundred people.[1211] One of her responsibilities included the coordination of manufacturing with contracting vendors. She found the work exhilarating and during this two-year project she garnered knowledge as to the business practices of the US government, along with learning the strategies from large aerospace corporations.

Consequential world events occurred that changed the relationship between the United States and Russia. President George H. Walker Bush met Mikhail Gorbachev in Malta on December 2nd and 3rd, 1989, for a major conference that resulted in the end of the Cold War, after the fall of the Berlin Wall.[1212] "When Harry Met Sally" and "Indiana Jones and the Last Crusade" hit the big screen with huge audiences while Garth Brooks shook the stage with his live performances.[1213] The couple came back to Houston during these momentous times, including when Microsoft Office was released. Whiteley engaged in several occupations at candy giant M&M/Mars, Incorporated.[1214] She worked as an industrial engineer for what was at the time Uncle Ben's, Incorporated—now branded as Ben's Original—located on Harvey Wilson Drive; and later, she worked as a logistics manager for a business unit of Mars.[1215] M&M/Mars owned the company, Uncle Ben's, and its rice product, and the company was a combination of Forest Mars' Food Products Manufacturing and Mars, Incorporated, his father's candy company. M&M candies, named for the younger Mars and his business partner, Bruce Murrie, hence the name of the candy, received a patent in 1941.[1216] The Mars family has owned the company for over a hundred years and it has a major presence in the US and overseas companies; Mars consists of a wide variety of products from candy to pet food.[1217] Whiteley, while at the rice company, participated in new food product launches. She learned that a highly orchestrated team enriched the company and was crucial to the success of a product line. As a logistics manager, she oversaw ship, rail, and over-the-road deliveries to global ports, including distribution centers and warehouses throughout the US After Whiteley recommended the Houston, Texas manufacturing plant of the business be combined with the plant in Mississippi, she later decided a relocation was not favorable to her career plan. After seven years of working for a large globally connected company, she decided to expand her ongoing business education.[1218]

After years in the food industry, Whiteley gained experience running a smaller company, owned by a California pharmaceutical concern, called Allergy Free, in Houston, that focused on allergy avoidance products. On her first day as General Manager, she learned of a major drawback at the time that concerned a new product the company advertised on the popular Paul Harvey radio show. Orders arrived and the company had not designed and manufactured the product—an air filtration system. As a problem solver, she gathered experienced vendors from around the country and, working as a team, they designed, tested and created not one but two new products. Then, Whiteley employed her engineering skills to design specialized manufacturing equipment, had it built and shipped to Houston with production starting within eight weeks of her first day. Her last goal, after two years there, became fulfilled when the company proved they were strong enough, financially, to be sold.[1219]

Whiteley, with a solid work history behind her, ventured outside the US in May of 2000 to become Chief Operating Officer (COO) for Wholesome Sweeteners, Inc., a subsidiary of Edward Billington and Sons located in Reading, United Kingdom.[1220] She found the employment ad online and chose to seek the position, as she never used services of employment agencies or high-level headhunters. As the first female executive hired in

America, some of her efforts, on behalf of the organic sweeteners business meant that she would spend expansive periods of time in Paraguay and other Central and South American countries, where acceptance of women as bosses was met with a degree of male skepticism. While she never let on that she understood Spanish, she found that the Paraguayans believed she was a secretary, so she affirmatively stated that her role was as "la hefa," meaning the leader or boss. While in this role of Chief Operating Officer, Whiteley assisted one of the largest sugar mills in Paraguay to become certified as a food grade manufacturing facility meeting the standards of the United States. This sugar mill was the first food grade manufacturing company in South America to ever achieve this status; also as Whiteley noted, the sugar mill owner began to hire and promote women resulting in a more smoothly running operation. Seeing women in new roles made her happy. After seven years with the company, she proceeded to evaluate about a thousand potential companies with the intent to buy her own.

Whiteley chose AGS Solutions, Inc., a Houston-based entity that had recently marked 25-years in business. Not risk adverse, her business personality bloomed as Whiteley based her future on the strength of her past. Finding a business that would remain a stable and a staple entity had been instrumental in her decision-making processes. She did not accidently buy the industrial chemical cleaning company.[1221] The company had developed "green" responsible biodegradable cleaners from the get-go, before "green" became a buzz word. They have excellent products and services, a reputation of providing excellent customer service and have blue chip customers. As she often states about her company, "We may be the small dog on the porch, but we hang with the big dogs." Bringing responsibly, environmentally-sound, cleaning products to market remain an ever-constant goal. At the time, she never considered herself a pioneer when women in Texas and in the South did not normally work in the chemical industry. What she realized was that regardless of any other factors in a business, all companies had to clean. She purchased shares that gave her a majority; her husband became a minority shareholder.[1222] For thirteen years, she has operated a federally certified, woman owned, business as the President and owner. As stated by Whiteley, "AGS makes proprietary biodegradable industrial specialty cleaners for companies such as Exxon-Mobil and Chevron to clean process equipment, degass tanks, pipelines and refineries and many other applications in the downstream oil & gas market."[1223] She is "proud to also have developed Environmental Protection Agency Schedule N surface washing agents and dispersants for oil spills in salt water such as in oceans."[1224]

Whiteley never operated in a business or personal vacuum; she cultivated several mentors who guided her through business practices that worked for her. Her first mentor was a vice president at Uncle Ben's, Incorporated who had not volunteered to assist her; still, she persisted until he caved. She noted, "He was tough as nails and I admired that; he was tough but fair."[1225] She adapted the leadership styles learned from him and found her own style. After she bought AGS, a female in the procurement department at ExxonMobil became her go-to person for discussions and ideas. Although this mentor has since retired, they remain friends. Also during her long-term career, Whiteley fostered professional relationships with three male mentors who also owned businesses. The four of them worked well together, and their roles expanded to that of sounding boards for one another. As a result of their mutual trust, they "would help each other no matter what." She never assumed, or felt, as though gender influenced this special gathering with her three colleagues, where trust, faith, and loyalty remained paramount. Whiteley, after some reflection, thought that being female in a male dominated world allowed her some advantages. She focused on the human rapport dynamic that meaningful relationships made good business sense, because at some point in time, there will be rough spots and it will be the personal and professional associations "you build that get you through it."[1226] On occasion, she dealt with some difficult men that attempted to build roadblocks to her success; however, regardless of harassment, she went around them or above them. Truly, she found most male colleagues supportive. Nothing impeded her dreams.[1227]

By the turn of the century, younger generations of women might have been exposed to the Feminist Movement of the 1960s and 1970s during college classes, or from their own female relatives. Whiteley believed, when she began her career out of college, that no barriers existed that could prevent her from fulfilling her goals. Instead of believing that women should lament the idea of a metaphorical glass ceiling, they instead should create a new mindset that what path they desire is the path they can take, if willing to work hard and exercise sheer determination. According to her, "The only glass ceilings out there are the ones that we create ourselves...there are no glass ceilings."[1228] She believes that successful companies benefit from having diverse employees able to interact in meaningful ways that ultimately contribute to the bottom line.

By the new century, women voted in great numbers, served on juries, ran for office, purchased homes, opened brokerage accounts, signed up for 401-K plans, received credit cards based on their own financial status, and joined clubs once exclusive to men. Companies provided health insurance to female employees, once limited to male employees in many cases. The purpose of any corporation is to make money, and women-owned businesses proved success comes with an understanding of both finance and the importance of the bottom line.

The new century had been full of surprises, some good and others tragic. Terrorists hijacked airliners that crashed into the World Trade Center, bringing both buildings down, including an attack on the Pentagon, and a field in Shanksville, Pennsylvania on September 11, 2001. In October of the same year, Apple Computer delivered the first iPad.[1229] The Space Shuttle Columbia broke apart while attempting reentry, killing seven astronauts on February 1, 2003. Hurricane Rita, a strong, deadly, and devastating cyclone in September of 2005, prompted the evacuation of about two million residents from Southeast Texas; from Beaumont to Houston, the storm slammed the coast near Sabine Pass, killing 120 persons overall, of which, 107 were Texans.[1230] The storm was the fourth most intense Atlantic hurricane in history.[1231] Barack Obama won the election for the presidency on November 4, 2008, eventually becoming a two-term leader of the free world. Donald Trump defied all odds to win the presidency in 2016 with his slogan of "Make America Great Again." Of all the changes during the first two decades of the new century, perhaps the most overwhelmingly disturbing and ubiquitous event that stunned the world—the Pandemic of 2020–21—affected all aspects of life. The COVID-19 virus swept across the world from China to almost every country in the world, apart from some small island atolls and a couple inland locations, such as Turkmenistan.[1232] Small and independent businesses closed when the first lockdown, "to flatten the curve," occurred. Whiteley immediately used her creative heft to pivot toward providing necessities available to a wide variety of companies needing disinfectant wipes and hand sanitizer. She wrote her adaptive strategies down as an effort to save her own company and shared what she called the "Pivot Principle," attaching an easily identifiable logo to the concept.[1233] These principles needed to succeed against the odds during the Pandemic, included the following ideas:[1234]

1. Examine the strengths that you as a leader have and what your business excels at doing. Then, determine what you can do for your customer by applying your strengths in a different manner.
2. Adopt an attitude that anything is possible.
3. Commit to persevere until a viable and sustainable solution is secured.
4. Be willing to step far out of your comfort zone.
5. Explore opportunities to collaborate with other small businesses who have different areas of expertise to add to your own skills.
6. Explore opportunities to collaborate with other vendors and suppliers to support your customers in different ways.
7. Engage your customers to better understand their needs to determine if your business can deliver a solution—even if that solution is not one you previously offered.

The Pivot Principle of products and services was developed by Whiteley at a time of desperate need. "This collection includes success strategies, webinars, workshops, and books designed to equip and empower businesses, sole practitioners, and individuals to outlast and overcome adversity."[1235]

Whiteley shared her principles with struggling company leaders and as evidenced by Bloomberg's business wire news story, she garnered national attention as "the little company that could."[1236] At the beckoning of a manager at ExxonMobil's diversity team, Whiteley provided disinfectant wipes for them. While not a standard offering at AGS Solutions, she vetted known suppliers, quickly becoming a distributor. Using her logistics skills and her warehousing relationships, the company began selling disinfectant wipes and hand sanitizer. Her quick thinking led to the growth of the company and AGS became one of the largest US distributors; new customers abounded. Whiteley, like many other owners of both large and small businesses, experienced the Covid-19 Pandemic; she adjusted her business plan to meet the crisis and her pivoting principles led the way. Her customers come from a variety of businesses, including airlines, rail lines, and medical research facilities.[1237] She saved her company, gained a stronger, broader reputation, preserved her employees' jobs, and kept the future alive with new prospects.

American volunteerism dates to the pre-Revolution days and has always been an American trait. Rapid economic and social changes would continue the need for advocating for those vulnerable segments of society that are without advantages and resources necessary to improve lives. Volunteering improves the well-being of the less fortunate and provides a sense of wellness to those who give time or monetary support. Whiteley volunteers at the Beaumont Texas Workforce Commission and her contributions consist of teaching job interviewing skills and resume building. She chose Beaumont because the unemployment rates are higher than many Texas cities, and she is from Port Arthur, a city close by. She noted those without jobs suffer self-doubt and lack of self-esteem. The time proved so worthwhile for her as she helped unemployed people turn their skills into plans of action. Whiteley worked with a homeless man who walked several miles to attend the class she taught. He had nothing and was without an address. They identified his skills and created a resume; he went door-to-door in downtown Beaumont until he ultimately obtained a job. Giving people a purpose, guiding them in a positive direction, and instilling self-worth were important factors that she taught and.[1238]

As the newer generations begin their business careers, many will become aware that they will not work at the same company for thirty to forty years and retire with a pension or 401K retirement fund. As exampled by Whiteley, she represents a 'breakaway" female that created her own path through strategic planning; this included gaining a variety of helpful business skills at different companies, whereby her career culminated in the ownership of a business she chose that met her criteria for success. She built her dream based on a useful education that opened many doors for her. However, she chose those doors, plotting and planning the direction of her life. She went about her goals by exercising good communication skills, applying logic when adapting to new and unexpected problems, and knowing the importance of building solid relationships. A female entrepreneur takes full ownership and responsibility for one's business and nurtures her employees. Whiteley's choices provide a guide for younger, highly driven women that want to own successful Texas businesses. Her words for younger women entering the workforce, "The sky's the limit, just make it happen."[1239]

Chapter Fourteen
Concluding Thoughts

A great pivot to freedom of choice for working women has emerged in Texas. Women in the state, by the twenty-first century, had disrupted the male confrontational, Social Darwinian environment in the business world by circumventing the Glass Ceiling. Much of this new success percolates from fresh generations of young women who have never been told "No." From the heady days of the Feminist Movement of the 1960s, to the idea that the only avenue to the top meant cracking the glass ceiling, women innovate and create their own business enterprises as Texas females entered a Texas-styled post-feminist period. Women have now embraced education as mandatory and they flock to Texas institutions of higher learning, obtaining degrees that propel them forward. Although the fight for equality is far from finished in the Western World, and incipient in many struggling countries, great strides have been realized. Women feel the sense of pride and accomplishment when they write the title, "chief executive officer" or "president" on their corporation filing papers. Governments at any level that facilitate "doing business" without gender restrictions means the more opportunities all women of the world will have to live a life; such that allows them the choices men have exercised throughout much of humankind's story from the cave to the penthouse.[1240]

Texas presently represents an example of a place where women can create their own futures. Breaking or cracking the glass at the top can, and should, be a laudable goal, but entrepreneurship should remain a strong and viable path for women. While war may never vanish from the planet, women provide the counterbalance needed for a stable earth. Wars, while devastating and lamentable, have broken the barriers that isolated and insulated women from the working and political world and gave women the impetus to break from traditional roles. There exists no exclusivity on suffering by either sex during times of crises, as wars have enveloped and disrupted whole populations, damaging both males and females.[1241] The warrior ethic amplified perceptions by men that women were the weaker sex. War victories in Texas produced euphoric feelings of overall superiority that had permeated workplace attitudes for many years. Women, presently, are providing a standard of living that comes with the ownership of businesses that deliver prosperity and happiness for more inhabitants of our small planet. A woman's reach should be far wider than her role as a mother or wife should she desire a position beyond the home.[1242] Many of the women described in this book did both successfully by raising strong children and "bringing home the bacon." Truly, all women should choose their individual path that meets their personal expectations of a life well lived. Women work, whether at home, nurturing their children, operating a small business, or running a large corporation; one can hope their lives are reflected by their choices. Recognizing societies produce better results when both men and women can dream their dreams, and realize both their individual and collective aspirations to the fullest capacity, remains a worthy goal. Men, and many women, in Texas have replaced their horses with the Ford F-150 pickup, driving around the big state that brags about producing the world's largest rodeo, and remembers the Alamo. Men are learning to share the benefits of a promising business environment in a state that is certainly large enough for both sexes to succeed. Romantically, though, some of the cultural expectations remain, as falling in love should always bring happiness and excitement. As Ella Bird Dumont, a brave frontier lady, stated when beholding the man she would marry, "I beheld, mounted on the most beautiful big black horse I had ever seen, a man, yes, a man, in full Western attire, that of a Texas Ranger, gallant, and brave in appearance."[1243] They lived a happy marriage in what she described as a love nest.[1244] She noted that the four men working on their ranch, which included her husband, treated her well and with a great deal of respect. However, at his death, she barely survived and her dreams of being a sculptor were dashed, except for designing monuments for graves.[1245] Women want respect for their talents and, through the excersice of them, a chance to avoid the poverty of widowhood and old age. And they can do so without "cracking their heads" into a glass ceiling. "As New York-based finance wizard and Wall Street trailblazer Alexandra Lebenthal, 54," hated to admit, "You're not really supposed to step out of the mold," in traditionally "buttoned-up workplaces." [1246] Those places represent corporations most often originated by men, based on their rules. Women with creative minds can explore a variety of diverging business ideas leading to novel concepts that set precedents for future success. Women are part of that victory, and their business endeavors represent a new model of expectation where power between men and women is presently being diffused.[1247]

The foundation for changes that will ensure economic power for women suggests necessities such as stable governments; good education systems; strong women-to-women and men-to-women mentoring; and require societies and economic structures no longer steeped in the patriarchal, patrilineal, patrilocal pattern of cultural practices, where primogeniture represents the mainstay of inheritance. Men are adjusting to "sharing the pie" and can no longer view women within a zero-sum game construct. Governments that pass laws that encourage ease of business formation can rise and shine economically, making their respective countries and their people strong, equal, and happy. The talents of all women combined can and should create a better planet where all humans flourish and succeed. Texas, presently, regardless of the long struggle experienced by the women of the state, represents an economic model worth duplicating. These women that circumvented the Glass Ceiling and broke the control men had in the state are the foundation of a new business paradigm. The variety of women highlighted in this narrative indicates that fame never dilutes the significance of all women striving to support themselves, in a way that hopefully allows them security and overall happiness. Although Frederick Jackson Turner's Frontier Thesis never as much mentioned the role of women in the growth and expansion of America from sea to shining sea, women forged Texas; and regardless of the statement by the Census Bureau that the frontier had officially closed by 1890, women in the state continued the advancement of Texas in the true meaning of the "next frontier."[1248]

1 Caroline Sutton, "Texas ranked No. 1 State for Women Entrepreneurs," Central Texas News Now, 25 ABC News, assessed January 11, 2019. http://www.kxxv.com/story/39759721/texas-ranked-no1-state-for-women-entrepreneurs; Glenn Hegar, "Texas Ranks High Nationally for Women-Owned Businesses," accessed December 7, 2018. https://comptroller,texas.gov/about/media-center/news/2017/170508-fiscal-notes.php.
2 "The 2018 State of Women-Owned Businesses Report," accessed September 20, 2018. https://about.americanexpress.com/files/doc_library/file/2018-state-of-women-owned-businesses-report.pdf.
3 GDP by State, US Bureau of Economic Analysis (BEA). Accessed January 20, 2019. https://www.bea.gov/data/gdp/gdp-state.
4 Dale Buss, "Best and Worst States for Business in 2018," Chief Executive, accessed August 8, 2019, https://executive.net/be-worst-state-business-2018/; Devlin, Cynthia Marshall. "Bypass the Glass Ceiling: Texas Women Disrupt Traditional Male-Dominated Business Models. Journal of Academic Perspectives. No. 4 (2019): 2,3.
5 Handbook of Texas Online, Thomas W. Cutrer, "Roberts, Daniel Webster," accessed January 6, 2019, http://www.tshaonline.org/handbook/online/articles/fro11.
6 Lucy A. Sponsler, *The Status of Married Women Under the Legal System of Spain*, 42 La. L. Rev. (1982). Available at: https://digitalcommons.law.lsu.edu/lalrev/vol42/iss5/9.
7 Ibid.
8 Ibid.
9 Claude Morin, "Age at Marriage and Female Employment in Colonial Mexico," accessed April 5, 2021. Age at marriage in Colonial Mexico (umontreal.ca). Paper read at the International Conference "Women's Employment, Marriage-Age and Population Change," University of Delhi, Developing Countries Research Center, March 3-5, 1997.
10 Ibid.
11 Ibid.
12 Ibid.
13 Ibid.
14 Ibid.
15 "Hard Road to Texas: Texas Annexation 1836-1845," Texas State Library and ArchiveCommission, accessed April 4, 2021. Texas Annexation Questions and Answers | TSLAC.
16 Ibid.
17 *Handbook of Texas Online*, Cynthia E. Orozco, "MEXICAN-AMERICAN WOMEN," accessed February 19, 2020, http://www.tshaonline.org/handbook/online/articles/pwmly.
18 Robert McCaa, "The Population of Mexico from Origins to Revolution," accessed February 20, 2020. users.pop.umn.edu/~rmccaa/mxpoprev/cambridg3.htm.
19 Ibid.
20 Richard Salvucci, "Mexico: Economic History" EH.Net Encyclopedia, edited by Robert Whaples. December 27, 2018. accessed February 21, 2020. http://eh.net/encyclopedia/the-economic-history-of-mexico/.
21 Ibid.
22 Ibid.
23 Ibid.
24 Ibid.
25 Ibid.
26 Richard Salvucci, "Mexico: Economic History" EH.Net Encyclopedia.
27 Ibid.

28 Ibid.
29 Ibid.
30 Ibid.
31 Joe S. Graham, *El Rancho in South Texas: Continuity and Change from 1750*, 1st ed. (Denton, Texas: University of North Texas Press, 1994) 13, 27, 59.
32 *Handbook of Texas Online*, Cynthia E. Orozco.
33 Ibid.
34 "Ester Boserup and Boserupian Theory: Boserup's thesis and status of women," March 11, 2019, accessed January 13, 2020. https://article 1000.com/boserup-thesis-status-women; Alberto f. Alesina, Paola Giuliano, Nathan Nunn, "On the Origins of Gender Roles: Women and the Plough," Working Paper 17098, 2.
35 Claude Morin, "Age at Marriage and Female Employment in Colonial Mexico.
36 Frances Spears Cloyd, "Facets of Texas Legal History," 52 SMU Law Review 1653, 1999, accessed October 21, 2012. http://web.lexis-nexis.com/universe. Article was based on her thesis for a Master of Law Degree in 1959. She practiced in Texas for fifty years.
37 Ibid.
38 Eugene A. Gittinger, "The Colonization of Texas: 1820-1830" (1940). Master's Theses, 51.
39 Ibid., 48.
40 Ibid., 62-63, 102, 103.
41 William Curry Holden, *Alkali Trails* (Dallas: The Southwest Press, c.1930), 21; Sandra L. Myers, *The Ranch in Spanish Texas, 1691-1800* (El Paso: Texas Western Press, 1969), 7.
42 Fred A. Shannon, *The Farmer's Last Frontier: Agriculture*, 1860-1897, 197.
43 Robert A. Calvert, Arnoldo De León, Gregg Cantrell, *The History of Texas*, 3rd ed. (Wheeling, Illinois: Harlan Davidson, Inc., 2002), 38.
44 Ibid.
45 Ibid., 31.
46 Ibid., 32, 33.
47 Ibid., 32.
48 Ibid., 33.
49 Fred A. Shannon, *The Farmer's Last Frontier: Agriculture*, 1860-1897, vol. V of *The Economic History of the United States* (New York: Holt, Rinehart, and Winston, 1963) 367.
50 Ibid.
51 Benjamin Moser, "Appellation Texas Contrôlée: The bloody history of the Lone Star State," Harper's Magazine (August 2004), 87.
52 Frances Spears Cloyd, "Facets of Texas Legal History."
53 John H. Lienhard, "Food In Early Texas," 1080. (Houston: University of Houston's College of Engineering, 1080), accessed February 19, 2020. https://www.uh.edu/engines/epi1080.htm.
54 Mary Austin Holley, *Mary Austin Holley: The Texas Diary, 1835-1846*. (Austin: University of Texas Press, 1965), 7.
55 John H. Lienhard, "Food In Early Texas."
56 Ibid.
57 1830 Fast Facts - History - US Census Bureau, accessed February 22, 2020. https://www.census.gov/history/www/through_the_decades/fast_facts/1830_fast_facts.html.
58 Ibid.
59 Ibid.
60 Past Patterns: 1830's - 1840's patterns, accessed February 19, 2020. www.pastpatterns.com/1830.html.

61 Women's Rights, ushistory.org, accessed Feb. 22, 2020. https://www.ushistory.org/Us/26c.asp.
62 Ibid.
63 Ibid.
64 Frederick Jackson Turner, "The Significance of the Frontier in American History, 1893." A paper read at the meeting of the American Historical Association in Chicago, July 12, 1893. It first appeared in the Proceedings of the State Historical Society of Wisconsin, December 14, 1893, http://www.nationalhumanitiescenter.org/pds/gilded/empire/text1/turner.pdf.
65 Sandra L. Myers, *The Ranch in Spanish Texas, 1691-1800* (El Paso: Texas Western Press, 1969), 5.
66 Frances Spears Cloyd, "Facets of Texas Legal History," 52 SMU Law Review 1653, 1999, accessed October 21, 2012. http://web.lexis-nexis.com/universe. Article was based on her thesis for a Master of Law Degree in 1959. She practiced in Texas for fifty years.
67 Ibid
68 Ibid.
69 Ibid.
70 Ralph S. Jackson, *Home on the Double Bayou: Memories of an East Texas Ranch*, (Austin: University of Texas Press, 1966), 17.
71 Mary Austin Holley, *Mary Austin Holley: The Texas Diary, 1835-1846*. 59.
72 Ibid., 13, 27.
73 Fred A. Shannon, The Farmer's Last Frontier: Agriculture, 1860-1897, Vol. V., The Economic History of the United States (New York: Holt, Rinehart, and Winston, 1963), 363.
74 Velasco Texas, Texas travel, Texas history, Texas cities, accessed February 23, 2020. www.texasescapes.com/TexasGulfCoastTowns/Velasco-Texas.htm.
75 Gene Fowler, Mavericks: A Gallery of Texas Characters, (Austin: University of Texas Press, 2008), 35, 36.
76 Cynthia Marshall Devlin, "Bypass the Glass Ceiling: Texas Women Disrupt Traditional Male-Dominated Business Models," Journal of Academic Perspectives Dec.- 4 (2019): accessed February 24, 2020. http://www.journalofacademicperspectives.com/.
77 Ibid.
78 Jo Ella Powell Exley, ed., 1st ed. *Texas Tears and Texas Sunshine: Voices of Frontier Women* (College Station: Texas A & M University, 1985), 205; Cynthia M. Devlin, "Bypass the Glass Ceiling."
79 Jo Ella Powell, 91-100; Cynthia M. Devlin.
80 Ibid.
81 Ibid.
82 Ibid.
83 Ibid.
84 Ibid.
85 Ibid.
86 Ibid.
87 Richard Salvucci, "Mexico: Economic History."
88 Ibid.
89 Stephanie E. Jones-Rogers, a history professor at the University of California-Berkeley, is compiling data on just how many white women owned slaves in the US; and in the parts of the 1850 and 1860 census data she has studied so far, white women make up about 40 percent of all slave owners. As adults, white women often tore black women away from their babies so they could nurse the white mistress' baby instead. To this end, white women placed thousands of advertisements in newspapers looking for enslaved "wet nurses" to feed

their own children and created a huge market for enslaved black women who had recently given birth. Why did these white women want black women to nurse their children? One complained "she felt like continuously having children and continuously nursing her children made her 'a slave' to her children—that's an actual quote," Jones-Rogers says.

90 Becky Little, "The Massive, Overlooked Role of Female Slave Owners" - HISTORY, accessed February 24, 2020. https://www.history.com/news/white-women-slaveowners-they-were-her-property, March 12, 2019. Stephanie E. Jones-Rogers, a history professor at the University of California-Berkeley, is compiling data on just how many white women owned slaves.

91 Debates of the Convention, assembled at the city of Austin on the Fourth of July,1845, for the purpose of framing a constitution for the State of Texas. Austin: Miner & Cruger, printers to the Convention, 1845.Tarlton Constitutions 1824-1876 accessed February 5, 2020. http://tarlton.law.utexas.edu/constitutions/.

92 Slavery in Texas: A brief overview of Slavery in Texas, accessed February 24, 2020. https://exhibits.library.unt.edu/httpsexhibitslibraryunteduslaverytexas/brief-overview.

93 Ibid.

94 Robert A. Calvert, Arnoldo De León, Gregg Cantrell, *The History of Texas*, 3rd ed. (Wheeling, Illinois: Harlan Davidson, Inc., 2002), 83.

95 Frances Spears Cloyd, "Facets of Texas Legal History,"

96 Ibid.

97 Jo Ella Powell Exley, editor., 1st ed., *Texas Tears and Texas Sunshine: Voices of Frontier Women*, (College Station: Texas A & M University Press, 1985), 93.

98 Ibid., 93.

99 Ibid., 90.

100 Ibid., 95.

101 Ibid.

102 Ibid.

103 Cynthia Marshall Devlin, "Bypass the Glass Ceiling: Texas Women Disrupt Traditional Male-Dominated Business Models," online "*Journal of Academic Perspectives*," 2019 Dec. – 4; Kevin Ladd, "The Winter Storm of 1863 and 1864 – Part 2 (March 2013), Local Writers' Columns, Stephen F. Austin State University, Center of Regional Heritage Research, accessed March 22, 2020. www.sfasu.edu/heritagecenter/7093.asp; Texas Hurricane History, accessed March 22, 2020. https://www.weather.gov/media/lch/events/txhurricanehistory.pdf.

104 Constitution of Texas (1845) (Joining the US), Constitution of the State of Texas, Article VII General Provisions, SEC. 19, adopted in Convention, at the City of Austin 1845. Austin: Printed at the Office of the 'New Era', 1845.Tarlton Law Library, Jamil Center for Legal Research, accessed February 2, 2020. https://tarltonapps.law.utexas.edu/constitutions/texas1845. Property rights are reiterated verbatim in the 1861 & 1866 Constitutions. The 1869 Constitution states in SEC. XIV: The rights of married women to their separate property, real and personal, and the increase of the same, shall be protected by law; and married women, infants and insane persons, shall not be barred of their rights of property by adverse possession, or law of limitation, of less than seven years from and after the removal of each and all their respective legal disabilities. The 1876 Constitution, Article XVI, SEC. 15. All property, both real and personal, of the wife, owned or claimed by her before marriage; and that acquired afterward by gift, devise or descent, shall be her separate property; and laws shall be passed more clearly defining the rights of the wife, in relation as well to her separate property as that held in common with her husband. Laws shall also be passed providing for the registration of the wife's separate property.

105 The Mexican American War, US History, Accessed March 23, 2020. https://

www,ushistory.org/us/29d.asp. The Mexican American War was formally concluded by the Treaty of Guadalupe-Hidalgo.

106 Ibid.

107 Women In Business, History, "Working Women, Women's Worth." Accessed February 21, 2007. http://www.referencefor business.com/encyclopedia/Val-ZWomen-in-Business.html.

108 Dwight W. Morrow, *American Economic History*, 5th ed. (New York: Harper & Brothers Publishers, 1943), 217.

109 Fred A. Shannon, *The Farmer's Last Frontier: Agriculture*, 1860-1897, Vol. V., The Economic History of the United States (New York: Holt, Rinehart and Winston, 1963), 35.

110 Ibid.

111 Ibid., 122.

112 Ibid., 122.

113 Paul H. Dué, Origin and Historical Development of the Community Property System, 25 La. L. Rev. (1964), accessed December 22, 2019. https://digitalcommons.law.lsu.edu/lalrev/vol25/iss1/17.

114 Charles Chamberlain, Lo Faber, "Spanish Colonial Louisiana, 64 Parishes," from the Historic New Orleans Collection, accessed January 23, 2020. https://64parishes.org/entry/spanish-colonial-louisiana.

115 Frances Spears Cloyd, "Facets of Texas Legal History," 52 SMU Law Review 1653, 1999, accessed October 21, 2012. http://web.lexis-nexis.com/universe. Article was based on her thesis for a Master of Law Degree in 1959. She practiced in Texas for fifty years.

116 Joseph W. McKnight, "Texas Community Property Law: Conservative Attitudes," 1993, accessed January 12, 2020. https://scholarship.law.duke.edu/cgi/viewcontent.cgi?article=4185&context=icp.

117 Journals of the Convention, assembled at the city of Austin on the Fourth of July, 845, for the purpose of framing a constitution for the State of Texas. Austin: Miner & Cruger, printers to the Convention, 1845. Tarlton Constitutions 1824-1876, accessed February 5, 2020. http://tarlton.law.utexas.edu/constitutions/.

118 Debates of the Convention, assembled at the city of Austin on the Fourth of July,1845, for the purpose of framing a constitution for the State of Texas. Austin: Miner & Cruger, printers to the Convention, 1845. Tarlton Constitutions 1824-1876, accessed February 5, 2020. http://tarlton.law.utexas.edu/constitutions/.

119 Ibid., 594-601.

120 Ibid.

121 Ibid.

122 Ibid.

123 Debates of the Convention.

124 Ibid.

125 Ibid.

126 Debates of the Convention, Aug. 16, 1845, p. 600.

127 Ibid.

128 Ibid.

129 Constitution of Texas (1845) (Joining the US), Constitution of the State of Texas, Article VII General Provisions, SEC. 19, adopted in Convention, at the City of Austin 1845. Austin: Printed at the Office of the 'New Era', 1845.Tarlton Law Library, Jamil Center for Legal Research, accessed February 2, 2020. https://tarltonapps.law.utexas.edu/constitutions/texas1845. Property rights are reiterated verbatim in the 1861 & 1866 Constitutions. The 1869 Constitution states in SEC. XIV. The rights of married women to their separate property, real and personal, and the increase of the same, shall be protected by law; and married women,

infants and insane persons, shall not be barred of their rights of property by adverse possession, or law of limitation, of less than seven years from and after the removal of each and all their respective legal disabilities. The 1876 Constitution Article XVI, SEC. 15. All property, both real and personal, of the wife, owned or claimed by her before marriage; and that acquired afterward by gift, devise or descent, shall be her separate property; and laws shall be passed more clearly defining the rights of the wife, in relation as well to her separate property as that held in common with her husband. Laws shall also be passed providing for the registration of the wife's separate property.

130 Jone Johns Lewis, "A Short History of Women's Property Rights in the United States," ThoughtCo. Accessed February 6, 2020. https://www.thoughtco.com/property-rights-of-women-3529578.

131 Article VII: General Provisions - Constitution of Texas (1845) - Tarlton Law Library at Tarlton Law Library (utexas.edu).

132 Fred A. Shannon, *The Farmer's Last Frontier: Agriculture*, 1860-1897, Vol. V, The Economic History of the United States (New York: Holt, Rinehart and Winston, 1963), 123.

133 Ibid.

134 Walter Prescott Webb, "Walter Prescott Webb's Great Plains," KRTS 93.5 FM Marfa, in his own words, accessed February 2, 2020. https://marfapublicradio.org/blog/nature-notes/walter-prescott-webbs-great-plains.

135 Ibid.

136 Sandra L. Myers, *The Ranch in Spanish Texas, 1691-1800* (El Paso: Texas Western Press, 1969), 7.

137 28-Star US Flag, Bullock Texas State History Museum, accessed February 2, 2020. https://www.thestoryoftexas.com/discover/artifacts/28-star-us-flag-spotlight-061215

138 "Ester Boserup and Boserupian Theory: Boserup's thesis and status of women," March 11, 2019, accessed January 13, 2020. https://article 1000.com/boserup-thesis-status-women.

139 Texas Hurricane History.

140 "Hard Road to Texas, Texas Annexation 1836-1845," Texas State Library & Archives Commission, accessed March 23, 2020. https://www.tsl.texas.gov/exhibits/annexation/part5/page2.html.

141 Women in the US Mexican War," accessed March 23, 2020. https://www.nps.gov/paal/learn/historyculture/women-in-mexican-war.htm.

142 Ibid.

143 Ibid.

144 Ibid.

145 Ibid.

146 Cynthia Marshall Devlin, "Bypass the Glass Ceiling: Texas Women Disrupt Traditional Male-Dominated Business Models, online *Journal of Academic Perspectives*, 2019 Dec. – 4; Archie P. McDonald, "Music in the Civil War," Guest at author's American history class, Stephen F. Austin State University, Nacogdoches, Tx. circa 2012.

147 The Texas Historical Commission, "Texas in the Civil War," accessed March 29, 2020. https://www.thc.texas.gov/public/upload/publications/tx-in-civil-war.pdf.

148 "The Home Front: Life In Texas During The Civil War" - Texas History, accessed March 29, 2020. https://texashistory.com/archives/thc-home-front.

149 Ibid. A hogshead was a standard of measurement for sugar in Louisiana and other locations in the 19th century.

150 Ibid.

151 Ibid.

152 Cynthia Marshall Devlin, "Bypass the Glass Ceiling: Texas Women Disrupt

Traditional Male-Dominated Business Models," online "*Journal of Academic Perspectives*," 2019 Dec. – 4.
153 Ibid.
154 Kevin Ladd, "The Winter Storm of 1863 and 1864 – Part 2," (March 2013), Local Writers' Columns, Stephen F. Austin State University, Center of Regional Heritage Research, accessed March 22, 2020. www.sfasu.edu/heritagecenter/7093.asp.
155 Ibid.
156 Ibid.
157 Ibid.
158 Ibid.
159 Ibid.
160 Ibid.
161 Devlin, "Bypass the Glass Ceiling," *Journal of Academic Perspectives*; Texas General Land Office, "Hardship on the Home Front---Texas Women during the Civil War," accessed November 2, 2018. https://medium.com/save-texas-history/hardship-on-the-home-front-texas-women-duringt. This information was from the Rufus Brooks Mann Civil War Letters donated by Ray and Doris Moore in 2008 and are in the GLO Archives.
162 "Civil War Letters", compiled by Doris Simmons Clark Moore, 2004. RBP 000009, p. 62–64. Rufus Brooks Mann Papers. Archives and Records, Texas General Land Office, Austin, Texas.
163 Ibid.
164 Devlin, "Bypass the Glass Ceiling," *Journal of Academic Perspectives*; Powell Exley, *Texas Tears and Texas Sunshine*, 155-175.
165 Texas Hurricane History, accessed March 22, 2020. https://www.weather.gov/media/lch/events/txhurricanehistory.pdf.
166 Devlin, "Bypass the Glass Ceiling;" Powell, *Texas Tears*.
167 Ibid.
168 Ibid.
169 Ibid.
170 Ibid.
171 Ibid.
172 Ibid.
173 Ibid.
174 Ibid.
175 Ibid.
176 Ibid.
177 Ibid.
178 Ibid.
179 Ibid.
180 Ibid.
181 Powell, *Texas Tears*, 175.
182 Ibid.
183 "What Percentage of Americans Died in the US Civil War?" accessed April 5, 2021. www.infobloom.com/what-percentage-of-americans-died-in-the-us-civil-war.htm.
184 Katie Whitehurst, "Civil War and Reconstruction 1861-1870," accessed April 5, 2021. Civil War and Reconstruction - Texas Our Texas (texaspbs.org).
185 Portraits of Texas Governors, Texas State Library and Archives Commission, "The Wild West," article on Richard Coke and Timeline, assessed April 5, 2021.The Wild West, 1874-1887 | TSLAC (texas.gov).
186 1870 Fast Facts - History - US Census Bureau, accessed February 22, 2020.

187 Texas Hurricane History accessed March 22, 2020. https://www.weather.gov/media/lch/events/txhurricanehistory.pdf.

188 Anya Jabour, ed., *"Corsets, Crinolines, and the Civil War: The Politics of Women's Fashion,"* accessed March 29, 2020. www.pbs.org/mercy-steet/blogs/mercy-street.

189 Fred A. Shannon, *The Farmer's Last Frontier: Agriculture*, 1860-1897, Vol. V., The Economic History of the United States (New York: Holt, Rinehart and Winston, 1963), 361.

190 Ibid.

191 Ibid.

192 Women In Texas History Timeline, accessed April 1, 2020. www.womenintexashistory.org.

193 Ibid.

194 Ibid.

195 Ibid.

196 Sara R. Massey, et al., eds., *Texas Women on the Cattle Trails* (College Station: Texas A & M University Press, 2008) 15.

197 *Handbook of Texas Online*, "Census and Census Records," accessed April 01, 2020, http://www.tshaonline.org/handbook/online/articles/ulc01.

198 Handbook of Texas Online, "Late Nineteenth-Century Texas," accessed April 6, 2020, https://tshaonline.org/handbook/online/articles/npl01.

199 J. David Hacker, Libra Hilde, and James Holland Jones, "The Effect of the Civil War on Southern Marriage Patterns," J. South Hist. 2010 Feb. accessed April 7, 2020. https://pdfs.semanticscholar.org/2229/c3b053e6d4846537169f7fb7c3979c5d7837.pdf.

200 Ibid.

201 Ibid.

202 Ibid.

203 Katherine M. Franke, Becoming a Citizen: Reconstruction Era Regulation of African American Marriages, 11 Yale Journal of Law and the Humanities 251-309, 251-258, 307-309 (Summer 1999).

204 Ibid.

205 Jo Ella Powell Exley, ed., 1st ed. *Texas Tears and Texas Sunshine: Voices of Frontier Women* (College Station: Texas A&M University Press) 123.

206 Jo Ella Powell Exley, Texas Tears and Texas Sunshine, 107-123.

207 Exley, *Texas Tears*, 107-123.

208 Jacob Beltran, "Cholera Epidemics Killed at Least 700 in 1800s," accessed April 21, 2020. https://www.expressnews.com/150years/education. After the epidemic, the Board of Health recommended reforms in San Antonio, such as paving the sidewalks and grading the streets to provide gutters that would drain stagnant waters. There had been a large floor in 1885.

209 Exley, *Texas Tears*, 107-123.

210 Ibid., 121

211 Ibid.

212 Keith Wheeler, text, *et al*, eds., *The Old West: The Chroniclers,* (Alexandria, VA: Time-Life Books, 2nd Revised Printing 1979), 163.

213 Ibid.

214 Ibid., 161.

215 Jo Ella Powell Exley, ed., 1st ed. *Texas Tears and Texas Sunshine: Voices of Frontier Women* (College Station: Texas A&M University Press) 209.

216 Ibid.,.210.

217 Ibid., 210.

218 Ibid., 211-224.

219 Ibid, 211-214
220 Ibid., 211-224.
221 Joseph Woodrow Hensley and Patricia B. Hensley, coordinator, *Trinity County Beginnings,* (Texas: Trinity County Book Committee, 1986), 510. Information on the Kasprzak family was from Stamford, Jones County, Texas Volume XXVII, March 24th, 1950 by Hazel Kasprzak.
222 Ibid.
223 Ibid.
224 Ibid.
225 Ibid.
226 Ibid.
227 Ibid.
228 Ibid.
229 Ibid.
230 Ibid.
231 Judith P. Rooks, "The History of Midwifery: Our Bodies Ourselves," accessed May 15, 2020. https://www.ourbodiesourselves.org/book-excerpts.
232 Ibid.; Joe S. Graham, *El Rancho in South Texas: Continuity and Change from 1750,* 1st ed. (Denton, Texas: University of North Texas Press, 1994) 27.
233 19th Century Midwives, History of American Women, accessed May 15, 2020. www.womenhistoryblog.com/2014/06/19th-century-midwives.html.
234 Gene Fowler, *Mavericks: A Gallery of Texas Characters,* (Austin: University of Texas Press, 2008), 123, 124.
235 Ibid.; "White Proclaims Mary Neely Day." *Comanche Chief,* January 2, 1986, unknown page.
236 Gene Fowler, *Mavericks*, 124.
237 "White Proclaims Mary Neely Day."
238 Gene Fowler, *Mavericks*, 124.
239 Ibid.
240 Ibid.
241 Kristen McPike, "Cotton, Cattle, and Railroad, 1850 – 1901," accessed May 16, 2020. https://texasourtexas.texaspbs.org/the-eras-of-texas/cotton-cattle-railroads/
242 CCRHistory - Calf Creek Ranch, accessed May 16, 2020. www.calfcreekranch.com/calfcreekranch_008.htm; Fane Downs and Nancy Baker Jones, eds. with Elizabeth Fox-Genovese, keynote essay, *Women and Texas History: Selected Essays*, (Austin: Texas State Historical Association, 1993), 123.
243 CCRHistory - Calf Creek Ranch.
244 Ibid.
245 Ibid.
246 Ibid.
247 Women in Texas History Timeline accessed May 16, 2020. www.womenintexashistory.org.
248 CCR History.
249 Ibid.
250 Ibid.
251 Ibid.
252 Ibid.
253 Ibid.
254 Ibid.
255 Andrew Beattie, "Hetty Green: The Witch of Wall Street," Investopedia, accessed

May 17, 2020. https://www.investopedia.com/articles/financialcareers/09/hetty-green-witch-wall-street.asp.
256 Ann Fears Crawford and Crystal Sasse Ragsdale, *Women in Texas*, 1st ed., (Burnet, Texas: Eakin Press, 1982) 123.
257 Andrew Beattie, Hetty Green; Crawford, *Women in Texas*, 126, 127.
258 Ibid.; Ibid. 127.
259 Crawford, Women in Texas, 127.
260 Ibid, 128.
261 Ibid. 123,130.
262 Ibid. 128.
263 Sara R. Massey, ed., *Texas Women on the Cattle Trails*, (College Station: Texas A&M Press, 2006) 194.
264 Crawford, Women in Texas, 131.
265 Ibid., 195.
266 Crawford, Women in Texas, 131, 132.
267 Women in Texas History Timeline.
268 Ibid.
269 Alwyn Barr, "Late Nineteenth-Century Texas," accessed May 16, 2020. https://tshaonline.org/handbook/online/articles/npl01.
270 Kristen McPike, "Cotton, Cattle, and Railroads, 1850 – 1901.
271 Ibid.
272 Texas Hurricane History, accessed March 22, 2020. https://www.weather.gov/media/lch/events/txhurricanehistory.pdf. Accessed March 22, 2020.
273 Ibid.
274 Ibid.
275 Ralph S. Jackson, *Home on the Double Bayou: Memories of an East Texas Ranch* (Austin: University of Texas Press, 1961) 17.
276 Ibid.
277 Ralph S. Jackson, *Home on the Double Bayou*, 19, 20.
278 Texas Hurricane History.
279 Ralph S. Jackson, *Home on the Double Bayou*, 17.
280 Theodore Roosevelt, (1899) 2018. *The Rough Riders*, New York: C. Scribner's. Republication, Mineola, New York: Dover Publications 12-15. Citations refer to the Dover edition.
281 Galveston and Texas History Center accessed May 18, 2020. https://www.galvestonhistorycenter.org/research/1900-storm.
282 1900 Fast Facts - History - US Census Bureau, accessed May 18, 2020.
283 Ibid.
284 History of Dr Pepper accessed May 18, 2020. https://drpeppermuseum.com/history/. (The period after Dr was dropped in the 1950s.)
285 Darla Stewart, "The History of Texas Cuisine," accessed May 18, 2020. https://texascultures.housing.utexas.edu/assets/pdfs/texas_cuisine.pdf.
286 Titanic Clothing, Fashion, Outfit Ideas, accessed May 18, 2020. https://vintagedancer.com/1900s/what-to-wear-titanic-event/
287 Women In Texas History Timeline, accessed April 1, 2020. www.womenintexashistory.org.
288 Gene Fowler, *Mavericks: A Gallery of Texas Characters,* (Austin: University of Texas Press, 2008), 125.
289 Ibid., 126.
290 Ibid., 125.

291 Ibid., 125. (Chatelaine Definition of Chatelaine by Merriam-Webster, accessed May 18, 2020. https://www.merriam-webster.com/dictionary/chatelaine. (1a: the wife of a castellan: the mistress of a château. b: the mistress of a household or of a large establishment.)
292 Cynthia Marshall Devlin, "Bypass the Glass Ceiling: Texas Women Disrupt Traditional Male-Dominated Business Models," *Journal of Academic Perspectives* Dec.-4 (2019): accessed February 24, 2020. http://www.journalofacademicperspectives.com/. Gravestone of Ichabod David Driver, Jr., Aug. 2, 1817- Nov. 27, 1910, Saint's Rest Cemetery, Nacogdoches, Texas; Gravestone of Joseph Columbus Franklin, Confederate States of America, Oct. 2, 1887, Homer Cemetery, Angelina County, Texas; Carolyn Pearson Genealogy, Roots Web's WorldConnect Project: Kathy's Kin, Joseph Columbus Franklin, accessed May 30, 2009. http://www.wc.rootsweb.ancestry.com/cgi-bin/igm.cgi? op=GET&db-gonefishin&id=1000389, Lufkin Genealogical and Historical Society, *History of Angelina County, Texas 1846-1991* (Dallas, Texas: Curtis Media Corp., 1992), 262-263; Patricia B. Hensley and Joseph W. Hensley, eds. *Trinity County Beginnings*, vol. 1 (Dallas: Curtis Media Corp, 1986), 357-359.
293 Ibid.
294 Janiece Chambers Marshall, Interview by author, November 5-6, 2018.
295 Helen Juanita Chambers Hill, Interview by author, January 2007.
296 *Handbook of Texas Online*, Megan Biesele, "NANCY, TX," accessed May 24, 2020, http://www.tshaonline.org/handbook/online/articles/hvn03.
297 Gravestone of Chas. (Charles) A. Chambers, M.D., 1854-1926, Chambers Cemetery, Angelina County, Texas.
298 Janiece Chambers Marshall, Interview.
299 Janiece Chambers Marshall, Interview.
300 *Handbook of Texas Online*, Mary L. Cox, "MOUNT BLANCO, TX," accessed May 25, 2020, http://www.tshaonline.org/handbook/online/articles/hrm54.
301 Elizabeth Boyle Smith - Cowgirl Hall of Fame & Museum, accessed May 25, 2020. www.cowgirl.net/portfolios/elizabeth-boyle-smith.
302 Ibid.
303 Ibid.
304 Ibid.
305 Postal History – USPS, accessed May 26, 2020. https://about.usps.com/who-we-are/postal-history/women-postmasters.pdf.
306 Ibid.
307 Ibid.
308 Cynthia Marshall Devlin, "Bypass the Glass Ceiling: Texas Women Disrupt Traditional Male-Dominated Business Models," *Journal of Academic Perspectives* Dec.- 4 (2019).
309 Downs, Fane & Jones, Nancy Baker. Women and Texas History: Selected Essays, book, 1993; Austin, Texas. (https://texashistory.unt.edu/ark:/67531/metapth296850/: accessed May 26, 2020), University of North Texas Libraries, The Portal to Texas History, https://texashistory.unt.edu; crediting Texas State Historical Association. Essay by Diana Davids Olien, titled "Domesticity and the Texas Oil Fields: Dimensions of Women's Experience, 1920-1950."
310 Ibid.
311 Ibid.
312 Ibid.
313 Andrea Borghini. "How Do Philosophers Think About Beauty?" ThoughtCo., accessed May 28, 2020. https://www.thoughtco.com/how-do-philosophers-think-about-beauty-2670642.
314 Ibid.
315 Devlin, "Bypass the Glass Ceiling; Hollace Ava Weiner, "Carrie Marcus Neiman,"

Jewish Women's Archive, accessed October 29, 2015. http://jwa.org/enclycolpedia/article/neiman-carrie-marcus.
316 Cynthia Marshall Devlin, "Bypass the Glass Ceiling"; Hollace Ava Weiner, "Carrie Marcus Neiman."
317 Ibid.
318 Ibid.
319 Ibid.
320 Ibid.
321 Gene Fowler, *Mavericks: A Gallery of Texas Characters*, 126.
322 Ibid., 126.
323 Ibid., 126 Baylor University was chartered February 1, 1845. accessed May 20, 2020. https://www.baylor.edu/about/index.php?id=88778)
324 Clay Coppedge, "Desdemona," accessed May 22, 2020. http://texasescapes.com/ClayCoppedge/Desdemona.htm
325 Ibid.
326 Ibid.
327 Ibid.
328 Ibid.
329 Ibid.
330 Gene Fowler, *Mavericks: A Gallery of Texas Characters*, 126.
331 Ibid.
332 Ibid.
333 Charles Butt & Family - Forbes, accessed May 24, 2020. https://www.forbes.com/profile/charles-butt/#7746acf65054.
334 Ibid.
335 Ibid; Neal Morton, "H.E.B. Started as a Small Store 110 Years Ago," https://www.expressnews.com/150years/economy-business/article/H-E-B-started-in-small-Kerrville-store-110-years. (*The San Antonio News* Archives contributed to his report.)
336 Ibid.
337 Joe Herring, Jr., "Florence Thornton Butt: A History of HEB Grocery, Comanche Trace Blog, August 1, 2011. accessed May 27, 2020. http://www.comanchetrace.com/florence-thornton-butt-a-history-of-heb-grocery.
338 Charles Butt & Family.
339 Cynthia Marshall Devlin, "Bypass the Glass Ceiling: Texas Women Disrupt Traditional Male-Dominated Business Models," *Journal of Academic Perspectives* Dec.- 4 (2019); Darwin Payne, *Texas Chronicles: The Heritage and Enterprise of the Lone Star State*, (Encino, California: Jostens Publishing Group, 1994), 88-89.
340 Ibid.
341 Ibid.
342 Ibid.
343 Helen Thrope, "Bad News Baird's," *Texas Monthly*, Aug. 1996, accessed May 25,2020. https://www.texasmonthly.com/articles/bad-news-bairds/.
344 Fane Downs and Nancy Baker Jones, eds. with Elizabeth Fox-Genovese, keynote essay, Women and Texas History: Selected Essays, (Austin: Texas State Historical Association, 1993), 118.
345 Ibid.
346 Brief History of TWU, accessed June 12, 2020. https://twu.edu/about-twu/brief-history-of-twu/. The institution after several iterations became Texas Woman's University in 1957.
347 Ibid.

348 John Haywood, Paul Garwood, *Atlas of Past Times*, (Ann Arbor Michigan: Borders Press, 2003),183.
349 Justices of Texas 1836-1986, Texas Law, Tarlton Law Library, Jamail Center for Legal Research, Hortense Ward, accessed January 29, 2021. Hortense Sparks Ward (utexas.edu).
350 Kathleen Elizabeth Lazarou. "Concealed Under Petticoats: Married Women's Property and the Law of Texas 1840-1913." (1980) Diss., Rice University. accessed June 12, 2020. https://hdl.handle.net/1911/15561.
351 Carol Boyd Leon, "The life of American workers in 1915," *Monthly Labor Review,* US Bureau of Labor Statistics, February 2016, https://doi.org/10.21916/mlr.2016.5.
352 "A glimpse at your expenses 100 years ago," *US News and World Reports*, January 2, 2015, http://money.usnews.com/money/personal-finance/articles/2015/01/02/a-glimpse-at-your-expenses-100-years-ago.
353 Ibid.
354 Teresa Tomkins-Walsh, From the Archives, "Remembering Foley's," Special Collections, University of Houston, accessed June 12, 2020. https://houstonhistorymagazine.org/wp-content/uploads/2014/07/Remembering-Foleys.pdf.
355 A Brief History of Texas Electricity, Veteran Energy, accessed June 12, 2020. https://www.veteranenergy.us/blog/brief-history-texas-electricity
356 History.com Editors, "Women's Suffrage Amendment Ratified," History, A&E Television Networks. accessed June 13, 2020. https://www.history.com/this-day-in-history/woman-suffrage-amendment-ratified.
357 American Tanker *Gulflight*, accessed June 14, 2020. https://southtynesidehistory.co.uk/archive/river-tyne-and-maritime/ships/boats-and-ships/622616-american-tanker-gulfl.
358 *Handbook of Texas Online*, Katherine Kuehler Walters, "WORLD WAR I," accessed June 15, 2020, http://www.tshaonline.org/handbook/online/articles/qdw01.
359 History.com Editors, Zimmermann Telegram published in United States - HISTORY, accessed June 15, 2020. *https://www.history.com/this-day-in-history/*; Laura Rice, "Why Texas Was One Big Reason The US Entered World War I," Austin: National Public Radio, KUT 90.5, 2017, accessed June 15, 2020. https://www.kut.org/post/why-texas-was-one-big-reason-us-entered-world-war-1.
360 Michael Hagerty, "How an Infamous Telegram Spurred American Involvement in WWI," Houston Public Media, University of Houston, accessed June 28, 2020. https://www.houstonpublicmedia.org/articles/shows/houston-matters/2019/04/15/329183/how-an-infamous-telegra.
361 Thomas A. Garrett, "Economic Effects of the 1918 Influenza Pandemic: Implications for a Modern-day Pandemic," accessed June 26, 2020. https://www.stlouisfed.org/~/media/files/pdfs/community-development/research-reports/pandemic_flu_report.pdf?la. The article was written in 2007. Mr. Garrett is an assistant vice president and economist with the Federal Reserve Bank of St. Louis.
362 Ibid.
363 Ibid.
364 Ibid.
365 Women in World War I - National WWI Museum and Memorial, accessed June 21, 2020. https://www.theworldwar.org/learn/women.
366 Texas Military Forces Museum, "36th Division in World War 1," accessed June 23, 2020. http://www.texasmilitaryforcesmuseum.org/36division/archives/wwi/white/chap1.htm.
367 Walter B. Pitkin, Roscoe Conkling, Ensign Brown, eds., *Columbia War Papers Series* 1 No. 1-4, 7-8, 10, 12, 17, (New York: Columbia University Division of Intelligence and Publicity of Columbia Univ., 1917). Digitized July 13, 2006, accessed June 17, 2020. https://

books.google.com/books?id=pKsBAAAAMAAJ&source=gbs_navlinks_s.
368 Women in World War I - National WWI Museum and Memorial, accessed June 17, 2020. https://www.theworldwar.org/learn/women.
369 Walter B. Pitkin, *Columbia War Papers.*
370 Ibid.
371 Dallas Historical Society, "Remember Dallas' past builds, accessed June 20, 2020. www.dallashistory.org/caring-for-dallas-a-history-of-our-hospitals. The local Dallas chapter of the American Red Cross has been serving communities in the area since 1911. In 1918, members of the Red Cross played an essential role in caring for the sick during the "Spanish Flu" pandemic; The Red Cross of Houston - Square Cow Movers, accessed June 20, 2020. *https://squarecowmovers.com/community-happenings/the-red-cross-of-houston*. The American Red Cross Greater Houston Area Chapter was established in 1916.
372 Ibid.
373 History - The Salvation Army, accessed June 21, 2020. *https://www.salvationarmydfw.org/p/about/history.*
374 Lorraine Boissoneault, World War 1: 100 Years Later: "The Women Who Fried Donuts and Dodged Bombs on the Front Lines of WW1," accessed June 19, 2020. https://www.smithsonianmag.com/history/donut-girls-wwi-helped-fill-soldiers-bellies-and-get-women-vote-18096.
375 Ibid.
376 Amanda Sawyer, "Camp MacArthur," *Waco History*, accessed June 21, 2020. https://wacohistory.org/items/show/48.
377 Ibid.
378 Texas State Library and Archives Commission World War 1 Records, located at https://www.tsl.texas.gov/sites/default/files/public/tslac/exhibits/ww1/2-22-868_001_001.jpg, accessed June 27, 2020. https://www.tsl.texas.gov/news/2017/ww1_tda.
379 Dawn Mitchell, "How Peach Pits Helped Us Win the War," *IndyStar*, accessed Jun 27,2020. https://www.indystar.com/story/news/history/retroindy/2018/04/20/how-peach-pits-helped-us-win-great-war/519.
380 Ibid.
381 Marion Moser Jones, "American Nurses in World War One: Under-Appreciated and Under Fire," accessed June 20, 2020. https://www.pbs.org/wgbh/americanexperience/features/the-great-war-american-nurses-world-war-1.
382 Colonel Elizabeth A. P. Vane, RN, CNOR, MS, Army Corps Historian and Sander Marble, PhD., Senior Historian of the Office of Medical History, "Contributions of the US Army Nurse Corps in World War 1," Office of the Chief of Staff, US Army Medical Command, San Antonio, Texas. The article was written for the June 2014 issue of the French journal *Soins: La revue de référence infirmiéra* which featured medical care in World War 1. The Army Nurse Corps (ANC) was established in 1901 and was seventeen years old at the time the US entered WWI on April 16, 1917. The Corps was small (403 nurses on active duty and 170 reserve nurses). accessed June 21, 2020. https://e-anca.org/History/Topics-in-ANC-History/Contributions-of-the-US-Army-Nurse-Corps-in-WWI.
383 Women in World War I - National WWI Museum and Memorial, accessed June 21, 2020. https://www.theworldwar.org/learn/women.
384 Brian M. Simmons, "Women on the Warfront: Central Texas Women in World War 1 and World War 2," Baylor University, The Texas Collection, accessed June 21, 2020. https://blogs.baylor.edu/texascollection/2013/03/21/women-on-the-war-front-central-texas-women.
385 Ibid.
386 Kathryn Sheldon, "Brief History of Black Women in the Military," Women in Military Service For America memorial Foundations, Inc. accessed June 27, 2020. https://www.

womensmemorial.org/history-of-black-women.
387 Ibid.
388 Janice Brown, "100 Years Ago: 'Gold Star Women' Nurses of World War 1," New Hampshire's History Blog, Cow Hampshire, accessed June 20,2020. http://www.cowhampshireblog.com/2017/05/04/100-years-ago-the-gold-star-women-nurses-of-world-war. The list was published in 1922 by the *Asbury Evening Press* on Friday, Nov. 10th. One source stated that seven Texas Gold Star nurses perished. Those names were absent from the list on the above blog.
389 Ibid.
390 Jones, "American Nurses in World War One; Brown, "100 Years Ago."
391 Budreau, Lisa M., and Prior, Richard M. *Answering the Call, The US Army Nurse Corps, 1917- 1919, A Commemorative Tribute to Military Nursing in World War I.* Falls Church, VA: Office of Medical History, Office of the Surgeon General, United States Army. 2008.
392 Nathaniel Patch, "The Story of the Female Yeomen during the First World War," National Archives, Prologue Magazine, Fall 2006, Vol. 38, No. 3, accessed June 28, 2020. https://www.archives.gov/publications/prologue/2006/fall/yeoman-f.html.
393 Women in World War I - National WWI Museum and Memorial, accessed June 21, 2020. https://www.theworldwar.org/learn/women.
394 Nathaniel Patch, "The Story of the Female Yeomen."
395 Women in World War I - National WWI Museum and Memorial.
396 Meg Jones, 'The Hello Girls' Documentary Celebrates World War 1 Female Operators, accessed June 28, 2020. https://www.military.com/off-duty/2018/02/12/hello-girls-documentary-celebrates-wwi-female-telephone-operato; Carl J. Schneider and Dorothy Schneider, American Women in World War 1, *Social Education* 58(2), 1994, pp. 83-85, National Council for the Social Studies, accessed June 29, 2020. http://www.socialstudies.org/sites/default/files/publications/se/5802/580206.html.
397 Ibid.
398 Ibid.
399 D. Cochrane and P. Ramirez, "Women is Aviation and Space History," Smithsonian Air and Space Museum, accessed June 29, 2020. https://airandspace.si.edu/explore-and-learn/topics/women-in-aviation/StinsonM.cfm; Lawrence Hargrave, "Katherine & Marjorie Stinson, Pioneer Aviatrices," accessed June 29, 2020. www.ctie.monash.edu/hargrave/stinson_bio.html.
400 Ibid.
401 Ibid.
402 Ibid.
403 Ibid.
404 Ibid.
405 Ibid.
406 Ibid.
407 Ibid.
408 Texas State Library and Archives Commission World War 1 Records, located at https://www.tsl.texas.gov/sites/default/files/public/tslac/exhibits/ww1/2-22-868_001_001.jpg , accessed June 27, 2020
409 Smithsonian National Museum of History, Behring Center, "Building Ships for Victory," accessed June 18, 2020. https://americanhistory.si.edu/onthewater/exhibition/6_2.html.
410 Robert H. Peebles, *Handbook of Texas Online*, "Shipbuilding," accessed June 29, 2020, http://www.tshaonline.org/handbook/online/articles/ets03
411 Historic Fort Crockett and Galveston Laboratory, NOAA, accessed June29, 2020. https://www.fisheries.noaa.gov/southeast/historic. Information on this site on Fort Crockett was

paraphrased from information provided by the Galveston Historical Foundation and researched by Betty Hartman.
412 Women In Texas History Timeline, accessed April 1, 2020. www.womenintexashistory.org. Nonprofit Profile - DonorHouston, https://donorhouston.guidestar.org/profile/1148765/children's-center.aspx. In 1923, Charlie and Albertine Yeager purchased a home on the island of Galveston. The Yeager›s used the home initially as a day nursery and kindergarten. By 1930, the home became an orphanage dedicated to African American children in the community. In 1970 in response to the growing number of runaway and youth on the streets and beaches of Galveston, the YWCA of Galveston established an outreach effort. One assumes that the Yeager's bought a larger home in 1923, or perhaps they were renting a home in 1917.
413 Carl J. Schneider and Dorothy Schneider, "American Women in World War 1," *Social Education* 58(2), 1994, pp. 83-85, National Council for the Social Studies, accessed June 29, 2020. http://www.socialstudies.org/sites/default/files/publications/se/5802/580206.html.
414 Kimberly Amadeo, "The Economic Impact of World War 1," accessed June 30, 2020, https://www.thebalance.com/world-war-i-4173886 has 20 years of experience in economic analysis and business strategy. She writes about the US Economy for *The Balance*.
415 Ibid.
416 Americans Killed in Action, Numbers, American War Library, accessed June 30, 2020. www.americanwarlibrary.com/allwars.htm.
417 *Handbook of Texas Online*, Katherine Kuehler Walters, "WORLD WAR I," accessed June 30, 2020, http://www.tshaonline.org/handbook/online/articles/qdw01.
418 Carl J. and Dorothy Schneider, "American Women in World War 1."
419 *Handbook of Texas Online*, Norman D. Brown, "Texas in the 1920s," accessed July 01, 2020, http://www.tshaonline.org/handbook/online/articles/npt01.
420 Barton C. Hacker, "Women and Military Institutions in Early Modern Europe: A Reconnaissance," *Signs* 6, no. 4 (Summer 1981): 644.
421 Kimberly Amadeo, "The Economic Impact of World War 1."
422 David Roos, "When WW1, Pandemic and Slump Ended, Americans Sprung Into the Roaring Twenties," accessed July 1, 2020. https://www.history.com/news/pandemic-world-war-i-roaring-twenties.
423 Patricia B. Hensley and Joseph W. Hensley, eds. *Trinity County Beginnings*, vol. 1 (Dallas: Curtis Media Corp, 1986), 488.
424 US Department of Labor, *Women's Bureau History An Overview 1920-2020*, accessed July 20, 2020. https://www.dol.gov/agencies/wb/about/history.
425 Ibid.
426 History.Com Editors, "The Roaring Twenties History," accessed July 5, 2020. https://www.history.com/topics/roaring-twenties/roaring-twenties-history.
427 PBS, accessed July 18, 2020.https://www.pbs.org/wgbh/evolution/library/08/2/l_082_01.html.
428 Cooley, Winnifred Harper, excerpt from "The New Womanhood," Digital Public Library of America, accessed July 3, 2020. http://dp.la/item/af7f6384e00bf7d4a761164a851e91fd.
429 Bordin, Ruth Birgitta Anderson, excerpt from "Alice Freeman Palmer: The Evolution of a New Woman," Digital Public Library of America, accessed July 2, 2020.http://dp.la/item/61122e6aa1279a1b82af4add9cf9c814.
430 The Editors of Encyclopaedia Britannica, "Gertrude Stein," Publisher: Encyclopaedia Britannica, Inc., January 30, 2020, accessed July 2, 2020. https://www.britannica.com/biography/Gertrude-Stein.
431 Bordin, excerpt from "Alice Freeman Palmer."

432 Ibid.
433 Ibid.
434 Heziel Pitogo, "How the Great War Changed Fashion for Women," War History Online, accessed July 6, 2020. https://www.warhistoryonline.com/war-articles/great-war-changed-women-fashion.html.
435 Ibid.
436 Ibid.
437 Ibid.
438 Ibid.
439 Ibid.
440 Christopher Klein, "WWI Inventions, From Pilates to Zippers, That We Still Use Today Small inventions made life easier during—and after—the war," accessed July 3, 2020. https://www.history.com/news/world-war-i-inventions-pilates-drones-kleenex.
441 Ibid.
442 Ibid.
443 Ibid.
444 Ibid.
445 This information came from the docent's tour of the Kent House Plantation, Alexandria, LA, 2011, Cynthia Devlin visit. "Kent Plantation House, listed in the National Register of Historic Places, is an authentic Creole plantation house built circa 1796 prior to the Louisiana Purchase. The plantation house is one of the oldest standing structures in the state of Louisiana." Founded: 1796, accessed July 11, 2020 https://kenthouse.org.
446 Ibid.
447 "A History of Cosmetics from Ancient Times," accessed July 14, 2020. https://www.cosmeticsinfo.org/Ancient-history-cosmetics#the_roaring_twentys.
448 Ibid.
449 Ibid.
450 Ibid.
451 Ibid.
452 "The Rise of Hair Salons Through the Ages," accessed July 26, 2020. https://www.curioushistory.com/the-rise-of-hair-salons-through-the-ages/.
453 Emily Bobrow, "Jane Goodall." *The Wall Street Journal*, Saturday/Sunday, July 11-12, 2020.
454 "The Historical Background Of Human Resource Management," accessed July 25, 2020. http://www.whatishumanresource.com/the-historical-background-of-human-resource-management.
455 Encyclopaedia Britannic, Gertrude Stein.
456 Cooley, Winnifred Harper, excerpt from "The New Womanhood,"
457 Louise Benner, "A New Woman Emerges," Women in the 1920s in North Carolina, article reprinted online with permission from the *Tar Heel Junior Historian*. Spring 2004. Tar Heel Junior Historian Association, NC Museum of History, accessed July 5, 2020. https://www.ncpedia.org/history/20th-Century/1920s-women.
458 Ibid.
459 Ibid.
460 Ibid.
461 Department of Labor, Women's Bureau, "Data and Statistics: 100 Years of Working Women," accessed July 20, 2020. https://www.dol.gov/agencies/wb/data.
462 Biggest Texas Cities in 1920 - Historical Population Data, accessed July 5, 2020. https://www.biggestuscities.com/tx/1920.
463 "San Antonio and Southern Fashion and Style in the Model A Ford Era," accessed

July 15, 2020. https://alamomodela.com/fashion.php.
464 Department of the Interior, C.E. Ellsworth, "The Floods In Central Texas In September 1921," In cooperation with the State of Texas, Washington, D.C. Printing Office, 1923.
465 Vincent T. Davis, "Historic African American neighborhood evolved into San Antonio's East Side," *San Antonio Express News*, accessed July 29, 2020. https://www.expressnews.com/sa300/article/Historic-African-American-neighborhood-evolved-12432112.php.
466 Batz, Richard Charles. "The Development of Fort Sam Houston and its Impact on San Antonio." M. A. Thesis, Trinity University, 1972.Although the military has a prominent place in San Antonio history, the first permanent post for the U. S. army was not established until 1876. The appearance of the railroad was vital to the establishment of a major military post. The city donated the 40 acres that now comprise the Fort's Quadrangle
467 Office of Historic Preservation, "Military and Postwar Development in San Antonio," https://www.sanantonio.gov/Mission-Trails/Prehistory-History/History-of-San-Antonio/Military-and-Postwar-Devel.
468 City of San Antonio Economic Development, Office of Military Affairs, Steve Nivin, "San Antonio Military Impact Study," accessed August 9, 2020. https://www.sanantonio.gov/Portals/0/Files/OMA/JBSAEconReportFINAL.pdf. Dr. Nivin is Director and Chief Economist of the Strategic Alliance for Business and Economic Research (SABÉR) Institute—an economic research collaborative between the San Antonio Hispanic Chamber of Commerce and St. Mary's University.
469 Ibid.
470 Betty Trapp Chapman, "A System of Government Where Business Ruled," from When There Were Wards: A Series, accessed August 9, 2020, https://houstonhistorymagazine.org/wp-content/uploads/2015/09/ward-system-of-government.pdf.
471 Ibid.
472 Ibid.
473 Ibid.
474 Greater Houston Partnership, Houston in the 1920s, accessed August 8, 2020. https://www.houston.org/timeline#1920s; The Heritage Society, The Saga of Henke & Pillot, accessed August 8, 2020. https://www.heritagesociety.org/henke-pillot.
475 Ginger Berni, curator of the Heritage Society of Houston, Texas confirmed via email on August 11, 2020 that she obtained this information from the Henke-Pillot scrapbook. A photo showed about 8-9 females included in a newspaper clipping. She relayed that a separate photo included black employees, however, they were all male.
476 Greater Houston Partnership, Houston in the 1920s, accessed August 8, 2020. https://www.houston.org/timeline#1920s.
477 *Handbook of Texas Online*, Roger M. Olien, "Oil and Gas Industry," accessed July 29, 2020, http://www.tshaonline.org/handbook/online/articles/doogz.
478 A.M. Boyle, "What is a Girl Friday?" accessed July 20, 2020. https://www.wisegeek.com/what-is-a-girl-friday.htm. "Daniel Defoe, the author of *Robinson Crusoe,* indirectly gave birth to the term Girl Friday. In the book, Crusoe rescues a native from cannibals and refers to him as "man Friday" because of the day of the week the rescue took place. Man Friday becomes Crusoe's loyal friend and assistant. In this way, the book gave rise to the term *man Friday,* which refers to a loyal and close male assistant."
479 Noah Tesch, Assoc. Ed., *Encyclopaedia Britannica*, "Internet." s. v. Dallas, Texas United States. "Internet." Accessed August 9, 2020. https://www.britannica.com/place/Dallas.
480 Peter Simek, "Lost Dallas," accessed August 9, 2020. https://www.dmagazine.com/publications/d-magazine/2018/march/lost-dallas-history-secrets/.

481 Deep Ellum Texas, accessed August 9, 2020. http://deepellumtexas.com/history/.
482 Charles Gay, "Delta's history: From dusting crops to connecting the world, s.v. Rural Roots: Crop Dusting to Passenger Service, accessed August 9, 2020. https://news.delta.com/deltas-history-dusting-crops-connecting-world.
483 Dallas Chain Grocery/Supermarket Locations, 1928-1986, accessed August 9, 2020. https://www.groceteria.com/place/texas/dallas/; Peter Simek, "Lost Dallas."
484 Peter Simek, "Lost Dallas."
485 Ibid.
486 Ibid.
487 Ibid.
488 Ibid.
489 Ibid.
490 Ibid.
491 Ibid; Noah Tesch, *Encyclopaedia Britannica.*
492 "History of College Education," Britannica ProCon.Org. accessed August 3, 2020. https://college-education.procon.org/history-of-college-education/.
493 Vassar Athletics, by Vassar Historian, accessed August 8, 2020. http://vcencyclopedia.vassar.edu/student-organizations/athletics/athletics-1865-1945.html.
494 *US News and World Reports*, Best Colleges in Texas, accessed August 9, 2020. https://www.usnews.com/best-colleges/tx.
495 Ibid.
496 Ibid.
497 Ibid.
498 Ibid.
499 Ibid.
500 Ibid.
501 Ibid.
502 Ibid.
503 University of Texas History accessed August 8, 2020. https://www.utexas.edu/about/history.
504 Ibid.
505 Ibid.
506 Ibid.
507 Alamo Colleges District: History, accessed July 9, 2020. https://www.alamo.edu/sac/history/#:~:text=San%20Antonio%20College%2C%20one%20of%20the%20oldest%20com.
508 Josephine Ragolia, Sutori, accessed Aug 7, 2020. https://www.sutori.com/story/huston-tillotson-university--zNk3n6X7X4TTaYwKp4pnyCuH.
509 Ibid.
510 Greater Houston Partnership, Houston in the 1920s, accessed August 8, 2020. https://www.houston.org/timeline#1920s.
511 *Handbook of Texas Online*, Eleanor L. M. Crowder, "Nursing Education," accessed August 08, 2020, http://www.tshaonline.org/handbook/online/articles/shn01.
512 History, Texas Board of Nursing, accessed August 4, 2020. https://www.bon.texas.gov/history.asp. Acknowledgements by the Texas Board of Nursing: Jim Willmann, Texas Nurses Association; Jennie Cottle Beaty, RN, The History of the Graduate Nurses Association 1907-1931; and Carl Disher, Texas Board of Nursing.
513 Committee on the Grading of Nursing Schools, *Nurses: production, education, distribution, and pay.* (New York: Published and signed by the Committee on the grading of nursing schools),1930, accessed August 10, 2020. https://catalog.hathitrust.org/Record/002072057/Cite.

514 Mike Cox, "Typing in Tyler: The Business School Model in East Texas," accessed August 5, 2020. http://www.texasescapes.com/MikeCoxTexasTales/Typing-in-Tyler-Business-School-Model-in-East-Texas.htm.
515 Allene Ray, IMBd, accessed July 7, 2020. https://www.imdb.com/name/nm0001076/bio.
516 Hans J. Wollstein, "Allene Ray Biography," accessed July 13, 2020/ https://www.allmovie.com/artist/allene-ray-p282016.
517 Ibid.
528 Ibid.
519 Joan Crawford, IMBd, accessed July 7, 2020. https://www.imdb.com/name/nm0001076/bio.
520 Ibid.
521 Ibid.
522 Ibid.
523 Ibid.
524 Ibid.
525 The Mob Museum, "Queens of the Speakeasies," accessed July 26, 2020. http://prohibition.themobmuseum.org/the-history/the-prohibition-underworld/queens-of-the-speakeasies/
526 Ibid.
527 Ibid.
528 Ibid.
529 Ibid.
530 Ibid.
531 Ibid.
532 Ibid.
533 Ibid.
534 Ibid.
535 Ibid.
536 Triple AAA, *Texas Journey*, March-April 2020, 34.
537 Pearl, Koehler Takes the Helm, accessed August 19, 2020. https://atpearl.com/about/history.
538 Kelsey Bradshaw, "The true little-known story of the Three Emmas of San Antonio's Pearl Brewery," accessed July 12, 2020. https://www.mysanantonio.com/news/local/article/The-true-story-of-San-Antonio-s-Three-Emmas-of-12326609.php; Emma Koehler's Story, Hotel Emma History, accessed July 12, 2020. https://www.thehotelemma.com/overview/history/.
539 Ibid.
540 Ibid.
541 Ibid.
542 Ibid.
543 Ibid.
544 Ibid.
545 Ibid.
546 Ibid.
547 Ibid.
548 Ibid.
549 Ibid.
550 Ibid.
551 Rebecca Salinas, "Vintage Photos Show How San Antonio Looked the Decade You Were Born," San Antonio Express News, accessed July 15, 2020. https://www.mysanantonio.

com/news/local/history-culture/article/Vintage-photos-show-how-San-Antonio-looked.
552 Vintage Fashion Guild, "Frost Brothers," accessed July 9, 2020. https://vintagefashionguild.org/label-resource/frost-brothers/.
553 *Frank W. Jennings,* "Popular Chili Queens Graced San Antonio Plazas," Popular Chili Queens Graced an Antonio Plazas - Journal of San Antonio, accessed July 15, 2020. https://www.uiw.edu/sanantonio/jenningschiliqueens.html.
554 Ibid.
555 Ibid.
556 Ibid.
557 Ibid.
558 *Handbook of Texas Online*, Juanita Luna Lawhn, "Blanco, Beatriz," accessed July 25, 2020. http://www.tshaonline.org/handbook/online/articles/fblcw.
559 Ibid.
560 Ibid.
561 Ibid.
562 Ibid.
563 Ibid.
564 Bessie Coleman Biography accessed April 15, 2018. www.notablebiogrpahies.com, accessed April 15, 2018.
565 Ibid.
566 Ibid.
567 Ibid.
568 Ibid.
569 Ibid.
570 Ibid.
571 Bessie Coleman Biography; Raymond Eugene Peters and Clinton M. Arnold, *Black Americans In Aviation*, (San Diego: Neyenesch Printers, Inc., 1975), 1-6.
572 *Women at the Forefront*. San Diego Air & Space Museum – Historical Balboa Park, San Diego; available from http://sandiegoairandspace.org/exhibts/online-exhibit-page/women-at-the-forefront, Internet; accessed 13 April 2018.
573 Ibid.
574 Ibid.
575 Ibid.
576 Ibid.
577 Enid Justin, Nocona Boot Company Collection, University of North Texas Special Collections.
578 Enid Justin, Nocona Boot Company; Enid Justin, "Born into Boots: An Interview with Enid Justin," interview by Floyd Jenkins, University of North Texas Oral History Program, Nov. 13, 1981, accessed July 27, 2020. https://www.humanitiestexas.org/news/articles/born-boots-interview-enid-justin.
579 Ibid.
580 Ibid; "Hurricanes: Science and Society: 1915- Galveston Hurricane," accessed July 31, 2020. hurricanescience.org/history/storms/1910s/Galveston.
581 Enid Justin, "Born into Boots."
582 Ibid.
583 Ibid.
584 Enid Justin, "Born into Boots: An Interview with Enid Justin," interview by Floyd Jenkins.
585 Enid Justin – Nocona Boot Company Collection.
586 Ibid.

587 Ibid.
588 Ibid.
589 Ibid.
590 Enid Justin, "Born into Boots."
591 Ibid.
592 Ibid.
593 Ibid.
594 Enid Justin, Nocona Boot Company Collection.
595 Ibid.
596 Patricia B. Hensley and Joseph W. Hensley, eds. *Trinity County Beginnings*, vol. 1, F915, s. v. Mary Eva Dominy Martin by Emma Dominy Bolling (Dallas: Curtis Media Corp, 1986), 556.
597 Ibid.
598 Ibid.
599 Ibid.
600 Ibid.
601 Patricia B. Hensley and Joseph W. Hensley, eds. *Trinity County Beginnings*, vol. 1, s. v. Carrie Harrison Poe Hensley by Joseph W. Hensley, (Dallas: Curtis Media Corp, 1986),835-836.
602 Ibid.
603 Ibid.
604 Ibid.
605 Ibid.
606 Ibid.,836.
607 Paul Schattenberg, "Women Agents Demonstrated Their Importance to Texas History," AgriLife Today, Texas A&M AgriLife Extension, Texas Extension Association of Family Consumer Sciences, accessed August 12, 2020. https://teafcs.tamu.edu/history/.
608 Ibid.
609 Ibid.
610 Ibid.
611 Ibid.
612 Ibid.
613 Ibid.
614 Ibid.
615 Patricia B. Hensley and Joseph W. Hensley, eds. *Trinity County Beginnings*, vol. 1, s. v. Kee Family, F820, by Bessie Mae Kee, (Dallas: Curtis Media Corp, 1986), 517, 518.
616 Ibid.
617 Ibid.
618 Ibid.
619 Ibid.
620 Ibid.
621 Ibid.
622 Ibid.
623 Paul Schattenberg, "Women Agents Demonstrated their Importance to Texas History."
624 Patricia B. Hensley and Joseph W. Hensley, eds. *Trinity County Beginnings*, vol. 1, s.v. Trinity Telephone Exchange, 1926-1929, T-41 by Mrs. J. B. Wooten (Dallas: Curtis Media Corp, 1986), 51.
625 Patricia B. Hensley and Joseph W. Hensley, eds. *Trinity County Beginnings;* Trinity County Texas, W.A. Belle House, accessed April 23, 2021. Trinity County, Texas - Lynne Peter Atmar (rootsweb.com).

626 Hensley, *Trinity County Beginnings.*
627 Ibid.
628 Telecommunications History Group accessed August 15, 2020. https://www.telcomhistory.org/operators.shtml.
629 Ibid.
630 National Cowgirl Museum and Hall of Fame,1976, accessed August 16, 2020. http://www.cowgirl.net/portfolio_tag/1976/.
631 Ibid.
632 Ibid.
633 Ibid.
634 Ibid.
635 Ibid.
636 Gerald D. Saxon, *Handbook of Texas Online*, Gerald D. Saxon, "CUELLAR, ADELAIDA," accessed August 17, 2020, http://www.tshaonline.org/handbook/online/articles/fcu50.
637 Ibid.
638 Ibid.
639 Ibid.
640 Ibid.
641 Ibid.
642 Ibid.
643 Ibid.
644 Hensley, *Trinity County Beginnings*, vol. 1, s.v. Mattie Hatcher, F614, by Mrs. David L. Oliver (Dallas: Curtis Media Corp, 1986), 422.
645 Hensley, *Trinity County Beginnings*; Diana J. Kleiner, Handbook of Texas Online, "Jasper, Tx," accessed August 18, 2020, http://www.tshaonline.org/handbook/online/articles/hfj02.
646 Hensley, *Trinity County Beginnings*; 422.
647 Ibid.
648 Ibid.
649 Ibid.
650 Ibid.
651 Ibid.
652 Ibid.
653 Ibid.
654 Ibid.
655 Hensley, *Trinity County Beginnings*, vol. 1, s.v. Hearn, Mattie Rosalie Terry Hood, F617, by Bernice Hood Weeks (Dallas: Curtis Media Corp, 1986), 423.
656 Ibid.
657 Ibid.
658 Ibid.
659 Ibid.
660 Ibid.
661 Ibid.
662 Ibid.
663 Ibid.
664 Ibid.
665 Ibid.
666 Ibid.
667 Ibid.

668 Ibid.
669 Ibid.
670 Ibid.
671 Ibid.
672 Ibid.
673 Historic Homes in Beaumont accessed August 17, 2020. https://www.beaumontcvb.com/things-to-do/museums-historic-sites/.
674 Ibid.
675 Ibid.
676 Ibid.
677 Ibid.
678 Ibid.
679 Ibid.
680 Robert L. Foster, "Black Lubbock: A History of Negroes in Lubbock, Texas, to 1940," Thesis, Texas Tech, 1974, accessed August 16, 2020. https://ttu-ir.tdl.org/bitstream/handle/2346/23878/31297000606956.pdf?sequence.
681 Ibid.
682 Ibid.
683 Ibid.
684 Ibid.
685 The Woman's Club of El Paso accessed August 17,2020. http://wcoep.org/history/.
686 Ibid.
687 Gracious Quotes, "60 Best Jack Welch Quotes On Leadership (Wining)," accessed August 20, 2020. https://graciousquotes.com/jack-welch/.
688 History.com Editors, "Stock Market Crash of 1929," A&E Television Networks, May 10, 2010, updated April 6, 2020, accessed August 20, 2020. https://www.history.com/topics/great-depression/1929-stock-market-crash.
689 Sarah Jacobs, "20 rarely seen images that show the struggle of America's farmers during the Great Depression," photo by Dorothea Lange, accessed August 21, 2020. https://www.businessinsider.com/20-rare-images-of-the-great-depression-2015-10.
690 Upper Texas Coast Tropical Cyclones in the 1930s, accessed August 21, 2020. https:/www.weather.gov/hgx/hurricans_climatology_1930s.
691 Last Hired, First Fired: Women and Minorities in the Great, accessed September 19, 2020. https://saylordotorg.github.io/.../s10-02-last-hired-first-fired-women-a.html.
692 From the title of the book by Jerome H. Farber, *Houston Where 17 Railroads Meet the Sea.*
693 US Census Bureau, 1930 Census, Vol 3, Population Reports by States, accessed September 13, 2020. https://www.census.gov/library/publications/1932/dec/1930a-vol-03-population.html.
694 US Department of Labor, Women's Bureau, Data and Statistics, 100 Years Women Working, accessed August 8, 2020. https://www.dol.gov/agencies/wb/data/occupations-decades-100.
695 "Radio In The 1930s," History Detectives, PBS, accessed August 21, 2020. *https://www.pbs.org/opb/historydetectives/feature/radio-in-the-1930s.*
696 Swing, Editors of Encyclopaedia Britannica, accessed September 14, 2020. https://www.britannica.com/art/swing-music.
697 1930s Fashion: What Did People Wear? accessed September 14, 2020; Characteristics of Fashion in the 1930s, accessed September 14, 2020. http://fashion.just-the-swing.com/1930s-womens-fashion. https://www.retrowaste.com/1930s/fashion-in-the-1930s/; Characteristics of Fashion in the 1930s, accessed September 14, 2020. http://fashion.just-the-

swing.com/1930s-womens-fashion.
698 Vintage Dancer, 1930s Fashion History, "What Did Women Wear in the 1930s?" accessed August 20, 2020. https://vintagedancer.com/1930s/women-1930s-fashion/.
699 History of the Bra (Brassiere), accessed September 14, 2020. http://fashion.just-the-swing.com/history-of-the-bra.
700 Patricia Reaney, "Sales of Beauty Products Get Boost from Recession," quote by Sarah E. Hill, an assistant professor of social psychology at Texas Christian University in Fort Worth.accessed September 14, 2020. https://www.reuters.com/article/us-beauty-sales-recession-idUSBRE86417C20120705.
701 Lady Bird Johnson. AZQuotes.com. Wind and Fly Ltd., 2020, accessed September 17, 2020. https://www.azquotes.com/author/7507-Lady Bird Johnson.
702 1930s Fashion: What Did People Wear?
703 Vintage Dancer, 1930s Fashion History.
704 National Museum of American History, Feedsack Dress, accessed September 14, 2020. https://americanhistory.si.edu/collections/search/object/nmah_1105750.
705 What Technology Was Available During the 1930s? accessed September 14, 2020. https://www.reference.com/history/technology-available-during-1930s-15f1ae59dbae6d4c.
706 Marshall, Janiece Chambers. Interview by author. November 5-6, 2018.
707 Courtney Strader, "All About the Servel Gas Refrigerators," Warehouse Appliance Blog, posted April 1, 2019, accessed September 28, 2020. https://www.warehouseappliance.com/blog/all-about-the-servel-gas-refrigerators/#:~:text=Gas%20refrigerators%2.
708 Ibid.
709 Emma Grahn, "Keeping your (food) cool: From ice harvesting to electric refrigeration," National Museum of American History Blog, April 29, 2015, accessed September 27, 2020.
710 Ibid.
711 Victor Fleming, *Gone With the Wind* (1939), accessed September 19, 2020. https://archive.org/details/gonewiththewind1939bluray.
712 LBJ Presidential Library, "Lady Bird Johnson," accessed September 21, 2020. http://www.lbjlibrary.org/lyndon-baines-johnson/lady-bird-johnson/.
713 Ibid.
714 Ibid.
715 Jan Jarboe Russell, "Alone Together," *Texas Monthly,* August 1999, accessed September 24, 2020. https://www.texasmonthly.com/politics/alone-together/.
716 What Was Education Like in the 1930s? accessed September 24, 2020. https://www.reference.com/history/education-like-1930s-c7ae4262b986c0e4.
717 Ibid.
718 Jan Jarboe Russell, "Alone Together."
719 Texas Association of Broadcasters, "Lady Bird Johnson: 2007 Pioneer Broadcaster of the Year, https://www.tab.org/convention-and-trade-show/ladybird-johnson.
720 Ibid.
721 Ibid.
722 Ibid.
723 Ibid.
724 Ibid.
725 Ibid.
726 Ibid.
727 Ibid.
728 Ibid.
729 Ibid.

730 Ibid.
731 Ibid.
732 Ibid.
733 Ibid.
734 Ibid.
735 Ibid.
736 Paul Burka, "Lady Bird Blog," *Texas Monthly*, July 12, 2007.
737 Ruth Roach, woman champion trick rider, c. 1920s, photograph, 1925~; (https://texashistory.unt.edu/ark:/67531/metapth21068/m1/1/: accessed September 21, 2020), University of North Texas Libraries, The Portal to Texas History, https://texashistory.unt.edu; crediting UNT Libraries Special Collections.
738 Ibid.
739 Ibid.
740 Ibid.
741 National Cowboy & Western Heritage Museum, Explore the West, "Early Rodeos in the Extreme Sports," accessed September 21, 2020. https://nationalcowboymuseum.org/explore/early-rodeos-extreme-sports-tradition/.
742 Patricia B. Hensley and Joseph W. Hensley, eds. *Trinity County Beginnings*, vol. 1, s. v. Woodlake, T273, by Joseph W. Hensley, (Dallas: Curtis Media Corp, 1986), 157-158.
743 Ibid.
744 Ibid.
745 Ibid.
746 "Brother Can You Spare a Billion? The Story of Jesse H. Jones," PBS KAMU, Texas A & M, accessed September 10, 2020. https://www.pbs.org/jessejones/jesse_bio1.htm.
747 Ibid.
748 Ibid.
749 Hensley, *Trinity County Beginnings*.
750 Ibid.
751 Ibid.
752 Ibid.
753 Ibid.
754 Ibid.
755 Ibid.
756 Ibid.
757 Hensley, *Trinity County Beginnings*, vol. 1, s. v. Bell, Gertie Pool, F105, by Fay Collier and Joy LeMasters, (Dallas: Curtis Media Corp, 1986), 198.
758 Ibid.
759 Ibid.
760 Ibid.
761 Ibid.
762 Ibid.
763 Hensley, *Trinity County Beginnings*, vol. 1, s. v. James, Isicetta Nicholds, F767, by Isicetta Nicholds James, (Dallas: Curtis Media Corp, 1986), 489-90.
764 Ibid.
765 Ibid.
766 Ibid.
767 Ibid.
768 Ibid.
769 Ibid.
770 Ibid.

771 Ibid.
772 Ibid.
773 Ibid.
774 Ibid.
775 Ibid.
776 Ibid.
777 Ibid.
778 Ibid.
779 Ibid.
780 Ibid.
781 Ibid.
782 Ibid.
783 Ibid.
784 Willie Atkinson Thorp, "W.P.A. in Chireno," in *Memories of Chireno*, Chireno Historical Society (n.p.: Kline Printing, 1994), 86.
785 Elsie Frankfurt Pollock, Obituary, *Los Angeles Times*, January 8-9, 2011. accessed October 29th, 2015. http://www.legacy.com/obituaries/latimes/obituary.aspx?pid=147663147; Cynthia Marshall Devlin, "Bypass the Glass Ceiling: Texas Women Disrupt Traditional Male-Dominated Business Models Cynthia Marshall Devlin, Stephen F. Austin State University," US, *Journal of Academic Perspectives*, Volume 2019 No 4.
786 Ibid.
787 Ibid.
788 Pollack, Elsie Frankfurt, Obituary, *Los Angeles Times*; Cynthia Marshall Devlin, *Journal of Academic Perspectives.*
789 Hensley, *Trinity County Beginnings*, vol. 1, s. v. Miles, Wyatt S., M.D., by Mary Aloise Miles, F986, 577.
790 Ibid.
791 Ibid.
792 Ibid.
793 Ibid.
794 *Blue Bell Ice Cream: A Century at the Little Creamery in Brenham, Texas, 1907-2007,* (Austin: Published in partnership with Texas Monthly Custom Publishers, distributed by Texas A&M Univ. Press, College Station), 59.
795 Ibid.
796 Ibid.
797 Ibid.
798 Ibid.
799 Ibid.
800 Andrew Knighton, "Blitzkrieg Tactics: Lightning Conquest of Poland," War History Online, accessed July 7, 2020.https://www.warhistoryonline.com/world-war-ii/blitzkrieg-tactics-poland.html.
801 Ibid.
802 Nancy Macdonell, "A Century Old, the Sweatsuit Prevails," The *Wall Street Journal*, June 27-28, 2020, Weekend Edition.
803 David Roth, "Texas Hurricane History," National Weather Service, accessed September 28, 2020. https://www.weather.gov/media/lch/events/txhurricanehistory.pdf.
804 *Texas Almanac*, "Significant Weather 1940s," Texas State Historical Association, (Austin: Published TSHA, distributed in partnership with the University of Texas) 2018. accessed October 10, 2020. https://texasalmanac.com/topics/environment/significant-weather-1940s.

805 WWll Ration Books, Arts & Sciences Department of History, University of Delaware, accessed October 19, 2020. https://www.history.udel.edu/about/history-media-center/wwii-ration-books#:~:text=War%20ration%20books%20w.
806 US Department of Labor, Women's Bureau, Data and Statistics, 100 Years Women Working, accessed August 8, 2020. https://www.dol.gov/agencies/wb/data/occupations-decades-100.
807 Annette McDermott, "How World War II Empowered Women: How did women's service in World War II inspire their fight for social change and equality? Accessed October 12, 2020. https://www.history.com/news/how-world-war-ii-empowered-women.
808 Ibid.
809 Anonymous, "Census and Census Records," *Handbook of Texas Online*, accessed October 12, 2020, https://www.tshaonline.org/handbook/entries/census-and-census-records. Published by the Texas State Historical Association.
810 Kimberly Amadeo reviewed by Somer G. Anderson, Unemployment Rate by Year Since 1929 Compared to Inflation and GDP, accessed October 26, 2020. https://www.thebalance.com/unemployment-rate-by-year-3305506
811 National Archives, Women in the Workforce during World War II, War Manpower job flyer promoting women to register for War Jobs., 1942 National Archives Identifier 281500, accessed October 18, 2020. https://www.archives.gov/education/lessons/wwii-women.html.
812 Ibid.
813 Ibid.
814 Sara Sundin, "Make It Do: Clothing Restriction in World War II," Blog, Wednesday March 8, 2017, accessed October 12, 2020. https://www.sarahsundin.com/make-it-do-clothing-restrictions-in-world-war-ii/.
815 Ibid.
816 Ibid.
817 Ibid.
818 Ibid.
819 Ibid.
820 Ibid.
821 James H. Madison, "Wearing Lipstick to War: An American Woman in World War II in France and England, Prologue Magazine, Fall 2007 Vol. 39, No. 3, National Archives, accessed October 16, 2020. https://www.archives.gov/publications/prologue/2007/fall/lipstick.html.
822 Stevie McGlinchey, "A Brief History of 1940s Vintage Makeup," Glamour Daze, accessed October 16, 2020. https://glamourdaze.com/history-of-makeup/1940s.
823 Ibid.
824 Jane Thynne, "Fashion and the Third Reich," *History Today,* March 12, 2013, accessed October 16, 2020. https://www.historytoday.com/fashion-and-third-reich.
825 Steve McGlinchey, "A Brief History of 1940s Vintage Makeup."
826 Spring, Kelly, «Oveta Hobby» National Women›s History Museum. 2017. Accessed October 28, 2020. www.womenshistory.org/education-resources/biographies/oveta-hobby.
827 Judith A. Bellafaire, "The Women's Army Corps: A Commemoration of World War II Service, CMH Publication 72-15, update February 17, 2005, accessed November 2, 2020. https://history.army.mil/brochures/WAC/WAC.HTM.
828 Ibid.
829 Kelly Spring, "Oveta Hobby."
830 Judith A. Bellafaire, "The Women's Army Corp."
831 Kelly Spring, "Oveta Hobby."
832 Ibid.
833 Ibid.

834 Ibid.
835 Ibid.
836 Ibid.
837 Pamela Marshall, "A Real Rosie the Riveter," Daughters of the American Revolution, accessed January 11, 2019. txdar.org/a-real-rosie-the-riveter.
838 Ibid.
839 Hensley, *Trinity County Beginnings*, vol. 1, s. v. Russell, George Dallas and Annie Lee, F1204, by Annie Lee Nutt., 678.
840 Ibid.
841 Ibid.
842 Ibid.
843 Ibid.
844 Ibid.
845 Ibid.
846 Ibid.
847 Ibid.
848 Ibid.
849 Ibid.
850 Ibid.
851 Find A Grave, *Lufkin Daily News*, Dec. 22, 1992, Col. James Doyle "Jim" Nutt, accessed October 17, 2020. https://www.findagrave.com/memorial/49119279/james-doyle-nutt.
852 Find A Grave, Annie Lee Jones Russell Nutt, Glenwood Cemetery, Groveton, Texas, Memorial ID 49488007, maintained by tisanders, contributor 47050864, accessed October 17, 2020. https://www.findagrave.com/memorial/49488007/annie-lee-russell.
853 Hensley, *Trinity County Beginnings*, vol. 1, s. v. Bayless, George William, F96, by V. Wayne Bayless Reynolds, 194-195.
854 Ibid.
855 Ibid.
856 Ibid.
857 Ibid.
858 Ibid.
859 Ibid.; Walker County History, "Camp Hunt[s]ville World War II Prisoner of War Camp," Walker County Historical Commission. accessed October 18, 2020. http://walker-countyhistory.org/camphuntsville.php. "Camp Huntsville was one of the first prisoner of war camps built in the US during World War II and the first in Texas. It was built in the spring and summer of 1942 and included facilities to accommodate 4,800 prisoners. It consisted of more than 400 buildings, including a cafeteria, gymnasium, laundry, and hospital. There were clubs for commissioned and noncommissioned officers, and separate barracks for the American and prisoner personnel. The first prisoners to use the camp were members of Germany's Afrika Korps who arrived in the spring of 1943. By the fall of the same year, the camp's population hit its peak at 4,840. Two years later, it became a branch camp for Camp Hearne where its prisoners were sent to make way for the arrival of a small group of Japanese prisoners. The Army closed the camp in December 1945, and all prisoners were repatriated."
860 John Bush, "All Music Review," accessed October 18, 2020. https://www.allmusic.com/album/gi-jukebox-songs-from-world-war-ii-mw0000044898.
861 Patricia B. Hensley and Joseph W. Hensley, eds. *Trinity County Beginnings*.
862 Ibid.
863 Ibid.
864 Ibid.
865 Ibid.

866 Patricia B. Hensley and Joseph W. Hensley, eds. *Trinity County Beginnings*.
867 Sir Denis Brogan as quoted in Carl Solberg, *Conquest of the Skies: A History of Commercial Aviation in America* (Boston: Little, Brown and Co., 1979) p. 262.
868 Air Mobility Command, Scott AFB, "Civil Reserve Air Fleet," accessed December 20, 2004. http://www.af.mil/factsheet_print.asp?fsID=173&page=1.
869 Interview with A.J. High by Cynthia Devlin, March 17, 2005, Houston, Texas; Interview with Lamar Muse by Cynthia Devlin, February 23, 2005 Nacogdoches, Texas; "Trans-Texas Airways Marks 20th Year," *Dallas Morning News*, October 11, 1967.
870 Ibid.
871 Ibid.
872 Ibid.
873 "The Fifinella Gazette," No. 1, February 10, 1943, from On the Record, accessed March 25, 2005. http://waso-wwii.org/wasp/scrao2.htm.
874 Interview, A.J. High.
875 Nell S. Stevenson Bright collection: Veterans History Project Library of Congress, Experiencing War: Stories from the Veterans History Project. accessed November 4, 2020. https://memory.loc.gov/diglib/vhp-stories/loc.natlib.afc2001001.60871/.
876 Ibid.
877 Ibid.
878 Ibid.
879 Ibid.
880 Ibid.
881 Ibid.
882 Ibid.
883 Ibid.
884 Ibid.
885 Ibid.
886 Women Airforce Service Pilots, Remembered by those who knew them, 1995-2014, accessed October 26, 2020. https://www.wwii-women-pilots.org/the-38.html.
887 Ibid.
888 Ibid.
889 Ibid.
890 Ibid.
891 Ibid.
892 Ibid.
893 Ibid.
894 Ibid.
895 Ibid.
896 Ibid.
897 Ibid.
898 Ibid.
899 Lorena Oropeza, "Proving Valor in War Seeking Equality Back Home," National Park Service's, Latino in the Military, accessed November 1, 2020. https://www.nps.gov/articles/latinoww2.htm.
900 Ibid.
901 Ibid.
902 The Buffalo Soldier Educational and Historical Committee, "Women of the 6888th Central Postal Directory Battalion," accessed October 30, 2020. https://www.womenofthe6888th.org/list-of-6888th-veterans.
903 Alexis Clark, "These Black Female Heroes Made Sure US World War II Forces Got

Their Mail: The 6888th Central Postal Delivery Battalion helped boost the morale of millions of Americans during World War II, February 1, 2019, updated September 24, 2020, History.com, accessed November 1, 2020. https://www.history.com/news/black-woman-army-unit-mail-world-war-ii.

904 Ibid.

905 Ibid.

906 Ibid.

907 Ibid.

908 Ibid.

909 Judith A. Bellafaire, "The Women's Army Corps: A Commemoration of World War II Service, CMH Publication 72-15, update February 17, 2005, accessed November 2, 2020. https://history.army.mil/brochures/WAC/WAC.HTM.

910 Alexis Clark, "These Black Female Heroes Made Sure US World War II Forces Got Their Mail."

911 Ibid.

912 Ibid.

913 Ibid.

914 Ibid.

915 Ona B Reed, Living Stories, "Texas Women and World War II," by Louis Mazé, Collection of the Baylor University Institute for Oral History, Original Airdates on KWBU-FM August 17,18, 20 of 2010.

916 Ibid.

917 Ibid.

918 Ibid.

919 Ibid.

920 Ibid.

921 Texas Historical Commission, "Texas in World War Two," accessed November 10, 2020. https://www.thc.texas.gov/public/upload/publications/tx-in-wwII.pdf.

922 Women In Texas History Timeline, accessed April 1, 2020. www.womenintexashistory.org.

923 Alice K. Leopold as quoted from the Labor Department, Changes in Women's Occupations 1940-1950, Part 1 – Major Occupation Groups, p. 1. accessed September 30, 2024. https://fraser.stlouisfed.org/files/docs/publications/women/b0253_dolwb_1954.pdf.

924 History.com Editors, John F. Kennedy marries Jacqueline Bouvier in Newport, Rhode Island, A&E Television Networks, November 16, 2009, updated September 10, 2020. Accessed November 28, 2020. https://www.history.com/this-day-in-history/john-f-kennedy-marries-jacqueline-bouvier-in-newport-rhode-island; Explore Jackie O's Mansion In Martha's Vineyard Hit The Market With A Listing Price Of $65 Million, Trendchaser, accessed November 28, 2020. Jackie O's Mansion In Martha's Vineyard Sold For Over Half A Billion Dollars - Trend Chaser (trend-chaser.com).

925 Michael Rich, Fifties WEB, accessed November 8, 2020.https://fiftiesweb.com/fashion/1950s-fashion/.

926 Ibid.

927 Women In Texas History Timeline, accessed April 1, 2020. www.womenintexashistory.org.

928 "Census and Census Records," *Handbook of Texas Online*, accessed October 12, 2020, https://www.tshaonline.org/handbook/entries/census-and-census-records.Published by the Texas State Historical Association.

929 US Department of Labor, Women's Bureau, Data and Statistics, 100 Years Women Working, accessed August 8, 2020. https://www.dol.gov/agencies/wb/data/occupations-decades-100.

930 Ibid.
931 Kimberly Amadeo reviewed by Somer G. Anderson, Unemployment Rate by Year Since 1929 Compared to Inflation and GDP, accessed October 26, 2020. https://www.thebalance.com/unemployment-rate-by-year-3305506
932 Jeremy Greenwood and Nezih Guner. "Marriage and Divorce since World War II: Analyzing the Role of Technological Progress on the Formation of Households." PSC Working Paper Series PSC 08-01, 2008.
933 Ibid.
934 United States. Bureau of Labor Statistics, Occupational Wage Survey: Houston, Texas, January 1952 Bulletin of the United States Bureau of Labor Statistics, No. 1084, 1952, accessed November 28, 2020. Titles | # | FRASER | St. Louis Fed.
935 Ibid.
936 Ibid.
937 Ibid.
938 Ibid.
939 John Burnett, "How One Drought Changed Texas Agriculture Forever." NPR, KAMU, accessed November 29, 2020. How One Drought Changed Texas Agriculture Forever: NPR.
940 Ibid.
941 Ibid.
942 Ibid.
943 Ibid.
944 Ibid.
945 Ibid.
946 Ibid.
947 Ibid.
948 Ibid.
949 Sue Birdwell-Alves, Interview by author, July 5, 2007.
950 Cynthia Devlin, "Twice Through the Glass Ceiling: Sue Birdwell-Alves," *East Texas Historical Journal*, XLIX, No. 2 (Fall 2011), 24 – 40; Sue Birdwell-Alves, Interview by author, July 5, 2007; Cynthia Marshall Devlin, "Bypass the Glass Ceiling: Texas Women Disrupt Traditional Male-Dominated Business Models," Journal of Academic Perspectives Dec.- 4 (2019), accessed February 24, 2020. http://www.journalofacademicperspectives.com/.
951 Ann Fears Crawford and Crystal Sasse Ragsdale, *Texas Women Frontier to Future,* (Austin: State House Press, 1998), 187.
952 Ibid., 189.
953 Ibid., 189.
954 Ibid., 188.
955 Ibid., 190.
956 Ibid., 189, 192.
957 Ibid., 188.
958 Ibid., 188.
959 Ibid., 189.
960 Ibid., 189.
961 Ibid., 189.
962 Ibid., 189.
963 Ibid., 189.
964 Ibid., 189.
965 Ibid., 189.
966 Ibid., 190.
967 Ibid., 190.

968 Ibid., 190.
969 Ibid., 190.
970 Ibid., 191.
971 Ibid., 191.
972 Ibid., 191.
973 Ibid., 191.
974 Ibid., 191.
975 Ibid., 192.
976 Ibid., 192.
977 Ibid., 192.
978 Ibid., 192.
979 Ibid., 193
980 Ibid., 193.
981 Ibid., 193.
982 Ibid., 193.
983 Ibid., 194.
984 Ibid., 194.
985 Ibid., 195.
986 Ibid., 196-197.
987 Ibid., 198.
988 Ibid., 199.
989 Ibid., 199.
990 Ibid., 198-199.
991 Ibid., 199
992 Ibid., 199.
993 Prudence Mackintosh, *Taste Maker of the Century-- Helen Corbitt*, Texas Monthly, Dec. 1999, accessed December 26, 2020. Tastemaker of the Century—Helen Corbitt – Texas Monthly.
994 Ibid.
995 Ibid.
996 Ann Fears Crawford and Crystal Sasse Ragsdale, 199-203.
997 Ibid.
998 Ibid.
999 Ibid.
1000 Ibid.
1001 Ibid.
1002 Ibid.
1003 Cynthia Marshall Devlin, "From the Lone Goose to the Golden Tail: A History of Trans-Texas Airways," Master's thesis, Stephen F. Austin State University, 2005, 43,44.
1004 Ibid., 43.
1005 Ibid., 22.
1006 Ibid., 43.
1007 Lanelle Diggles Edwards on "Texas International Airlines," interview by author.
1008 Cynthia Marshall Devlin, "From the Lone Goose to the Golden Tail, " 43-48.
1009 Ibid., 42.
1010 Ibid., 46.
1011 Ibid., 48.
1012 Ibid., 52.
1013 Ibid.
1014 Cynthia Marshall Devlin, "From the Lone Goose to the Golden Tail, " 52.

1015 Nancy Hendricks, Gail Davis (1925 -1997), Encyclopedia of Arkansas, University of Arkansas, accessed November 11, 2020. https://encyclopediaofarkansas.net/entries/gail-davis-2745/#:~:text=Gail%20Davis%20was%20an%20Arkansas-bor.
1016 Ibid.
1017 Jess Catcher, "1950s Secretaries: 11 Rules Women Were Forced To Follow At The Office," accessed December 28, 2020. 11 Rules 1950s Secretaries Were Forced To Follow | LittleThings.com.
1018 Ann Fears Crawford and Crystal Sasse Ragsdale, *Texas Women Frontier to Future,* (Austin: State House Press, 1998), 49.
1019 Ibid., 50.
1020 Ibid., 49.
1021 Ibid., 50.
1022 Tanya Tarr, "How This former Secretary Built a Multi-Million Dollar Corporation (Without any Capital," ForbesWomen, April 22, 2020, accessed December 29, 2020. https://www.forbes.com/sites/tanyatarr/2020/04/22/how-this-secretary-built-a-multi-million-dollar-corporation-wi.
1023 Ibid.; Mary Bellis, Biography of Bette Nesmith Graham, Inventor of Liquid Paper: Graham used a kitchen blender to create correcting fluid, ThoughtCo., accessed December 29, 2020. Bette Nesmith Graham, Inventor of Liquid Paper (thoughtco.com).
1024 Ibid.
1025 Ibid.
1026 Crawford and Ragsdale, *Texas Women Frontier to Future*, 51.
1027 Famous Women Inventors, "Bette Nesmith Graham: Liquid Paper Inventor," accessed December 28, 2020. Bette Nesmith Graham: Liquid Paper Inventor (women-inventors.com).
1028 Find a Grave, database and images, accessed December 29, 2020, https://www.findagrave.com, memorial page for Bette Claire McMurray Nesmith Graham, March 23, 1924, May 1980, Grave memorial no. 13208394, maintained by lola contributor 46780914, cremated, location of ashes is unknown.
1029 Ibid.
1030 Crawford and Ragsdale, *Texas Women Frontier to Future*, 51.
1031 Bellis, Biography of Bette Nesmith Graham, Inventor of Liquid Paper
1032 Ibid.
1033 Cynthia Marshall Devlin, "Bypass the Glass Ceiling: Texas Women Disrupt Traditional Male-Dominated Business Models," Journal of Academic Perspectives Dec.- 4 (2019), accessed February 24, 2020. http://www.journalofacademicperspectives.com/.
1034 American Foreign Relations, "Oil: The Seven Sisters," Accessed January 14, 2019. https://www.americanforeignrelations.com/O-W/Oil-The-seven-sisters.html#ixzz5ccH78OHz; Mira Wilkins, *The Journal of Economic History* 36, no. 3 (1976): 789-90. http://www.jstor.org.steenproxy.sfasu.edu:2048/stable/2118895.
1035 Cynthia Marshall Devlin, "Bypass the Glass Ceiling."
1036 US Department of Labor, Women's Bureau, Data and Statistics, 100 Years Women Working, accessed August 8, 2020. https://www.dol.gov/agencies/wb/data/occupations-decades-100.
1037 US GNP 1962 – 2020, Macro Trends, accessed November 28, 2020. US GNP 1962-2020 | MacroTrends.
1038 Ibid.
1039 Cynthia Marshall Devlin, "Bypass the Glass Ceiling."
1040 "What Commercial Involved the Phrase "I Can Bring Home the…, accessed January 14,2019. www.reference.com › Cooking. The Enjoli perfume commercial's jingle contained the iconic line, "I can bring home the bacon, fry it up in a pan." Charles of the Ritz launched the ad

in 1978."Bring home the bacon" refers to earning a living. "Fry it up in a pan" represents her attention to her domestic responsibilities. The ad represented the feminist "superwoman" of the 1970s.

1041 Cynthia Marshall Devlin, "Bypass the Glass Ceiling."

1042 Clem Reid, interview by author via email, "HL&P Remembrances," December 23, 2018; Cynthia Marshall Devlin, "Bypass the Glass Ceiling."

1043 Ibid.

1044 "The Pill and Women's Liberation Movement," PBS, accessed January 22, 2021. The Pill and the Women's Liberation Movement | American Experience | Official Site | PBS; Alexandra Nikolchev, "A brief history of the birth control pill," PBS, accessed January 22, 2021. https://www.pbs.org/wnet/need-to-know/health/a-brief-history-of-the-birth-control-pill/480/#:~:text=1960%20The.

1045 Alex Dixon, "July Marks 40 anniversary of all-volunteer Army," July 3, 2013, accessed January 24, 2021. https://www.army.mil/article/106813/July_marks_40th_anniversary_of_all_volunteer_Army/#:~:text=But%20the%20Ar.

1046 Frederick Jackson Turner, "The Significance of the Frontier in American History, 1893," A paper read at the meeting of the American Historical Association in Chicago, July 12, 1893. It first appeared in the Proceedings of the State Historical Society of Wisconsin, December 14, 1893, http://www.nationalhumanitiescenter.org/pds/gilded/empire/text1/turner.pdf.

1047 25 Best "The Mary Tyler Moore Show," accessed January 21, 2021. www.msn.com/en-us/entertainment/news/25-best-e2-80-98the-mary-tyler-moor; Lydia Hutchinson, "The Mary Tyler Theme Show Song," written by Sonny Curtis, accessed January 21, 2021.

1048 Amanda Weinstein," When More Women Join the Workforce, Wages Rise--Including for Men," *Harvard Business Review*, accessed January 8, 2021. https://hbr.org/2018/01/when-more-women-join-the-workforce-wages-rise-including-for-men#:~:text=In%20the%.

1049 James Hefley, Cleveland Historical Society, "A Look Back: Popular Hangouts of the 1950s and 60s, accessed November 29, 2020. https://www.chron.com/neighborhood/cleveland/news/article/A-look-back-Popular-hangouts-of-the-1950s-60s-939.

1050 Patricia B. Hensley and Joseph W. Hensley, eds. *Trinity County Beginnings*, vol. 1, s. v. Young, Clyde Edward, F1501 by Shirley Baker and Donia Young (Dallas: Curtis Media Corp, 1986), 823.

1051 Carole Marie Bloomquist, Interview by author, December 23, 2020. Answers to written questions via correspondence through mail in writing due to Covid-19 Virus.

1052 Ibid.

1053 Ibid.

1054 *New York Times*. "Galveston, Tex., Jan. 20 (AP)—Four college students from Beaumont, Tex., were found dead of carbon monoxide poisoning," *New York Times Archive*. January 21, 1964, Page 14. https://www.nytimes.com/1964/01/21/archives/4-students-die-of-gas-poison.html.

1055 Bloomquist, Interview by author.

1056 "1979 Iran Hostage Crisis Recalled," National Security Archive, The George Washington University, accessed January 7, 2021. 1979 Iran Hostage Crisis Recalled | National Security Archive (gwu.edu)

1057 Ibid.

1058 Ibid.

1059 Ibid.

1060 History.com editors, "Iran Hostage Crisis," accessed January 7, 2021. Iran Hostage Crisis - Definition, Results & Facts - HISTORY.

1061 William B. Royer, Jr., 1979-1981, Dolph Briscoe Center for American History, The University of Texas at Austin. William B. Royer, Jr., 1979-1981, Dolph Briscoe Center for

American History, The University of Texas at Austin.
1062 Ibid.
1063 Emma Hinchliffe, "Restitution deal renews painful time for local figure in Iran hostage crisis" *Houston Chronicle*, accessed January 8, 2021. https://www.houstonchronicle.com/news/houston.
1064 "The Former Hostages: Where They are Now," *Washington Post Archive*, accessed January 8, 2021. https://www.washingtonpost.com/archive/politics/1982/01/20/the-former-hostages-where-they-are-now/aa18c0.
1065 Ibid.
1066 Ibid.
1067 Bloomquist, Interview by author.
1068 Richard Dunham, "Ronald Reagan: How he changed Texas politics forever, Houston Chronicle, February 6, 2011, accessed January 7, 2021. Ronald Reagan: How he changed Texas politics forever - Texas on the Potomac (chron.com).
1069 Ibid.
1070 Bloomquist, Interview by author.
1071 Ibid.
1072 Cynthia Marshall Devlin, "From the Lone Goose to the Golden Tail: A History of Trans-Texas Airways." Master's Thesis, Stephen F. Austin State University, 2005, p. 26.
1073 Ibid.
1074 Linda K. Stone, "Women's Retirement Challenges," accessed January 15, 2021. https://www.soa.org/news-and-publications/newsletters/pension-section-news/2013/may/psn-2013-iss80/womens-.
1075 E. Mazareanu, "Employment in the US Aviation Industry---Statistics & Facts," Nov. 16, 2020. accessed January 15, 2021. Employment in the US aviation industry - Statistics & Facts | Statista.
1076 Ashikaga, "Shakey's Pizza," Houston's Original Social Network, accessed January 22, 2021. Shakey's Pizza - Historic Houston - HAIF - Houston's original social media (houstonarchitecture.com).
1077 Ninfa Laurenzo's Biography accessed January 21, 2021. Ninfa Laurenzo's Biography/ Ninfa Laurenzo's Biography (houstonisd.org).
1078 Author frequented various Ninfa's Restaurants and met her, as she often mingled with her patrons. Ninfa Laurenzo's Biography.
1079 Ibid.
1080 Ibid.
1081 Donald Payton, "Black Dallas Since 1842: A Concise History of Black Dallas," *D Magazine*, June 1998, accessed January 24, 2021. A Concise History - D Magazine. Juanita last name was spelled Kraft instead of Craft in this source.
1082 The Juanita Craft Foundation, History of 20th Century Freedom Movements in Texas, accessed January 24, 2021. The Juanita Craft Foundation | History of 20th Century Freedom Movements in Texas (wordpress.com).
1083 City of Dallas, Office of Arts and Culture, Juanita J. Craft Civil Rights House, accessed January 24, 2021. Juanita J. Craft Civil Rights House - City of Dallas Office of Arts and Culture (dallasculture.org); National Park Service, Person: Juanita J. Craft, accessed January 24, 2021. Juanita J. Craft (US National Park Service) (nps.gov); National Park Service, Place: Texas: Juanita J. Craft Civil Rights House, accessed January 24, 2021. Texas: Juanita J. Craft Civil Rights House (US National Park Service) (nps.gov).
1084 Ibid.
1085 Donald Payton, "Black Dallas Since 1842: A Concise History of Black Dallas," *D Magazine*, June 1998, accessed January 24, 2021. A Concise History - D Magazine.

1086 Ibid.
1087 Ibid.
1088 City of Dallas, Office of Arts and Culture, Juanita J. Craft Civil Rights House, accessed January 24, 2021. Juanita J. Craft Civil Rights House - City of Dallas Office of Arts and Culture (dallasculture.org); National Park Service, Person: Juanita J. Craft, accessed January 24, 2021. Juanita J. Craft (US National Park Service) (nps.gov); National Park Service, Place: Texas: Juanita J. Craft Civil Rights House, accessed January 24, 2021. Texas: Juanita J. Craft Civil Rights House (US National Park Service) (nps.gov).
1089 Ibid.
1090 Ibid.
1091 Ibid.
1092 Ibid.
1093 Texas Black History Calendar, Texas Black History Preservation Project, accessed January 24, 2021. Texas Black History Preservation Project—This Week (tbhpp.org).
1094 City of Dallas, Office of Arts and Culture, Juanita J. Craft Civil Rights House, accessed January 24, 2021. Juanita J. Craft Civil Rights House - City of Dallas Office of Arts and Culture (dallasculture.org); National Park Service, Person: Juanita J. Craft, accessed January 24, 2021. Juanita J. Craft (US National Park Service) (nps.gov); National Park Service, Place: Texas: Juanita J. Craft Civil Rights House, accessed January 24, 2021. Texas: Juanita J. Craft Civil Rights House (US National Park Service) (nps.gov).
1095 Ibid.
1096 Ibid.
1097 Ibid.
1098 Ibid.
1099 Cynthia Marshall Devlin, "From the Lone Goose to the Golden Tail: A History of Trans-Texas Airways." Master's Thesis, Stephen F. Austin State University, 2005, 1.
1100 Ibid.
1101 Jae Jones, "Jill Elaine Brown: First African-American Woman to Serve as a Pilot for Major US Airline, posted May 4, 2018 accessed January 15, 2021. Black Then | Jill Elaine Brown: First African American Woman to Serve as a Pilot for Major U.S Airline.
1102 "Jill E. Brown-Hiltz," San Diego Air & Space Museum, available from http://sandiegoairandspace.org/exhibts/online-exhibit-page/women-at-the-forefront, Internet; accessed April 13, 2018.
1103 E. Mazareanu, "Employment in the US Aviation Industry---Statistics & Facts."
1104 Texas Economic Development Corporation, Texas Enters 2021 As World's Ninth Largest Economy, accessed February 6, 2021. Texas enters 2021 as world's 9th largest economy by GDP - Texas EDC (businessintexas.com).
1105 Ibid.
1106 Texas Economic Development Corporation, Building & Attracting the World's Best, accessed February 6, 2021. Texas enters 2021 as world's 9th largest economy by GDP - Texas EDC (businessintexas.com).
1107 Ibid.
1108 2010 Fast Facts-History-US Census Bureau accessed February 14, 2021.
1109 Census Bureau Reports at Least 350 Languages Spoken in US Homes, United States Census Bureau, November 3, 2015, Release Number CB15-185, accessed February 14, 2021. https://www.census.gov/newsroom/press-releases/2015/cb15-185.html#:~:text=Houston%20 metro%20area%20At%.
1110 *What Was It Like to Fly?* | America by Air, available from https://airandspace.si.edu/exhibitions/america-by-air/online/..., Internet; accessed 26 April 2018; "History of Dallas, Texas, available from http://www.u-s-history.com/pages/h3878.html, Internet; accessed 16

May 2018; Aeroweb, "Top 100 US Airports," available from http://www.fi-aeroweb.com/Top-100-US-Airports.html, Internet; accessed 16 May 2018; "Here are the Busiest Airports in the World, 2017, available from www.businessinsider.com/20-busiest-airports-in-the-world-2017-5, Internet; accessed 16 May 2018.

1111 Kerry Hannon, "Sidepreneurship: The Booming Trend for Women," *Forbes*, October 14, 2019, accessed March 14, 2021. https://www.forbes.com/sites/nextavenue/2019/10/24/sidepreneurship-the-booming-trend-for-women/?sh=50651

1112 Bureau of Labor Statistics, US Department of Labor, *The Economics Daily*, Women in the labor force, 1970–2009, accessed February 14, 2021; 1980 Fast Facts - History - US Census Bureau, accessed May 18, 2020. https://www.bls.gov/opub/ted/2011/ted_20110105.htm.

1113 US Department of Labor, Women's Bureau, Data and Statistics, 100 Years Women Working, accessed August 8, 2020. https://www.dol.gov/agencies/wb/data/occupations-decades-100.

1114 Ibid.

1115 Ibid.

1116 Ibid.

1117 Ibid.

1118 "The 2018 State of Women-Owned Businesses Report," accessed September 20, 2018. https://about.americanexpress.com/files/dc_library/file/2018

1119 Glenn Hegar, Women in the Workforce, Texas Comptroller's Office, accessed March 8, 2021. Statewide Snapshot - Women in the Workforce (texas.gov).

1120 Ibid.

1121 Ibid.

1122 "The 2018 State of Women-Owned Businesses Report."

1123 Ibid.

1124 Ibid.

1125 Ibid.

1126 Glenn Hegar, Women in the Workforce, Texas Comptroller's Office, accessed March 8, 2021. Statewide Snapshot - Women in the Workforce (texas.gov).

1127 Irma Gonzalez Galvan, Irma's Original, a restaurant in Houston, information under "Our Story," accessed January 14, 2019. https://irmasoriginal.com.

1128 Irma Gonzalez Galvan, Irma's Original.

1129 Ibid.

1130 Ibid.

1131 Rob D'Amico, "Living Maya: Austin Become a Hotbed of Past and Future Maya Knowledge," The Austin Chronicle, May 2, 2008, accessed March 15, 2021. Living Maya: Austin becomes a hotbed of past and future Maya knowledge - News - The Austin Chronicle.

1132 Cynthia Marshall Devlin, "Schele, Linda Dean Richmond," *Handbook of Texas Online*, accessed October 21, 2021, https://www.tshaonline.org/handbook/entries/schele-linda-dean-richmond.Published by the Texas State Historical Association; University Communications, "Maya Historian Linda Schele Dies," UT News, April 20, 1998, accessed March 16, 2021. Maya historian Linda Schele dies - UT News (utexas.edu).

1133 Devlin, "Schele, Linda Dean Richmond." *Handbook of Texas Online*.

1134 Ibid.

1135 Ibid.

1136 Ibid.

1137 Ibid.

1138 Devlin, "Schele, Linda Dean Richmond." *Handbook of Texas Online*; University Communications, "The Tradition of Dr. Linda Schele Lives On," UT News, March 2, 1999, accessed March 16, 2021. Tradition of Dr. Linda Schele lives on with Maya Meetings - UT

News (utexas.edu).
1139 University Communications, "Maya Historian Linda Schele Dies;" Devlin, "Schele, Linda Dean Richmond." *Handbook of Texas Online.*
1140 University of Texas, Arts & Humanities, "Maya historian Linda Schele dies," April 20, 1998, accessed October 4, 2024. Maya historian Linda Schele dies - UT News (utexas.edu.).
1141 Devlin, "Schele, Linda Dean Richmond." *Handbook of Texas Online.*
1142 Ibid.
1143 University Communications, "The Tradition of Dr. Linda Schele Lives On;" Devlin, "Schele, Linda Dean Richmond." *Handbook of Texas Online.*
1144 Dawn Rosenberg McKay, "Careers for Women in the Military," accessed March 2, 2021. Careers for Women in the Military (thebalancecareers.com).
1145 Ibid.
1146 Ibid.
1147 Texas Veterans Commission, Women Veterans, accessed March 2, 2021. Texas Veterans Commission – Claims, Education, Employment, Grants, Health Care Advocacy. These women veterans self-attested.
1148 Ibid.
1149 Ibid.
1150 Ibid.
1151 Ibid.
1152 Ibid.
1153 Ibid.
1154 Ibid.
1155 Ibid.
1156 Ibid.
1157 Giselle Phelps and Jihad Hassan Muhammad, "This Girl is on Fire: Dallas' Black Women in Business," accessed October 9, 2018, https://www.dallasweekly.com/business/article_57acb084-b410-11e2-b...
1158 "The Story of Mary Kay," accessed January 9, 2019, "M**arykay**museum.com/images/museum/TheStory**OfMaryKay**.pdf.
1159 Ibid.
1160 Angelo Andaloro, "Tanya Tucker Reflects On Her Storied Country Music Career 48 years After Her First Hit Song," accessed March 15, 2021. Tanya Tucker Reflects On Her Career & How Much Touring Means To Her | LittleThings.com.
1161 Bethany Reed, "Wise Words from Double D Ranch's Audrey Franz and Cheryl McMullen: The sisters behind the Western couture brand pull back the curtain," *Cowgirl,* August 12, 2019, accessed March 14, 2021. Wise Words from Double D Ranch's Audrey Franz and Cheryl McMullen - COWGIRL Magazine; Andrea Thorp, "30 Years of Double D Ranch," *Cowboys & Indians*, November/December 2020, pp. 81-83.
1162 Ibid.
1163 Peyton Waldrip, "The Story of a 'Texas Rancher Girl,'" IBBA Communications, accessed April 8, 2021. TRG_Dec2016.pdf (texasranchergirl.com).
1164 Ibid.
1165 Ibid.
1166 Ibid.
1167 Ibid.
1168 Ibid.
1169 Ibid.
1170 Ibid.
1171 Ibid.

1172 Ibid.
1173 Live Science Staff, " Wild Facts About the Texas Drought," accessed April 10, 2021. Wild Facts About the Texas Drought | Live Science.
1174 Ibid.
1175 Jim Forsyth, "Texas' 2011 drought costliest in state history: researchers," Reuters, March 21, 2012, accessed April 10, 2021. Texas' 2011 drought costliest in state history: researchers | Reuters.
1176 Ramit Plushbnick-Masti, "Texas Ranchers use Business Wile to Weather Drought," accessed April 10, 2021. https://news.yahoo.com/texas-farmers-business-wile.
1177 Ibid.
1178 Ibid.
1179 Ibid.
1180 Ibid.
1181 Ibid.
1182 Ibid.
1183 Ibid.
1184 Ibid
1185 Ibid.
1186 Ibid.
1187 Linda Elane Barras Whiteley, Interview by author, April 6, 2021. Answers to written questions via correspondence through mail in writing due to Covid-19 Pandemic
1188 Angela Woo, " The Forgotten Generation: Let's Talk About Generation X," November 14, 2018, accessed April 11, 2021. https://www.forbes.com/sites/forbesagencycouncil/2018/11/14/the-forgotten-generation-lets-talk-about-generation.
1189 "Women's Roles VS. Social Norms," Archives of *The New York Times*, accessed April 11, 2021. WOMEN'S ROLES VS. SOCIAL NORMS - The New York Times (nytimes.com).
1190 Linda Elane Barras Whiteley, Interview by author.
1191 Ibid.
1192 Ibid.
1193 Max Berger and Lee Wilborn, "Education," *Handbook of Texas Online*, accessed April 11, 2021, https://www.tshaonline.org/handbook/entries/education. Published by the Texas State Historical Association.
1194 Carlos J. Ovando, "Bilingual Education in the United States: Historical Development and Current Issues," accessed April 12, 2021. Untitled-3 (nd.edu).
1195 Linda Elane Barras Whiteley, Interview by author.
1196 Ibid.
1197 Ibid
1198 Ibid.
1199 Arya Min, "The Past, Present and Future of Women in STEM," July 10, 2019, Blog, accessed April 12, 2021. The Past, Present and Future of Women in STEM – PCS Edventures.
1200 Ibid.
1201 The People History accessed April 18, 2021. What Happened in 1986 inc. Pop Culture, Prices Significant Events, Key Technology and Inventions (thepeoplehistory.com).
1202 Michael Frontain, "Compaq Computer Corporation," *Handbook of Texas Online*, accessed April 15, 2021, https://www.tshaonline.org/handbook/entries/compaq-computer-corporation.Published by the Texas State Historical Association.
1203 Ibid.
1204 Ibid.
1205 Mary Bellis, "The History of Laptop Computers," accessed April 12, 2021. https://www.thoughtco.com/history-of-laptop-computers-4066247#:~:text=1988%3A%20Compaq%20

Computer.
1206 Linda Elane Barras Whiteley, Interview by author.
1207 The People History accessed April 18, 2021. What Happened in 1986 inc. Pop Culture, Prices Significant Events, Key Technology and Inventions (thepeoplehistory.com).
1208 Ibid.
1209 Linda Elane Barras Whiteley, Interview by author.
1210 John T. Correll, "History of Stealth: From Out of the Shadows," Air Force Magazine, September 1, 2019, accessed April 15, 2021. History of Stealth: From Out of the Shadows - Air Force Magazine.
1211 Linda Elane Barras Whiteley, Interview by author, via email.
1212 The People History.
1213 Ibid.
1214 The People History; Interview with Linda Whiteley.
1215 Amanda Drane, "Mars Foods says 'uncle,' rebrands Ben's rice brand," Houston Chronicle, September 23, 2020, accessed April 16, 2021. Mars Foods says 'uncle,' rebrands Ben's rice brand (houstonchronicle.com).
1216 Mary Bellis, "Forest Mars and the History of M&Ms Candies: A Legacy of the Spanish Civil War," accessed April 16, 2021.The Invention of M & Ms Candies (thoughtco.com).
1217 All About Mars, accessed April 23, 2021. All About Mars | Mars, Incorporated.
1218 Linda Elane Barras Whiteley, Interview by author.
1219 Linda Elane Barras Whiteley, Interview by author.
1220 The Billington Group, History and Heritage, Criddle, accessed April 21, 2021. History and Heritage (Billington Group) | Criddle & Co Ltd (criddles.co.uk).
1221 Linda Elane Barras Whiteley, Interview by author.
1222 Ibid.
1223 Linda Elane Barras Whiteley, Interview by author.
1224 Ibid.
1225 Ibid.
1226 Ibid.
1227 Ibid.
1228 Ibid.
1229 Fast Facts - History - US **Census** Bureau, accessed April 21, 2021. https://www.census.gov/history/www/through_the_decades/fast_facts/2000_new.html#:~:text=POP%20Culture%3A%2020.
1230 National Weather Service, Hurricane Rita, accessed April 18, 2021. ttps://www.weather.gov/hgx/hurricanes_climatology_1980s.
1231 Ibid.
1232 Kaia Hubbard, "Places Without Reported COVID-19 Cases, A handful of countries and territories are the few places left with no reported cases from the coronavirus pandemic" February 22, 2021. accessed April 21, 2021..Countries Without Reported COVID-19 Cases | Best Countries | US News.
1233 Houston-based Small Business Owner Linda Whiteley Introduces The Pivot Principle™ and Offers Recommendations to Help Peers Survive and Thrive During the COVID-19 Pandemic. Accessed April 21, 2021. Laura M. Pennino, senior PR consultant for The Pivot Principle. https://www.businesswire.com/news/home/20201116005954/en/.
1234 Houston-based Small Business Owner Linda Whiteley Introduces The Pivot Principl.™
1235 Ibid.
1236 Bloomberg Business Wire, "The Little Company That Could: Houston-Based

Certified Woman-Owned AGS Solutions Gets Creative to Fulfill Special Order of Disinfectant Wipes for Long-Term Customer ExxonMobil by Becoming a Distributor for Dreumex USA," accessed April 21, 2021. https://www.bloomberg.com/press-releases/2020-10-26/the-little-company-that-could-houston-based-certified-w.

1237 Linda Elane Barras Whiteley, Interview by author.

1238 Ibid.

1239 Linda Elane Barras Whiteley, Interview by author.

1240 Cynthia Marshall Devlin, "Bypass the Glass Ceiling: Texas Women Disrupt Traditional Male-Dominated Business Models," Journal of Academic Perspectives Dec.- 4 (2019), accessed February 24, 2020.

1241 Mary Beth Norton, *Liberty's Daughters: The Revolutionary Experience of American Women 1750-1800* (Ithaca: Cornell University Press, 1996), 297.

1242 Ibid.

1243 Powell Exley, *Texas Tears and Texas Sunshine*, 209, 210, 213, 218.

1244 Ibid.

1245 Ibid., 224.

1246 Rory Satran, "Seize the Gray," *Wall Street Journal*, Sat.-Sun., Jan 19-20, 2019.

1247 Devlin, "Bypass the Glass Ceiling."

1248 Ibid.

tent.com/pod-product-compliance
LLC
224
MB/12

9 781622 882724